# ACADEMIC WRITING

# ACADEMIC WRITING

Writing and Reading
Across the Disciplines

*Second Edition*

Janet Giltrow

broadview press

**Canadian Cataloguing in Publication Data**

Giltrow, Janet Lesley
    Academic writing: writing and reading across the disciplines
2nd ed.
Includes index

ISBN 1-55111-055-5

1. Report writing.  2. English language -- Rhetoric.  3. Exposition
(Rhetoric).  I. Title.

PEI408.G55  1995   808'.042   C95-931112-2

Broadview Press Ltd., is an independent, international publishing house, incorporated in 1985.

North America:
P.O. Box 1243, Peterborough, Ontario, Canada K9J 7H5
3576 California Road, Orchard Park, NY 14127
TEL: (705) 743-8990; FAX: (705) 743-8353;
E-MAIL: 75322.44@compuserve.com

United Kingdom:
Turpin Distribution Services Ltd.,
Blackhorse Rd., Letchworth, Hertfordshire SG6 1HN
TEL: (1462) 672555; FAX (1462) 480947; E-MAIL: turpin@rsc.org

Australia:
St. Clair Press, P.O. Box 287, Rozelle, NSW 2039
TEL: (02) 818-1942; FAX: (02) 418-1923

www.broadviewpress.com

Broadview Press gratefully acknowledges the financial support of the Book Publishing Industry Development Program, Ministry of Canadian Heritage, Government of Canada.

Text and cover design and composition by George Kirkpatrick

Canadä

# Contents

# 4 Portrait of a reader 110

# 5  Definition and Comparison   174

# 6  Academic styles   213

# 7  The state of knowledge: positions, conditions, limits   260

# Preface

This book develops from a strong claim: namely, that style is meaningful. A textbook may not be the best place to advance a strong claim, so, to make this claim less conspicuous, I could downgrade it by describing it as in keeping with established views. I could point out that few authors of composition textbooks deny the importance of style, and most offer advice on words and sentences. And I could point out that many researchers, especially those working in English for Special Purposes, have analyzed style in the scholarly genres. In turn, these inquiries could be seen as developing the long standing sociolinguistic idea of "register," the condition which indexes language for use in definable social settings.

Both the textbook tradition and the research tradition could absorb the claim that style is meaningful, and thus make it less outstanding. But I prefer that this claim about style remain conspicuous. I prefer that it not be absorbed into customary ideas about the decorum or efficiency of writing smoothly, or even into the more exacting observation of the distribution of linguistic features across social groups and social roles. I prefer that the meaningfulness of style be taken seriously, and not be allowed to slip into peripheral vision, where it becomes only a marker of appropriateness, or a factor in readability.

Writing teachers may intuit the meaningfulness of style when they read a certain kind of student essay. This is the essay that is coherent by generalized measures — an identifiable introduction and conclusion govern a discussion that would seem logical to a sensible person. It is "correct" by most measures of Standard English. It demonstrates that the author has done the assigned reading, listened to lectures, and worked studiously. Yet, despite these virtues, it fails to speak to an academic audience, or enter into the discourse of the discipline. Its way of speaking locates it out of earshot of scholarly interests.

Often it is hard to respond helpfully to such an essay. Pressed, some might refer its failure to address academic interests to a lack of "original" thinking, or to another condition equally resistant to overt correction: some might observe "surface" shortcomings — maybe something like a naïve plainness, or an undue bloom on sentences. But I would argue that there is no "surface" to writing, and that the stylistic qualities which tax our capacity to name them are more than skin-deep. And, moreover, I would suggest that the "originality" academic readers value *depends on style* — on the typical ways of speaking that produce certain kinds of knowledge of the world. A writer involved in the characteristic wordings of a discipline is involved in its practices and perspectives and its procedures for interpreting the world. A discipline's typical wordings embody its representation of the world, what Kenneth Burke (1966) called "tribal [idiom]," this idiom being in a sense a set of tacit instructions for understanding the world and making statements about it. Style constitutes a position in the world, and shared methods for thinking about it. Without access to scholarly ways of speaking, student writers cannot occupy scholarly positions, or use scholarly methods for producing statements, or speak to academic interests.

A strong stand on the matter of style can be supported by deliberately broad definitions of style. Such definitions would include global conditions of coherence and connectedness — how elements of a text make themselves available for the reader's construction of meaning. They would include conditions of assertion and presupposition — how texts deliver some propositions explicitly but leave others assumed rather than asserted, and how these patterns configure a discourse community's ground of shared knowledge. The analyses offered in this book not only respect these larger conditions as features of style but also observe their effect on areas more traditionally regarded as the domain of style: the character of phrases and sentences. The distinctive grammar of scholarly writing provides the footings for larger schemes.

Broad definitions of style are useful, but can still beg the question. After all, if style is everything, it must be important. So this book's approach to academic writing offsets the enlargement of style to universal (and thus tautological) proportions by insisting that style is both a representation of and a guide to practice. Borrowing Carolyn Miller's (1984) motto "genre as social action," and grafting onto it Carol Berkenkotter and Thomas Huckin's (1992) characterization of genre as "socio-cognitive," I suggest that *style* is "socio-cognitive action." The social and cognitive agency of style is often invisible to us, and the very efficacy of style as an instigator lurks in its tacitness, its low profile in our consciousness, and its tendency to naturalize itself. But we can coax it out for inspection by taking one relatively noticeable example of style representing and guiding practice: parenthetical citations. These expressions distinguish scholarly writing, displaying a scholarly stance. They represent a scholarly practice: the way researchers systematically consult other research, and estimate its relevance and proximity to their work, these activities being stylized as a summoning of voices to substantiate, by accord or contrast, the individual speaker's utterance. Through the semiotics of style, parenthetical expressions represent the research community's routines of association. At the same time, these typical wordings not only represent but also *guide* practice. They instruct a writer in the research genres to read other writers, and to read them in a particular way, so as to be able to construct gist compactly and dialectically. Parenthetical citations — a feature of style — constitute for the writer a position in the world, one contingent on other positions.

Other stylistic features — nominalization, for example, or expressions of indeterminacy — also constitute a position, and instructions for thinking about the world. These are among features I take to be *salient* to research writing: that is, they are the genre's distinguishing insignia, the linguistic-pragmatic features which make it recognizable, and which particularly define its service to the equally recognizable research and knowledge-making situations of academic life, guiding people to the kinds of thinking that are productive in those situations.

One might ask whether students can acquire scholarly know-how simply by mastering scholarly wording. Common sense could suggest that students would acquire only a surface glibness, an empty compliance with form. But the strong claim about the meaningfulness of style suggests, first, that there are no "surfaces" to language, and, second, that language is constitutive of experience. The social and cognitive behaviors which attend the production of scholarly utterance are scholarly behaviors.

Moreover, this book doesn't simply prescribe the wordings characteristic of scholarly writing. Rather, it convenes a colloquy of voices from the academic disciplines, speaking in their characteristically scholarly ways, and assuming characteristically scholarly attitudes. It presents these voices to students, asking them to listen for the accents of the research genres, to interpret them as functional tokens of academic culture, and to adopt in their own writing those features which can represent their position as apprentice workers in knowledge-making settings. This book also asks them, in the process of developing an ear for the characteristic sounds of scholarly voices and developing their own positions as writers, to learn some things about how language constructs our experience of the world. Teachers in English departments may shy away from such direct attention to language. They may want to avoid the stigma associated with the teaching of "grammar" — a pedagogical focus with a bad reputation — or they may object to such direct attention to language as too technical, or too difficult. But both objections would be hard to sustain in the long run. First, the discourse on language — or the discourse on discourse — has transformed the intellectual climate of the end of the twentieth century, and it seems unreasonable to exclude the study of university writing from this transformation. And, second, other areas of study do not exempt students from learning complex or "technical" principles on the grounds of difficulty, and these disciplines survive and flourish despite the demands they make on students. Moreover, the linguistic-pragmatic principles which inform this book's analysis of research writing provide a basis for approaching the social and political implications of the research genres and their salient features: if style is meaningful, we should ask *what it means*, and if style is social action, we should ask *what it does*. We should ask by what principles a way of speaking organizes knowledge of the world, and organizes systems of association, solidarity, and advantage.

In its analysis of scholarly ways of speaking, this book locates style in new conceptualizations of genre which emphasize the reciprocity between, on the one hand, social context and its typical occasions and, on the other hand, the discursive practices which serve and maintain these recurring occasions. So it benefits from the work of a community of researchers who have developed powerful new ideas about genre: Carolyn Miller (1984), John Swales (1990), Carol Berkenkotter and Thomas Huckin (1992), Aviva Freedman (1993), Aviva Freedman and Peter Medway (1994), Richard Coe (1987, 1994). Exemplifying the best results of scholarly exchange, the discourse on genre has proceeded richly, and productively, and I am grateful for the contact I have had with these people and their ideas.

With others I have had only the remote contact of a respectful reader. M. A. K. Halliday and J. R. Martin's (1993) research into the language of science — research also mindful of reconceptualizations of genre — provided a boost for my analysis of the relation between abstraction and the kind of coherence peculiar to research writing; Greg Myers' (1989) analysis of "politeness" in science writing confirms my analysis of the pragmatics of indeterminacy; and in general my approach to the linguistic-pragmatics of the research genres is indebted to a company of theorists whose work offers instruments for measuring the subtle service of words and sentences to the maintenance of positions, attitudes, and relations in the social order. Members of this company include Ellen Prince (1981), Herbert Clark (1992) and Herbert Clark and Catherine Marshal (1981), Dan Sperber and Deirdre Wilson (1986), M. A. K. Halliday

(1985), Georgia Green (1989), F. R. Palmer (1990), Eve Sweetser (1990), Wallace Chafe (1986), Gennaro Chierchia and Sally McConnel-Ginet (1990). Readers of this book will also catch a glimpse of influence from celebrated thinkers whose reasonings have helped me postulate the character of the social order and its manifestations in both language and language learning: Michel Foucault, Mikhail Bakhtin, Pierre Bourdieu, Anthony Giddens.

Closer to home, I am indebted to the encouragement and inspiration I have received from co-workers — especially those with whom I have collaborated on teaching and research projects: David Stouck for his persistent faith (even in the face of others' doubt) in the idea that style is meaningful; Richard Coe for providing me with a privileged introduction to the ideas of Kenneth Burke; Michele Valiquette for her tireless commitment to the idea that the composition classroom can be a site of rigorous inquiry.

In the first edition of this book, I also referred to "the students who visited the Simon Fraser University Writing Centre during the six years that I . . . worked there. Face-to-face with these writers, I learned about the details of their struggles and achievements in making sense of the academic community and its intricate ways of communicating with itself." Nothing will surpass the insight those years gave me into the ground-level conditions of learning and composing at university. But subsequent years have brought along new generations of writers who have labored over exercises and assignments reproduced in this book, and from their intellectual resourcefulness — their sincerity and scepticism, and their ambitious intelligence — I have learned that, by asking a lot, we get a lot in return: fine papers, exciting discussion, and a renewal of scholarly traditions, in new terms.

# References

Berkenkotter, Carol, and Thomas Huckin 1992 Rethinking genre from a sociocognitive perspective. Paper presented at Colloquium on Rethinking Genre, Ottawa.

Bourdieu, Pierre 1984 *Distinction: A Social Critique of the Judgement of Taste*, trans. Richard Nice. Cambridge, Mass.: Harvard UP.

Burke, Kenneth 1966 *Language as Symbolic Action: Essays on Life, Literature, and Method*. Berkeley: U of California P.

Cameron, Deborah 1990 Demythologizing sociolinguistics: Why language does not reflect society. In *Ideologies of Language*, ed. John E. Joseph and Talbot J. Taylor. London: Routledge.

Chafe, Wallace 1986 Evidentiality in English conversation and academic writing. In *Evidentiality: The Linguistic Encoding of Epistemology*, ed. Wallace Chafe and Johanna Nichols. Norwood, NJ: Ablex.

Chierchia, Gennaro, and Sally McConnel-Ginet 1990 *Meaning and Grammar: An Introduction to Semantics*. Cambridge, Mass.: MIT Press.

Clark, Herbert H. 1992 *Arenas of Language Use.* Chicago: U of Chicago P.

Clark, Herbert H., and Catherine R. Marshall 1981 Definite reference and mutual knowledge. In *Linguistic Structure and Discourse Setting*, ed. A. K. Joshi, B. Webber, and I. Sag. Cambridge: Cambridge UP.

Coe, Richard 1987 An apology for form; or, who took the form out of the process. *College English* 49, 1: 13-28.

____. 1994 Teaching genre as process. In *Learning and Teaching Genre*, ed. Aviva Freedman and Peter Medway. Portsmouth, NH: Boynton/Cook, Heinemann.

Freedman, Aviva 1993 Show and tell? The role of explicit teaching in the learning of new genres. *Research in the Teaching of English* 27, 3: 222-51.

Freedman, Aviva, and Peter Medway 1994 Introduction. In *Learning and Teaching Genre*, ed. Aviva Freedman and Peter Medway. Portsmouth, NH: Boynton/Cook, Heinemann.

Green, Georgia M. 1989 *Pragmatics and Natural Language Understanding*. Hillsdale, NJ: Erlbaum.

Halliday, M. A. K. 1985 *An Introduction to Functional Grammar*. London: Edward Arnold.

Halliday, M. A. K., and J. R. Martin. 1993 *Writing Science: Literacy and Discursive Power*. Pittsburgh: U of Pittsburgh P.

Miller, Carolyn 1984 Genre as social action. *Quarterly Journal of Speech* 70, 2: 151-67.

Myers, Greg 1989 The pragmatics of politeness in scientific articles. *Applied Linguistics* 10: 1-35.

Palmer, F. R. 1990 *Modality and the English Modals.* London: Longman.

Prince, Ellen F. 1981 Toward a taxonomy of given-new information. In *Radical Pragmatics*, ed. Peter Cole. New York: Academic Press.

Sperber, Dan, and Deirdre Wilson 1986 *Relevance: Communication and Cognition.* Cambridge, Mass.: Harvard UP.

Swales, John 1990 *Genre Analysis: English in Academic and Research Settings.* Cambridge: Cambridge UP.

Sweetser, Eve E. 1990 *From Etymology to Pragmatics: Metaphorical and Cultural Aspects of Semantic Structure.* Cambridge: Cambridge UP.

# 1

## Chapter One:
## Introducing *genre*

### 1.1 Hearing voices

PASSAGE 1 Vokey and Read (1992) further extend their findings by applying a regression analysis to the general familiarity and memorability components to predict recognition discrimination, criterion, and hit and false alarm rates. They reason that if the effect of typicality on recognition is a function of both general familiarity and memorability, each of these should be a significant predictor of recognition performance. To do this, they derived a regression equation composed of differential additive weightings of the general familiarity and memorability components to predict discrimination performance. In fact, they found that both familiarity and memorability were significant predictors of discrimination performance, but not of criterion.[1]

PASSAGE 2     TALENTED, successful, good looking male, 30's, seeks attractive, intelligent, petite female, who knows authentic gems are rare. Toronto area. Box 000 ——————

PASSAGE 3     My husband and I spent a recent vacation driving along the spectacular California coast. One morning we stopped at Big Sky Cafe in San Luis Obispo for breakfast. Their menu includes a hash with delicious "glazed" eggs. What's the secret to the eggs?

Eileen Gilbert<br>
Casper, Wyoming

PASSAGE 4     Eugenics theory powerfully influenced late nineteenth- and early twentieth-century U.S. policies concerning the groups then known as "the dependent, defective, and delinquent classes" (Henderson 1901, U.S. Department of the Interior 1883). In essence, eugenicists held that the "fit" should be encouraged to reproduce ("positive" eugenics) and the "unfit" prevented from doing so ("negative" eugenics). Historians generally agree that between 1900 and 1920 this doctrine formed the basis for a full-fledged social movement with research centers, propaganda vehicles, and strong middle-class support (Haller 1963, Kevles 1985, Ludmerer 1972, Pickens 1968). Less commonly acknowledged is the fact that eugenics theory affected public policy for decades before becoming the social movement's foundation and that eugenic ideas long outlived the movement itself, in ways that a new generation of historians is just starting to explore (Dann 1991, Noll 1990, Reilly 1991). Even today, eugenics arguments occasionally make their way into debates about such matters as population growth and crime control (e.g., Wattenberg 1987, Wilson 1989; for a recent analysis see Duster 1990).[2]

PASSAGE 5     **PANORAMIC VIEW!**

Super 2 yr old 1 bedroom apartment in prime South Slopes, features 180 degree gulf island view, 9' ceilings, insuite laundry, 6 appliances, fantastic kitchen with oak cabinets, track lighting, balcony off living room & bedroom, gas f/p & more. Comes with 2 parking places. Unit located at 0000 Station Hill Court. Call now, priced to sell $147,900. Barry Wilson 000-0000, 000-0000, ——— ——— Realty.

PASSAGE 6     PROVIDED that the Mortgagor, when not in default hereunder, shall have the privilege of prepaying, at any time and without notice or bonus, the whole or any part of the Principal Amount. Where any such additional payment is made the Payment Dates of all remaining monthly instalments, if any, of the Principal Amount and interest thereon shall thereupon be advanced so that the Mortgagor shall pay the Amount of Each Periodic Payment in each and every month commencing with the month immediately following the month in which the additional principal is repaid and continuing until all the monies secured by this Mortgage shall have been fully paid.

These passages are all English. But what they have in common as English may be less important than the grounds on which they differ. Issuing from decidedly different moments in North American life, they voice different situations. No one could say which of these passages is "best," or which is proper English or which is not. But one can estimate the efficiency of each voice — each style of expression — in serving the situation from which it arises.

## I.2    Hearing genres

The passages above not only serve the situations in which they arise. They also embody them, representing certain recognizable occasions. So, when we hear these different voices, we also "hear" the setting in which they operate. The sounds of these passages signify typical moments which culture has produced: occasions of mating or marketplace, social distinction or professional publication. In each case, **situation** has **imprinted** English. It has pressed into the general shape of the language features which mark it for use in particular contexts. The imprint makes language characteristic — something we recognize as typical.

---

## exercise

Name the types of writing exemplified in Samples (1) - (6) in Section 1.1. Try to name the cultural situation which each serves.

---

To do the exercise above, you have to call on your knowledge of North American culture. Perhaps Sample 3 escaped you: your life experience may not have included contact with the situation which has produced a type of writing which we could call "request for recipe" and which appears in cooking magazines. (You may wonder why anyone would be interested in this person's holiday trip.) Or, if you are not from North America, you may be surprised by the boastfulness of the author of 2, and by his search for a person of a certain size. Hearing and speaking, reading and writing, we enact our experience of the world, as that experience has been shaped by culture.

As the diversity of the six samples shows, language is sensitive to situation. In recent years, this sensitivity has been captured and studied in new conceptualizations of **genre**. This textbook takes advantage of new reasoning about genre.

Before sketching the new genre theories, let us glance at the old. Chances are, if you have heard the term "genre" before, you heard it in connection with literary studies. Genre was, for instance, a way of saying poems, novels, and plays are different: they are different genres. So the notion of genre helped English departments keep courses separate, and made their curriculum orderly. For these purposes, **genre** was a docile concept, tending traditional ideas.

But then, as intellectual trends of the end of the twentieth century moved scholars in new directions, genre was wakened from its respectful service to study of forms and categories. These trends were moving people to take account of the social and political **contexts** of knowledge, and to calculate the degree to which the quality of statements about the world depended on who — in the world — was making the statement. Suddenly alert to new opportunities, genre offered itself as a way of thinking about the context-dependency of language.

While old ideas of genre had slipped into regarding only **form**, the new ideas insisted that it was not form alone that constituted genre, but form and situation:

$$\textbf{form} \quad + \quad \textbf{situation} \quad = \quad \textbf{genre}$$

Ways of speaking are webbed to their social context, and genres are routines of social behaviour: habits of acting in the world.

In this light, consider the thank-you note as a genre. People who know this genre not only know how to compose the note — what to mention, how much to say, how to begin, how to conclude, what kind of writing materials to use — but also when to do all this: soon after receipt of a certain type of gift from a person in a certain relation to the recipient. (So, in all probability, you would not send a thank-you note to your spouse for the gift of a laptop computer or to the local garage for the gift of a calendar or a window scraper. And if you delay sending a thank-you note where one is called for, you will feel — consciously or unconsciously — that you are failing to comply with the genre's norms, no matter how perfectly you compose the note itself.) The thank-you note genre is made up not only of a characteristic type of written expression but also of the *situation* in which it occurs. It is a way of acting in the world. People with know-how in this genre understand not only its form but also its situation. We could even say that, at some deep, unconscious level, these people also share an understanding of the role of the genre in larger social or cultural situations — systems of relationship amongst kin and friends, symbolized by the exchange of commodities and expressions of recognition.

Once wakened from its long servitude to the project of keeping poems and novels separate, genre no longer saw literary studies as its only — or even its best — place of work. It went abroad, and applied itself to many kinds of writing: auditors' reports, news accounts of violent crime, case reports in publications in veterinary medicine, architects' proposals, primary school show-and-tell sessions, and — most important to our interests — academic writing. At all these sites, genre was an avenue to investigating similarities in documents occurring in similar situations. The new conceptualizations of genre gave researchers a way of talking about these similarities not as rules but as signs of common ground amongst communities of readers and writers: shared attitudes, practices, positions in the world, habits of being.

So the style of Sample 5 comes about not because somebody followed rules, but because it embodies a widely recognized situation — property transaction in a market economy — through its conventional, list-like naming of qualities which the users of this genre recognize as valued and translatable into dollars. Views are good, so is newness, and so is a particular type of finishing on kitchen cabinets. The document assumes in readers a knowledge of local practices of transportation, and of laundering clothes. It assumes that readers will not interpret "6 appliances" as a sign of overcrowding in a small apartment, and that readers don't need to be told what these appliances are, or what they do. It also assumes in readers a knowledge of the customary practice of finding and disposing of a dwelling — contacting a broker specializing in this kind of transaction. In another culture, where people inherit their homes from their parents, or share them with co-workers, such a genre would not exist at all. Or some culture, somewhere, might value a home not for its appliances or parking spaces but for its human history: while in our culture we exchange homes with strangers, in some other place, dwellings might be identified with their residents. Then the genre accompanying property transactions might develop conventions for describing the dwelling's current occupant in appealing or prestigious terms.

Perhaps, a hundred years from now, scholars will examine personal ads or requests for recipes or mortgage documents to piece together vanished systems of association amongst people. Or they will look at the genres which report research in cognitive psychology or social history to understand the systems of relationship and production which held academic communities together in the 1990s.

## I.3  What is an essay, Alex?

Genre theory respects the diversity of expression and predicts that that diversity will reflect the complexities of the social order. Because people get together for a lot of different purposes, they will write and speak in a lot of different ways. And, as the world changes, so too will ways of writing and speaking change.

Writing instruction, however, has tended to focus on one type of writing: the schoolroom essay. Different kinds of assignments may produce slightly different versions of the essay — the "argument" essay, for example, or the "expository" essay — but, generally, when students arrive at college or university, they are experienced in producing a form of writing which serves schoolroom situations. Along with this experience, they absorb — from teachers, from handbooks, from public sentiments — ideas about writing. It should be "clear" and "concise," for example; it should not be "vague" or "wordy." Writing should also be "logical" and "well organized."

But then, at university, students encounter writing that would not be "clear" to most people, and writing that most people would not call "concise." And what seems to be "logical" in one discipline is not thought to be "logical" in another discipline. "Organization" in history is not "organization" in psychology, and neither resembles "organization" in an "argument" essay learned in composition class. After long experience in the schoolroom essay, and long contact with maxims about good writing, university students face many examples of expression which contradict the schoolroom tradition.

Genre theory tells us that the schoolroom essay — in its style — serves its situation. (Inspecting the situation, we might look for connections between the kinds of features prized in student essays and the larger function of the schoolroom itself. We might consider the schoolroom's role in socializing youth, in controlling the time of young people, in accrediting some and discrediting others, in scheduling some for further education — in well-paid occupations that structure and regulate social life — and scheduling others for poorly paid or low-prestige occupations.) Since the essay is a persistent genre, it must be doing an adequate job of serving and maintaining schoolroom situations. But the schoolroom situation and the university-classroom situation are different. Accordingly, the kind of writing that suits the schoolroom tends not to suit the university classroom.

The most important distinction between school situations and university situations is that the latter are located in research institutions. While students may see themselves as learners rather than researchers, they nevertheless do their learning under the direction of people who are trained as researchers and who read and write research publications. The knowledge students acquire is the kind of knowledge that comes from the techniques of inquiry developed by the various academic disciplines. We could go so far as to say that the very wording of the facts and concepts students must absorb derives from research practice: the routines, habits, and values which motivate scholars to do the work they do. This wording represents research communities' beliefs and their members' shared techniques for interpreting the world. At the same time, such wording is also the medium in which students must work.

If university students are not writing schoolroom essays, what are they writing? What wordings will represent the student's position in the university situation? While it would be too much to say that students should write research articles, it is not too much to say that their writing can share features of research writing. The style of the information they encounter in their university courses is shaped by the research situations which produced it. So, as students work with this information, producing knowledge themselves, the style of the research genres is the most appropriate wording for them to adopt. And while the wording of research writing shares some features with the schoolroom essay — both are, after all, English — the differences are perhaps more meaningful than the similarities. (Equally, as you may already have found out, the styles of the different disciplines share many features, but the differences can be meaningful, and can have consequences.)

This book puts student writers in touch with the wording of the research genres. It makes available to student writers salient features of scholarly expression — features which define the scholarly genres and represent academic situations.

# exercise

The styles of expression in Samples (1) to (6) differ in many respects. In the chapters which follow, you will acquire means of identifying and replicating salient features of (1) and (4) — the two samples from research genres. But you might begin to develop your awareness of style here by inspecting and comparing all six samples. First, and most broadly, what distinguishes (1) and (4) from the others? Second, and more narrowly, can you distinguish between the style of (1) and (4)? (Sample (4) is the first paragraph of the article's introduction; Sample (1) is the sixth paragraph of the article's introduction.) In approaching this task, you might take into account these features:

(a) ways the writers are represented in the text (most obviously, do they mention themselves?);

(b) words — their commonness (would they show up in, for example, conversation between neighbours?), their recurrence (to what degree do these writers repeat the same words?) — and sentences — their length, completeness;

(c) capitals, parentheses, names, numbers.

How would you describe the relation between writer and reader in each of these samples?

# Notes

1      Alice J. O'Toole, Kenneth A. Deffenbacher, Dominique
       Valentin and Hervé Abdi 1994 Structural aspects of face
       recognition and the other-race effect. *Memory and Cogni-
       tion* 22, 2, 209.

2      Nicole H. Rafter 1992 Claims-making and socio-cultural
       context in the first U.S. eugenics campaign. Social Prob-
       lems 39, 1, 17.

# 2

# Summarizing what you have read: Part One

## 2.1  The functions of summary

Summarizing something you have read may seem like a humble activity — neither a very creative thing to do nor one where you can show your independent thinking. But summary deserves respect, for several reasons.

For one thing, summary is not easy. It requires that you repeat someone else's ideas in a shorter form. At first, brevity can seem to be a benefit.

only 400 words? Easy! No problem!

But the process of reduction can turn out to be challenging, and students can find themselves attaching an apology to their summaries.

Even professional scholars can have a hard time composing a review (a form of summary) to fit an editor's prescribed word length. (They too are liable to attach an apology or excuse.) Also, the materials students and scholars summarize is often complicated. Getting an accurate summary can involve strenuous efforts of understanding.

So we can respect summary because it is hard. But there are other reasons for developing summarizing skills and practising summary. These have to do with the traditions of both the university classroom and the larger academic community.

Classroom experience depends heavily on turning reading into writing. Courses have reading lists; university libraries are full of more reading waiting to be turned into more writing. Assignments presume this process. In fact, this dependence is probably the most important distinction between the schoolroom essay and the academic essay. Whereas on many occasions a schoolroom composition can thrive on stand-alone argument — an authoritatively voiced "opinion" — an academic paper is far from alone in its voice. It depends on the sounds of other voices and, in certain ways we will be investigating, other authorities. Successful academic writing manages the sounds of the other voices — through skilful summary. Without summarizing skills, you can find yourself rambling on and on, long-windedly reproducing your reading, until your own voice is drowned out, and your own position engulfed. You will end up submitting a 15-page paper when an eight-page paper was assigned. And what your reader will remember is your essay's long repetition of what other writers say.

This dependence on reading may seem like a handicap peculiar to students — a reflection of their own lack of authority. This is not so. On the contrary, the relation between reading and writing in the classroom replicates conditions in the scholarly community. As writers themselves, your instructors depend on reading, just as you do. Actually, we could say that they are *more* dependent on reading than you are: while an assignment in itself gives you the right to speak, professional scholars must find in *what has already been written* justification for their own writing. In later chapters, we will be looking at the complexities of these justifications and their implications for student writing. We will also consider the social and political implications of these complex sanctions on speech. In the meantime, rest assured that your situation — as a writer positioned amongst even hundreds of pages of what has already been written — is an aspect of scholarly experience itself, and near its very heart.

## 2.2 Summary and the student writer

Setting aside some special forms of summary, such as the review-article or the abstract, or the bibliographical essay, we could say that, for the professional scholar, summary is not a **genre** as genre has been defined in Chapter One. If she is asked "What are you working on?" a professor is not likely to say "a summary." She will probably say "an article," "a paper," or "a book," or maybe "a proposal," naming one of the main genres in use in the scholarly community. For the professional scholar, summary is a kind of "sub-genre," an activity which contributes to the production of various genres. So, while at certain stages in the production of an article or a book, a scholar might be, in truth, "summarizing," her goal is not "summary." The scholarly community, at this point in its history, does not use summary as a genre.

Often, this is also the case for the student too. He is writing an **essay** or an **examination**, although summary will probably contribute to the final product. But sometimes the student, unlike the professional scholar, can be said to be writing summary as an end product: he is asked to account for a particular article or book. For the student, summary is one of the genres of academic writing.

So, if summary is a genre in the university classroom, we might ask what functions it serves, to better understand the features of successful summary.

First of all, we should admit that the genre serves as a form of test. The readers of your work not only read it but also explicitly judge it. A good summary shows a knowledgeable reader that the writer understands something important.

Next we should face the facts involved in that idea of the "knowledgeable" reader.

## 2.3    Where have I heard this before?

Your instructors not only mark your work, but also assign the reading preliminary to it. And they make a career of giving lectures and seminars on the topic. Your economics instructor knows all about the Canadian banking system; your philosophy teacher already knows about British Idealism. You could say that they have heard it all before.

These knowledgeable people can be difficult readers to address. How can you possibly capture their interest? You may imagine them as bored.

But we know that instructors can and do respond cheerfully and positively to writing on subjects with which they are very familiar.

One reason instructors don't mind (and even enjoy) reading what they already know is that they are used to it — and not just as readers of student writing. As scholars, they read many publications which summarize books and articles they themselves have read (and maybe even summarized in their own writing). Scholarly writing develops from other scholarly writing. When scholars come across good summary — whether in student writing or in publication — they appreciate its virtues. They recognize the sound of it, and admire efficient, accurate representation of other people's research and reasoning.

The rest of this chapter and the next chapter are about producing that kind of summary.

## 2.4    You and your sources

The relation between one person's speech and another person's representation of that speech is complicated. Some researchers specialize in studying the procedures by which someone says what someone else has already said; they look at the features which mark speech as not belonging to the speaker, and the conditions which prompt people to report others' statements. And this is not only a complicated topic but also an interesting one because many genres — news broadcasts, journalism, fiction, gossip — are made of reported speech.

Reported speech is also a central, defining feature of scholarly writing. We will begin to address its complications by thinking about the extreme case of the relation between the writer and his sources: copying. We will go back to a site where copying is indigenous.

Maybe in elementary school you were asked to do a "report" on South America, or the animals of Africa. You didn't know anything about either of these subjects. So you consulted the encyclopedia. And you copied out parts of it — but only parts, because you couldn't fit 10,000-word encyclopedia articles into a ten-page report.

Jason writes a report on South America

The copied parts sounded good. After all, they were written by grown-up experts. But, put together in this new document, they made strange reading. One page or paragraph would discuss the exports of Bolivia, while the next would send the reader into a surprisingly detailed description of the climate of Tierra del Fuego. And the same page might offer a neatly copied account of a harvest festival. Although the ten-page report was summary (it was shorter than the encyclopedia), and it was accurate in a sense (it was copied word-for-word from an authoritative source), it didn't really make sense.

Somehow, dressed up with maps and pictures, these documents served their purpose. They functioned as intended in the elementary-school classroom. The culture of the university classroom is different, of course, and what succeeded in the elementary schoolroom doesn't succeed there. Nobody expects that it would.

But still we can learn from this early and extreme case of dependence on sources. The process of writing the report on South America (a process cultivated in that particular social context) encouraged copying, and copying produced a certain text structure. That text structure, evidently suited to its context, was full of gaps and cracks: hard to read. Maybe the elementary-school report genre is not meant to be read in the ordinary way, so the fractures produced by copying didn't matter. But summaries produced at university *are* meant to be read, very attentively, and, at the same time, you are in a position not dissimilar to the author of the report on South America: dependent on sources. In that position, you are vulnerable to the same hazards of *copying* , although we may not use such a coarse term for the activity. Whenever you are dependent on sources, any word-for-word repetition of the original risks incoherence. In the next section, we will look at why this is so.

## 2.5   Your own words

From time to time in your schooling, you have probably been told to "use your own words" to express information gathered from written sources. Maybe your teacher told you this to prevent copying, or to see if you really understood what you had read, or to check on your writing skills. Whatever the motivation, this instruction turns out to be good advice. Follow it and you are more likely to produce readable texts.

Sometimes, however, when you are immersed in the reasoning of another writer's argument, copying may seem a very practical solution to the problems presented by the process of putting reading to use. The original author's sentences which express the point so well are tempting: why not just repeat them?

There is a good reason for not just repeating them. They are convincing and impressive *in context*, supported, explained, modified, extended and connected by all the material that surrounds them. *Out of context*, they are not nearly so powerful. Figure 1 shows important sentences (★★★★★★) occurring in the context of supporting ideas (〜〜〜). The arrow (⟶) yields a summary that copies the important sentences.

FIGURE 1     **Original source**           **Summary that copies important sentences**

〜〜〜★★★★★〜〜〜

〜〜〜〜〜〜〜   ⟶   ★★★★★ ★★★★★★ ★★★★★

★★★★★★〜〜〜〜

〜〜〜〜〜〜★★★★

*You* have read all the 〜〜〜〜. It is before you as you repeat that important sentence. But your reader doesn't have that material in mind. Consequently, the ★★★★★ nuggets that you have saved are stranded. Like a marooned sailor, they can seem eccentric. Just as a Grade-Six explanation of the climate of Tierra del Fuego sent an abrupt and erratic signal to the reader, who had no sense of the context it came from, these stranded sentences can be odd things, difficult to grasp.

It is important to get a sense of this situation from the reader's point of view. So we are going to set ourselves up as readers of copied-out points. Sample 1 below presents key sentences, just about word-for-word, from a 700-word passage by John Fiske and John Hartley which analyzes the nature of TV violence. (The original passage occurs in *Reading Television* [1982]; it appears as a whole in Chapter Three, where it is the basis for a summary exercise.) Sample 1 copies the important sentences in the order in which they appear; they occur at roughly equivalent intervals in the original passage. *In context*, they express important ideas — or parts of important ideas —

that Fiske and Hartley want to get across. But *out of context* they do not cooperate with one another; they make a difficult, disjointed text. As readers of Sample 1, we face a text that only copies important points from the original.

PASSAGE I    Violent figures are the most masculine, and the victims the least masculine and the oldest. The television message system is a system of "cultural indicators" by which the value structure of society is symbolically represented. Violence on television is not a direct representation of real-life violence. The criminal is distinguished from the hero primarily by his inefficiency and his social group.

The copying has taken Fiske and Hartley's words out of their habitat — out of the environment of repetition, explanation, examples, and logical connectives that made them intelligible and convincing to the reader of the whole passage. Stranded outside this habitat, the sentences are confusing rather than convincing: what is the connection between age and value structure? Between age and efficiency? Between efficiency and TV not being "real"?

As a copier, the summarizer may still have that connective material in mind, so he may not notice the discontinuities and gaps in what he offers his reader. But, as readers, we do notice the gaps. At best, we just skim over the passage as not worth the trouble. At worst, we object to its jumps from one notion to another. (In Chapter Three, we do a better job of summarizing the original, taking account of our readers' needs.)

We know, then, that the copying represented in Figure 1 and exemplified in Sample 1 doesn't work. In carrying forward material from another source, using *your own words* is more than just complying with a teacher's rule. It is a matter of making yourself intelligible to your readers, even when you are summarizing someone else's ideas.

Summary makes something new. The material from the original text takes on a new form to fit a new context. Whereas copying can be represented by Figure 1, Figure 2 schematizes the activity of summary. The material yielded by the arrow (→) is no longer just a repetition (****) of important sentences (****), but a new form (•••) of the original ideas.

FIGURE 2    **Original source**        **Summary that con-**
**veys important ideas**
**in a new form**

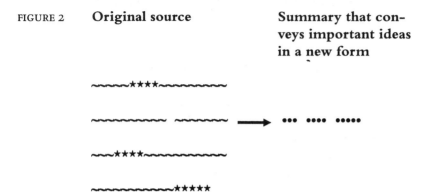

The rest of this chapter introduces ideas about prose structure that will help you make accurate, readable summaries. The
next chapter offers a method for summary that will help you
avoid copying and help you find your own words. Both sections
are devoted to providing you with some means of **control** over
the situation of being dependent on sources — control that the
author of the report on South America didn't have.

## 2.6   Up and down: levels in prose

To summarize effectively, you have to recover and express the
essential elements of what you have read, and get rid of the rest.
You have to distinguish between conceptually dominant and
conceptually subordinate material — roughly speaking, the
difference between a main point and a lesser point. As it happens, some genres are easier to summarize than others. I would
estimate that personal letters, auditors' reports, some kinds of
newspaper articles, and tourist brochures would be hard to summarize. Maybe surprisingly, in view of their length and complexity, scholarly publications are not so hard. Why is this?

The answer has to do with the typical structure of scholarly
writing. While it is probable that all genres can be analyzed for
their conceptual levels, scholarly prose exposes its conceptual

levels on the surface. We will continue to pursue this matter of conceptual levels in later chapters. We will consider its effects on readers and how they come to understand what is written. We will also consider how some conceptually dominant terms come to acquire high value in different disciplines. In the meantime, we will approach the system of levels as important in thinking about summary.

If you recognize the levels of information in your reading, and if you can discover the level of expression that dominates, you will have found a guide to making summary. You will have found a means of conserving essential material and trimming away less essential material, producing a summary that is both accurate and economical. Sample 1, which only copied from the TV violence passage, shows that this conserving and trimming is not simply a matter of keeping some things intact and throwing other things away. Instead, it is a matter of construction: making a text that conserves essentials in a new form.

## 2.6.1    *What the levels look like*

To put it simply, the highest level is the most general. It accommodates all the lower levels. Here is a brief passage with prominent levels of generalization. It begins at a high level of generality — ideas about individuals and institutions — and descends to a much lower level: reference to a particular clinic in London.

PASSAGE 2

Institutional buildings rise in people's neighbourhoods, marking the connection between public and private domains. The architecture of community hospitals expresses institutional health strategies addressed to individual patients. Like a family caring for its members, the hospital cares for members of the community. But the scale of care is not domestic and private, like family care, but civic and public. This conflict in scale can disorient and alienate the patient, confusing or coercing him, adding to his distress. The hospital building itself focusses these conflicts in scale at the interface between public presence and private life, and some hospital design now tries to rationalize the interface, making it readable and clear rather than confusing and imposing. At the Bethnal Green Health Centre in London, architectural design tries to harmonize the institutional prominence with personal outlook.

The passage begins by introducing its "highest" concepts: the connections between *private* and *public* domains, between *individuals* and *institutions*. These highest concepts generalize what comes next: *hospitals* (one kind of institution) and *patients* (one form that individuals can take); *conflicts of scale* (one kind of connection) and *rationalized interface* (another form of connection). Some of these second-level generalities are further specified before the passage descends to its lowest levels: conflicts of scale are narrowed to *disorientation, alienation, coercion*, while rationalized interfaces narrow to *clarity* and *readability*. Finally, at the lowest level of generality, the passage reaches its greatest specificity, mentioning one health-care building in particular: Bethnal Green Health Centre.

We can roughly diagram this descent through levels of generalization, constructing a picture of the up-and-down relationships among ideas and mentions:

FIGURE 3    connections        public presence        private life

| conflicts in scale | rationalized interface | institutional buildings | people's neighbourhooods |
|---|---|---|---|
| | | hospital | patient |
| | | Bethnal Green Health Centre | |

This diagram is only a rough sketch of the passage's structure. Other analysts might have found fewer levels or more, or used other words to identify the levels. But, even so, constructing and examining such diagrams can give us a feel for the patterns that shape our experience as readers, as we make our way from general claims to specific references and back again.

This passage about hospitals and patients might have extended itself even further through the range of generalization. The version which follows rises one level higher at the beginning, and descends to even more specificity at the end, mentioning site dimensions, holes in the wall, waiting rooms, and examination rooms.

PASSAGE 3    In the landscapes of modern urban communities, public systems connect with private lives; individual roles intersect with civic institutions. Institutional buildings rise in people's neighbourhoods, marking the connection between public and private domains. A school's facade, for example, expresses large-scale social priorities; its interior interprets those priorities in light of the needs of individual students. Similarly, the community hospital's architecture expresses institutional health strategies addressed to the individual patient. Like a family caring for its members, the hospital cares for members of the community. But the scale of care is not domestic and private, like family care, but civic and public. This conflict in scale can disorient and alienate the patient, confusing or coercing him, adding to his distress. The hospital building itself focusses these conflicts of scale at the interface between public presence and private life, and some hospital design now tries to rationalize the interface, making it readable and clear rather than confusing and imposing. At the Bethnal Green Health Centre in London, architectural design seeks to harmonize institutional prominence with personal outlook. The Centre's site itself blends domestic and public scale: while the site's depth is 14m — only a domestic expanse — its length is 60m, and the building spans this frontage with civic mass. To orient visitors to the arrangement of the building, circular holes in wing walls allow people to approach from the rear (actually on the main street) and see through to the building's front. In effect, the holes say, "Come around to the other side and you'll see the main entrance." Inside, three separate waiting rooms provide immediate and recognizable access to nurses' and specialists' examination rooms. From the waiting room, clients can see where they will be going, and, when they emerge from their consultation, they can quickly orient themselves and recognize the route back to the waiting room and exit.

A revision of the first diagram illustrates the reader's encounter with this stretched-out range of generality.

FIGURE 4                        urban communities

connection            public systems            private lives
conflicts    harmony       institutional buildings
in scale

                          schools    hospitals       students       patients
confusion  clarity        hospital buildings
                          London's Bethnal Green       Bethnal patients
                          Health Centre

                14x60m site, holes, waiting
                rooms, specialists' rooms

This diagram represents the passage's development: the system of assertions which support and expand one another. When your instructors ask that you "develop" your ideas further, they are reacting to the absence of such a pattern of levels in your writing. Sometimes they will be looking for more specific assertions to support high-level claims; other times they will be looking for more high-level claims to explain specific mentions.

Moreover, stretches across the range of generalization are characteristic of scholarly discourse. You will rarely encounter such stretches in the compact form of Passage 3, which is an example I made up from a series of articles. But you will often find yourself reading in the midst of this kind of movement through levels of generality.

Passages 2 and 3 are about how people feel when they go to a clinic or hospital — how a sick person feels about approaching a reception desk in a public building full of corridors and medical equipment. There are many ways to talk about feelings like that: a cartoon might make a joke of feelings of anxiety and alienation; a personal conversation might express the patient's distress or confusion; a letter to the editor might complain about the way patients are treated under a current government. Each of these genres has its own characteristics, and so do the scholarly genres have their own characteristics. But unlike the other genres, the scholarly genres typically stretch out across the range of generality, reaching high levels of conceptualization (concepts of public and private) and touching low levels of specificity (the position of a particular clinic's waiting rooms in relation to its examination rooms). This stretching across ranges of generality is one of the distinguishing features of academic writing, and it is involved with other important features, like citation and dependence on sources, and even sentence-level style.

This stretching is something you get used to in your university reading, and something you will develop in your own university writing. To help you acclimatize yourself to these conditions, we will reflect on what this system of levels means to us as readers of scholarly prose, and then as writers of summary.

## 2.6.2     *Reading through the levels*

Inspecting Figure 4, we notice that the descent in the centre of the diagram — from *urban communities* through *public systems* to *specialists' rooms* and *waiting rooms* — is deeper than elsewhere, dropping through seven levels of generality. If we diagram the same information another way, we get an idea of what such a descent feels like in the reading process. Taking into account the reading process, where things happen one after another, this diagram will show us making our way through the text, going from one level to the next.

Figure 5 shows what we could call the *landscape* or *topography* of the text, revealing the reader's experience of its up and downs. Figure 5 traces the *reader's path*. While the first kind of diagram showed the conceptual organization of the text as it exists all at once, the topography diagram shows that conceptual organization as the reader experiences it over time.

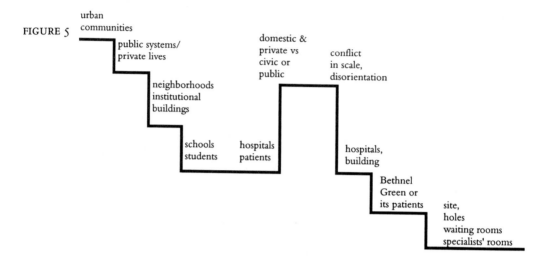

FIGURE 5

This topography of the text gives us some feeling of what happens to us as readers as we travel through a text's landscape. A fully developed passage will lead us up and down through several levels. And if we are going to get the whole picture, we are better off if we have some sense of where we are — at a summit, deep in a valley, lingering briefly on a plateau — as we make our way through our reading.

## 2.6.3 *Summarizing the levels*

Both kinds of diagram help us understand what happens to us as readers. Both help us understand the kind of work the text makes us do. But both kinds of diagram also help us understand our role as summarizers — as writers. Figure 4 shows how material *spreads* at the bottom, at the lowest levels of generality. Figure 5 shows us that getting down to and up from the lower levels is *time-consuming*. Summary, in its brevity, cannot accommodate this spreading, time-consuming material. To summarize, we will have to get rid of *waiting rooms*, *site dimensions*, and *holes* in the wall. Common sense will support what the diagrams tell us: a reader who came away from the health-care-architecture passage saying that the crucial issue was about going from the waiting room to the examination room would have missed the point.

Yet so too would the reader who hung on to only the highest level of generality have missed the point. The reader who claimed that the gist of the passage was the idea that there are connections in urban landscapes would not be summarizing accurately. That reader would have missed the point *this* passage makes about connections in the urban landscape. There are many things somebody could say about public and private meeting points in urban settings: the reader who got the point would be able to say what *this* writer claimed about such connections and meeting points. Since we can't simply repeat all the assertions this writer makes about urban connections (our writing then would not be summary), we have to reconstruct this material into a new form, using our own words.

## exercise

Write one or two sentences (50-60 words) which summarize passage (3). Compose your summary in such as way as to answer this kind of question:

A sample summary appears at the end of this chapter, along with an explanation of its features and their relationship to the original.

## 2.6.4 Selecting to communicate: between triviality and platitude

The concept of levels of generality tells us something about the selective nature of communication. At the lowest and most specific level, we could present **total information**: for example, an exhaustive description of every corridor, doorway, and examination room in the Bethnal Green hospital. Or a complete report of every visit made by every patient. But those kinds of descriptions would not communicate. Readers can't tolerate such completeness, except under rare and specialized circumstances (as, for example, when a commission of inquiry goes over every document in an organization's files). When these rare conditions are not in effect, expressions that dwells endlessly on specifics runs the risk of being trivial.

Working at the end of the scale opposite to triviality, we could go higher than the general claim that "[i]n the landscapes of modern urban communities, public systems connect with private lives." We could top that by saying something like, "In life there are many connections." Few people would disagree with this idea. But this kind of saying does not communicate information. Just as a description of every corridor and doorway and examination room in Bethnal Green Health Centre can't get through to the reader, neither can a big, loose claim about connections in life. It's a platitude.

Platitudes express what everybody already "knows" — or at least would not bother to actively dispute. Platitudes have little information value, although they can stimulate feelings of unanimity and rapport among members of social groups seeking to reaffirm their ties with one another. In conversation, for example, one speaker might express his acceptance of another speaker's anecdote by uttering a platitude: "Well, isn't life funny!" Or a valedictory speaker may utter predictable platitudes to arouse good feelings of affinity among members of the audience: "In future years, we will all look back on these days."

Academic writers try to avoid both platitudes and triviality, and work between the two extremes of *no information* (platitudes) and *total information* (triviality). But even professional scholarly writers, accustomed to the range between these extremes, can worry on the one hand that what they are saying is, at some level, self-evident ("My article is about how things change over time") or, on the other hand, that readers will not be able to stand going over all the details ("These are all the changes from 1946 to 1956").

## exercise

The following five passages give you an opportunity to practise investigating the levels of prose and to practise writing summaries. For each passage

1. construct a tree diagram like those in Figures (3) and (4), to show the arrangement of concepts from the highest level of generality to the lowest level;

2. construct a map like that in Figure (5), to show the reader's experience of the levels of generality;

3. write a summary.

### On the correctness of diagrams:

Sketching the diagrams and maps is only a way of encountering certain characteristics of writing which are good to think about from time to time. Practice in diagramming and mapping techniques is not meant to train you as an analyst, but only to make you aware of some of the sources of your experience as a reader, and, in turn, to help you locate the essentials that are the target of your own writing and summarizing. Moreover, you will find that the passages below are not as easy to schematize as the Bethnal

Green passage. "Bethnal Green" was concocted and compressed from a longer text, and cleaned up to demonstrate at a glance the range of generality. In the passages which follow, taken intact from published scholarship, some levels may seem very crowded, and hard to regulate. Do your best to sort them out, but don't feel obliged to produce such tidy schemes as those which represent "Bethnal Green." After all, the goal is to illuminate the actual structures of information in academic writing, and to pave the way to effective summary.

Your maps and tree diagrams may differ from those your classmates construct. Maybe they did a better job; maybe you did a better job, noticing things they missed. But it is also possible that the differences come from differences in your reading experiences. There is no reason to try to erase these differences as long as you can justify them from the original. (Differences can make you go back and check the original, to reconcile these natural diversities and understand their source. So it's good to compare your analyses with others'.) Moreover, just as any reading is a work of interpretation, so too analysis of this sort is also interpretive.

## On the length of summaries:

There is no single correct ratio between original and summary. In your reading, you may come across a single sentence that summarizes a whole book. Or, in your own writing tasks, you might fulfil an assignment by using 1000 words to summarize a 15-page article.

In this exercise, try to reduce the passages to 15%-25% of their original length.

PASSAGE A  **"Finsbury"**

Democracy . . . is surely to do with freedom of information, or, architecturally speaking, about legibility of organisation, explicitness of intention, in short, about the admission of causality. Finsbury Health Care Centre is saturated with such ideals. The entrance is unmistakable, surmounted by its municipal crest like a seal of guarantee — pro bono publico — and approached by a comfortable ramp that conveys you directly to reception, minimising the distance from the front door to a smiling face. The waiting area is self-evident, the lavatories at once visible but discreet. The circulation allows for easy mental mapping wherever you are in the building, so providing a simple reference system back to one's point of departure. The causal chain of interconnected decision leads on and on, through the structure, the servicing strategy, the curtain walling, providing a sort of continuous running commentary — "This is so because this is so. . . ." Even otherwise bare plaster is recruited to the cause, being originally adorned with murals by Gordon Cullen proclaiming such truths as "Chest Diseases are Preventable and Curable" as if to eradicate any lingering superstition that the cause of such afflictions was a divine mystery.

John Allan 1988 Finsbury at 50: Caring and causality. *Architectural Record*.

PASSAGE B ## "Creole"

Today, even in scientific spheres, a persistent stigma is attached to creole languages.[1] Because their formative period was relatively recent, the 17th and 18th centuries, they are often seen as not yet fully formed complex languages. The descriptions of creole languages in some linguistic circles are similar to the attitudes of many creole speakers toward their languages. These languages are described as "reduced," simple, and easy to learn; lacking in abstract terms, they are inadequate for scientific, philosophical, and logical operations. For most of their histories, creole languages have not been considered adequate for government, schooling or Western religious services.

The effect of pseudoscientific arguments or preconceived emotional ideas are evident in the negative attitudes lay persons generally hold toward creole languages and their speakers, and are revealed by the many pejorative terms used by both native and non-native speakers alike. Folk terminologies describe the French lexicon creoles as "broken French," "patois," "dialects," or "jargons," and many assume that creole languages are "diminished," "reduced," "deformed," "impoverished," "vitiated," "bastard" forms of the European standard languages that contributed to their birth.[2] Many educated and middle-class Haitians, members of the petite-bourgeoisie, as well as Haitian elites, view kreyòl [creole] as a simplified form of French at best. Many claim it is not a real language at all, but a mixture of languages without a grammar. The different varieties of kreyòl are viewed by Haitians of these social categories with a great deal of ambivalence. *Kreyòl rèk* [rough creole] and *gwo kreyòl* [vulgar creole] are often associated with pejorative connotations regarding the sounds (harsh, not harmonious, guttural, deformed), the grammatical features (debased, corrupted, elementary, lacking complexity), the social origin of the speakers (rural, lower class), and defects usually attributed to the speakers themselves (coarse, clumsy, stupid, illiterate, uneducated). On the positive side, the same varieties have been associated with national identity, authenticity, independence, sincerity, and trustworthiness. Much of this is connected to romantic notions about rural people — rough, coarse, but also authentic, real.

1   Diamond's (1991) article in *Natural History* titled "Reinventions of Human Language: Children Forced to Reevolve Grammar Thereby Reveal Our Brain's Blueprint for Language" includes the following:

> Between human languages and the vocalizations of any animal lies a seemingly unbridgeable gulf. . . . One approach to bridging this gulf is to ask whether some people, deprived of the opportunity to hear any of our fully evolved modern languages, ever spontaneously invented a primitive language . . . Children . . . placed in a situation comparable to that of the wolf-boy . . . hearing adults around them speaking a grossly simplified and variable form of language somewhat similar to what children themselves usually speak around the age of two . . . proceeded unconsciously to evolve their own language, far advanced over vervet communication but simpler than *normal* languages. These new languages were the ones commonly known as creoles. [p. 23, emphasis added]

2   Auguste Brun, a French scholar writing in the early part of the 20th century, claimed that "une langue est un dialecte qui a réussi. Un patois est un langue qui s'est dégradée" (quoted in Pressoir 1958:27). (A language is a dialect that has been successful. A patois is a language that

has deteriorated.) Such a view is still held by some educated Haitians today.

Bambi B. Schieffelin and Rachelle Charlier Doucet 1994 The "real" Haitian creole: ideology, metalinguistics, and orthographic choice. *American Ethnologist* 21 (1), 176-200, 181-82.

## "Taiwan"

Although there are exceptions, the small-to-medium size, single-unit firm is so much the rule in Taiwan that when a family business becomes successful the pattern of investment is not to attempt vertical integration in order to control the marketplace, but rather is to diversify by starting a series of unrelated firms that share neither account books nor management. From a detailed survey of the 96 largest business groups (jituanqiye) in Taiwan, we find that 59% of them are owned and controlled by family groups (Zhonghua Zhengxinso 1985). Partnerships among unrelated individuals, which, as Wong Sui-lun (1985) points out, will likely turn into family-based business organizations in the next generation, account for 38%. An example of such a family-controlled business group is the Cai family enterprise, until recently the second largest private holding in Taiwan.[1] The family business included over 100 separate firms, the management of which was divided into eight groupings of unrelated businesses run by different family members, each of whom kept a separate account book (Chen 1985, pp. 13-17).

1  The family enterprise was rocked by scandals in the early months of 1985. The scandal forced the family to open their books and to account for their economic success. For one of the better descriptions of the Cai family enterprise, see Chen (1985).

Gary G. Hamilton and Nicole Woolsey Biggart 1988 Market, culture, and authority: A comparative analysis of management and organization in the Far East. *American Journal of Sociology* 94, 252-294.

## "Vocal music"

"Humanization" was a pedagogical device which involved the development of capacities for feeling and moral behaviour. While these capacities were ethically and aesthetically pleasing to school reformers, they were also political instruments for the development of new modes of self-regulation. The "moral" attitude which this pedagogy sought was a way of relating to others and also an ethically-founded acceptance of and affection for existing political forms. The "humanist" pedagogy contains, to a large degree, the key to the explanation of Ryerson's curricular reforms — especially his adamant opposition to that instrument of rote learning par excellence, the spelling book. The thrust of pedagogy upon curriculum is perhaps nowhere more evident than in the matter of vocal music. "All men," Ryerson quoted in his argument for teaching vocal music in the elementary schools, "have been endowed with a susceptibility to the influence of music." [1] Vocal music was an important and intrinsically pleasing avenue to the faculties. Teaching children moral songs could displace the ribald and frivolous amusements they pursued, while turning their recreation into a means of instruction. "Music," if correctly used, could "refine and humanize the pupils." Ryerson approvingly quoted the English Privy Council Committee on Education which claimed that since the common schools of Germany had begun to teach workers to sing, "the 'degrading habits of intoxication' so common there had been much reduced."

Ryerson's humanistic and inductive pedagogy was an instrument and tactic aimed at developing the senses so they could be enlisted to make contact with human energy. Humanistic education was not a form of social control in any simple sense. It sought not to repress workers or students by feeding them doses of propaganda or ideology, but rather to develop their capacities for feeling and moral behaviour. Students were to become self-disciplining individuals who behaved not out of fear but because their experience at school had created in them certain moral forms for which they had a positive affection. In Ryerson's pedagogy, the student would have no desire to oppose the process of education and no grounds upon which to do so. Education would be intrinsically pleasing to the student and in consequence he or she would become the character sought by pedagogy. Education would produce in the population habits, dispositions and loyalties of a sort congenial to the state and to representative government. The problem of governance faced by generations of conservative educational critics would vanish: political rule would no longer be dependent upon "social control," coercion, terror, or bribery. One would be able to appeal to the "higher sentiments" of the subject formed by education; the state would rule by appeals to the emotions and intellect of the educated population.

1 Egerton Ryerson, Report on a System of Public Elementary Instruction for Upper Canada. 1847. All other quotations in the passage are also from this source.

Bruce Curtis 1987 Preconditions of the Canadian state: Education reform and the construction of a public in Upper Canada, 1837-1846. In *The "Benevolent" State: The Growth of Welfare in Canada*, ed. Allan Muscovitch and Jim Albert. Toronto: Garamond, 57-58.

PASSAGE E    **"Heterosexuality"**

Social practices, norms, and institutions are designed to meet heterosexual systems' need to produce sex/gender dimorphism — masculine males and feminine females — so that desire can then be heterosexualized. Gendered behaviorial norms, gendered rites of passage, a sexual division of labor, and the like produce differently gendered persons out of differently sexed persons. Prohibitions against gender crossing (e.g., against cross-dressing, effeminacy in men, mannishness in women) also help sustain the dimorphism necessary to heterosexualize desire.

Children and especially adolescents are carefully prepared for heterosexual interaction. They are given heterosexual sex education, advice for attracting the opposite sex, norms of heterosexual behavior, and appropriate social occasions (such as dances or dating rituals) for enacting desire. Adult heterosexuality is further sustained through erotica and pornography, heterosexualized humor, heterosexualized dress, romance novels, and so on.

Heterosexual societies take it for granted that men and women will bond in an intimate relationship ultimately founding a family. As a result, social conventions, economic arrangements, and the legal structure treat the heterosexual couple as a single, and singularly important, social unit. The couple is represented linguistically (boyfriend-girlfriend, husband-wife) and is treated socially as a single unit (e.g., in joint invitations or in receiving joint gifts). It is legally licensed and legally supported through such entitlements as communal property, joint custody or adoption of children, and the power to give proxy consent within the couple. The couple is also recognized in the occupational structure via such provisions as spousal health care benefits and restrictions on nepotism. Multiple practices and institutions help heterosexual individuals to couple and create families and support the continuation of those couples and couple-based families. These include dating services, match-makers, introductions to eligible partners, premarital counseling, marriage counseling, marriage and divorce law, adoption serv-ices, reproductive technologies, family rates, family health care benefits, tax deductions for married couples, and so on.

The sum total of all the social, economic, and legal arrange-ments that support the sexual and relational coupling of men with women constitutes heterosexual privilege. And it is privilege of a peculiar sort. Heterosexuals do not simply claim *greater* socio-po-litico-legal standing than nonheterosexuals. They claim as natural and normal an arrangement where *only* heterosexuals have socio-politico-legal standing. Lesbians and gay men are not recognized as social beings because they cannot enter into the most basic so-cial unit, the male-female couple. Within heterosexual systems the only social arrangements that apply to nonheterosexuals are elimi-native in nature. The coercive force of the criminal law, institution-alized discrimination, "therapeutic" treatment, and individual prejudice and violence is marshalled against the existence of lesbi-ans and gay men. At best, lesbians and gay men have negative so-cial reality. Lesbians are not-women engaged in nonsex with non-relationships that may constitute a nonfamily.

Cheshire Calhoun 1994 Separating lesbian theory from feminist theory *Eth-ics* 104, 558-581,579-80

## 2.6.5  *Styles of levels*

By analyzing and summarizing the passages above, you get a feel for how prose can move through levels of generality. You may have noticed as well that not all the passages made exactly the same kinds of moves. Passage (a) "Finsbury," for example, drops abruptly from very high conceptual levels — *democracy* — to very low levels — *lavatories* and *plaster.* The deepest descent to specifics in Passage (c) "Taiwan" occurs in a footnote, after passing through levels of statistics. The qualities of low levels differ, too: in "Creole" lows are made up of a series of terms people use to describe a language; in "Vocal music" the lowest point seems to be Ryerson's ideas about singing; in "Heterosexuality" the lows are lists of examples of particular social practices. The patterns of high levels also differ amongst the passages. Both "Vocal music" and "Heterosexuality" present a lot of high-level terms — *moral and political forms, self-regulation, pedagogy, education* and *political rule* in "Vocal music"; *social practices, norms, institutions, privilege, socio-politico-legal standing* in "Heterosexuality." While "Creole" could be said to be about *linguistic stigma*, at its highest level, the excerpted passage makes no explicit statement about this abstraction — only demonstrates it in relation to Haitian creole. These differences contribute to the particular style of each passage, and these styles in turn suit each passage to the discipline it addresses. And each "style of levels" presents a different kind of challenge to the summarizer.

Despite these differences, the passages nevertheless resemble one another in their routine descent through levels of generality. That resemblance constitutes one of the criteria of their shared membership in the academic genres. Other genres — that is, other types of writing serving other kinds of situations — don't necessarily behave this way. Their pattern of levels — their conceptual style — can differ noticeably from those you have just investigated.

The following exercise gives you a chance to explore other possible patterns of levels: non-academic ones. Knowing about these other possibilities can improve your sense of what scholarly style is — and isn't.

---

## exercise

---

Select one short article from each of the following:

- a tabloid daily or weekly newspaper
- a more conservative daily newspaper
- a news magazine.

(1) Construct a tree diagram and a map of each article.

(2) Compare these diagrams to each other and to those of the "academic" passages you worked on in the previous exercise. What system of differences and similarities can you describe?

(3) Write a one- or two-sentence summary of each of these articles. How does this writing experience resemble or differ from your summarizing of the "academic" passages?

## 2.7     A special case of summaries: stories

Some of the information in your university reading will arrive in narrative form: that is, as stories. The life of Trotsky, the events leading up to the War of 1812, the actions of the International Monetary Fund in 1982, the development of public-health legislation in western European countries — such information presents itself according to how it occurred in time. This information is organized chronologically: Event 1, Event 2, Event 3, etc.

Writers can find such material difficult to summarize, and nowhere is the difficulty more severe than in literature courses. On the one hand, your instructor insists, "Don't tell me the story." And, on the other hand, he complains that you haven't provided enough "context" or "proof" for your claims. These may seem like contradictory directives, but they're not. Both can be satisfied by accurate and economical summary.

It could be that the main source of difficulty in summarizing stories is the fact that narratives often don't carry those higher levels of generality which explained, for instance, the significance of details about a London hospital or a family business in Taiwan or the terms people use to describe Haitian creole. With no access to higher levels of generality, we are apt to get stuck at the lower levels of happenings. We have no easy means of climbing to broader, more economical levels where details can be collapsed into and represented by briefer statements. Once we get on the track of a series of happenings in recounting a story, we stay on it, and the track becomes a rut. This condition seems to be a common feature of the recounting humans do.

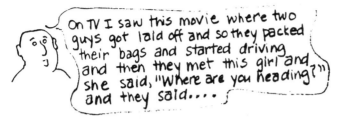

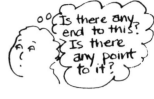

The way out of the rut is to supply the higher-level concepts that the original text doesn't provide — that is, give *names* to the story's episodes. This naming can turn plot summary (and other types of narrative summary) from writing-with-no-end-in-sight into writing that is creative and useful in support of larger arguments.

## 2.7.1    *Finding high-level names for events*

Passage 4 which follows is an imitation of a typical beginning to a certain kind of French-Canadian tale. (As in most stories of this kind, the narrator does not dwell on evocative settings. Things get off to a fast start.) Next to the narrative, I have given names to its elements, generalizing its details, finding a more compact and abstract expression of them.

PASSAGE 4

| | |
|---|---|
| Ti-Jean and his mother lived in the midst | |
| of a forest, vast and dark. Their cottage | ISOLATION |
| was little more than a shed — its floor | |
| only earth, its walls pierced by the weather. | |
| Once each day they sat down to their bowls of | POVERTY |
| thin soup, in which they dipped hard bread. | |
| Ti-Jean and his mother became ill. They | |
| suffered days and nights of fever. One dawn, | |
| before the stars faded, Ti-Jean's mother died. | LOSS |
| But the boy recovered, although in a weakened | WEAKNESS |
| condition. | |

I have condensed the 81-word fragment to four words, each of which gives a general name to the specific circumstances mentioned in the tale. I might have used other words instead of or in addition to the ones I chose: *misery*, *affliction*, or *hardship*, for example. You can probably think of some words that haven't occurred to me. The range of possibilities suggests that this stage of the summarizing process — this discovery of general names which will condense details — is not a routine, mechanical activity, but, on the contrary, one that challenges the summarizer's creative insight.

There is no one set of "right" names that will stand for this passage. The most we can say is that some names will work well as representatives of the story's details: these names will be plausible *interpretations* of the conditions and events reported in the narrative. Some other names might be less convincing and useful.

## 2.7.2    *Summarizing with the help of high-level names*

Once you have found those names, you can go on to put your reading to use, without getting stuck in the rut that makes you re-tell the whole story. Passage 5 uses the names I found for the Ti-Jean fragment, summarizing the fragment in one sentence.

PASSAGE 5       Ti-Jean's career begins in conditions of poverty and isolation, suddenly intensified by his own physical weakness and the loss that makes him an orphan.

The *naming* not only economizes, reducing the original substantially, but also makes something new. Instead of re-telling the story, the summary recreates the text in a new version for new purposes. The names you put to narrative episodes like the Ti-Jean one can enable you to approach main elements of your argument efficiently, without dragging the whole story behind you. In this case, we might now be prepared to talk more directly about some elements of the world view suggested by Québécois Ti-Jean tales: the way the stories are generated from conditions not simply of material deficit but of social deficit as well. The one-sentence summary provides a basis for an argument about the story — an interpretation, a claim about its significance.

### 2.7.3 Summary and presupposition: being told what we already know

It may be that literature teachers are especially sensitive to being told the story. Perhaps this sensitivity comes from reading lots of papers on the same novel or play. But their reaction to "plot summary" may also be simply a clear illustration of larger circumstances of human communication generally, and of scholarly communication in particular.

Generally, telling people what they already know can be risky. It can arouse bad feelings.

You have to get a passport form and fill it out and get a photo and hand it in at the passport office and wait three days and go and pick it up. You're leaving in three days.

I know. I know that.

Or it can make the listener question the speaker's motives or intentions.

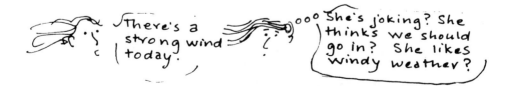

There's a strong wind today.

ooo She's joking? She thinks we should go in? She likes windy weather?

Or, by implying assumptions about the state of the listener's knowledge of the world, it can offend:

Whenever we speak or write, we represent, by the way we make our statements, information as already known, or as new and not known. These representations can have social consequences in any communicative setting. But they can have particularly important consequences in scholarly settings, where knowledge and its possession are the conditions for membership in the scholarly community. People who **know** are members in good standing. People who don't know are outsiders.

In your scholarly writing, you try to show that you *do* know things. But you are only part of the communicative action. Your reader is another part. And the way you represent your knowledge implicitly reflects your assessment of your reader's knowledge of the world. That's why a sentence like this, while true enough, at the beginning of a literature essay, can arouse a negative response:

*Charles Dickens was a nineteenth-century English novelist.*

Its form suggests that your reader doesn't know this. Moreover, and perhaps more important, its form suggests that this fact is, in general, not widely known — which, in turn, reflects on the writer of the statement as naive. In language study, the features which index a statement as known or not known are studied under the term **presupposition**. In Chapter 7 we will be investigating presupposition in more detail, for it turns out that academic readers are sensitive to the way statements represent propositions as widely known or not widely known.

In the meantime, we can see that presupposition can play a role in the summary of stories — so as to avoid appearing to tell the reader a story he already knows. In the one-sentence summary 5 of the Ti-Jean story, the phrase

*the loss that makes him an orphan*

presupposes

*his mother dies and he becomes an orphan.*

That is, it mentions the event without asserting it. Thereby, it avoids telling the reader what he already knows.

In a sense, handling knowledge as already known and presupposable or not known and assertible is a matter of sentence style. This element of sentence style seems to be important to academic readers and writers, and we will investigate it further, along with other matters of style to which it is related. For now, we can see that one way of summarizing story events can be more acceptable than another. A writer who tells a reader

*One afternoon, Nick visits Gatsby's mansion with Daisy.*

may seem to mistake this well-known event for something new and unknown, while a writer who presupposes this information may seem to have a better grasp on the state of knowledge in literary studies, where *The Great Gatsby* is very well known indeed:

> Nick's afternoon visit to Gatsby's mansion with Daisy turns from an interior moment, domestic and clandestine, to a vision of the larger world beyond, and the endless traffic of human migration.

Moreover, the presupposing structure of the sentence leaves a slot for a claim about the significance of the event.

# exercise

Below are two more narrative fragments. One of them you may recognize: it is the beginning of "Little Thumb," a long-enduring folk tale. The second is an excerpt from an account of conditions in Alert Bay, a small community on Vancouver Island.

Summarize each of the two fragments, reducing the original to 15%-25% of its original length. Begin by finding names which conceptualize the conditions described in the narrative. Use these high-level names to compose your summary.

While both passages are narrative (that is, both arranged according to the order of events), you will find that they are very different kinds of narrative. The second proceeds at a much higher level of generality, and at its highest levels you may find some of the generalizing and abstracting expressions you will need in your summary.

PASSAGE A  **"Little Thumb"**

There was once upon a time a man and his wife, fagot-makers by trade, who had seven children, all boys. The eldest was but ten years old, and the youngest only seven.

They were very poor, and their seven children incommoded them greatly, because not one of them was able to earn his bread. That which gave them yet more uneasiness was that the youngest was of a very puny constitution, and scarce ever spake a word, which made them take that for stupidity which was sign of good sense. He was very little, and when born no bigger than one's thumb, which made him be called *Little Thumb*.

The poor child bore the blame of whatsoever was done amiss in the house, and, guilty or not, was always in the wrong; he was, not withstanding, more cunning and had a far greater share of wisdom than all his brothers put together; and, if he spake little, he heard and thought the more.

There happened now to come a very bad year, and the famine was so great that these poor people resolved to rid themselves of their children. One evening, when they were all in bed, and the fagot-maker was sitting with his wife at the fire, he said to her, with all his heart ready to burst with grief:

"Thou seest plainly that we are not able to keep our children, and I cannot see them starve to death before my face; I am resolved to lose them in the wood tomorrow, which may very easily be done; for, while they are busy in tying up the fagots, we may run away, and leave them, without their taking any notice."

"Ah!" cried his wife; "and canst thou thyself have the heart to take thy children out along with thee on purpose to lose them?"

In vain did her husband represent to her their extreme poverty: she would not consent to it; she was indeed poor, but she was their mother. However, having considered what a grief it would be to her to see them perish with hunger, she at last consented, and went to bed all in tears.

*The Blue Fairy Book* 1969 Ed. Andrew Lang. New York: Airmont, 232-233.

PASSAGE B   **"Alert Bay"**

The first recorded European contact with the Kwakwaka'wakw was the arrival of Captain George Vancouver in 1792, who described his visit to a village at the mouth of the Nimpkish River, located directly across Johnstone Strait from Alert Bay. . . .

The Kwakwaka'wakw became actively involved in the fur trade during the first half of the nineteenth century and in 1849, the Hudson's Bay Company established Fort Rupert in the central Kwakwaka'wakw area. To the Kwakwaka'wakw, the new opportunities for trade and the increasing availability of European manufactured goods provided an opportunity for the elaboration of the central institution of aboriginal society: the potlatch. Potlatches became more frequent and access to, and the ability to accumulate, large amounts of European goods became a determining factor in achieving rank. During the fur trade era, such an elaboration of the potlatch did not directly conflict with the objectives of the Europeans, who were clearly interested in trade rather than settlement. Ships' logs and journals kept by traders testify to the fact that Native peoples on the Northwest Coast exercised significant control over the trade by such means as withholding furs to drive up prices, placing "advance orders" for specific trade goods, and refusing to trade unless satisfied with the good being offered in exchange.

The latter half of the nineteenth century brought with it the collapse of the European and Asian fur markets and, consequently, the decline of the fur trade. This corresponded to the advent of the Gold Rush and the beginning of intensive and permanent European settlement on the B.C. coast. These years mark the period during which basic colonial structures that continue to shape the relationship between Euro-Canadians and Native peoples came into being. On the [British Columbia] coast, as elsewhere, the decimation of the aboriginal population by epidemic diseases brought by Europeans played a major role in establishing the foundations of this relationship. Indigenous people found themselves rapidly becoming minorities in their own lands, and while a certain degree of economic independence could be maintained by continuing to live off the land, social demoralization, sickness, and dependence on European medical care to cure European diseases began to take their toll.

As early as 1787 epidemics of smallpox, influenza and measles had been recorded among the Native populations of B.C. However, with more and more Indians travelling to trading forts and camping around new cities like Victoria, these contagious diseases, against which the Indians had neither natural immunity nor effective medicine, began to threaten their very existence. [In 1862, a white man with smallpox arrived in Victoria from San Francisco. The disease reached the Native camps around the city, killing many people. The survivors returned to their coastal communities, taking the disease with them. The only medical aid available was provided by missionaries.]

The first census of the Kwakwaka'wakw was conducted by John Work around 1835 and he estimated the total population to be around 10,700. Fifty years later, in 1885, this figure had dropped by approximately 72 per cent, to around 3000.

Dara Culhane Speck 1987 *An Error in Judgement: The Politics of Medical Care in an Indian/White Community.* 70-72.

**Sample summary of passage (6), on Bethnal Green:**

In health care, we find one of modern life's connections between the public domain and the private — a connection with potential conflicts of scale. Trends in hospital architecture suggest that these conflicts can be resolved by design that familiarizes patients with the institutional environment, arranging settings in recognizable rather than disorienting ways.

The summary takes account of the fact that *school* as an institution is not a well developed point: whereas the *hospital* theme is developed right down to the details of design, schools are only mentioned as an example. This structural descent also justifies the summary's whole focus on health care and its elimination of higher level ideas about institutions and individuals in general. Bethnal Green itself, however, had to go: there wasn't room to introduce it and, at the same time, inform the reader of the point about Bethnal Green's particular characteristics.

# 3

## Summarizing what you have read: Part Two

### 3.1 Abstract words and concrete words

At the end of the last chapter we looked at the naming activities that can generalize circumstances or episodes, condensing them into concepts that represent or interpret their details. *Isolation*, for example, gathers up the circumstances of living in the middle of a forest and at the same time leads into the event of Ti-Jean losing his mother. *Poverty* and *weakness* were other names for occurrences and attributes reported in the story fragment. We might find still more words to name and interpret the sequence of happenings and conditions in Ti-Jean's life: *deficit, powerlessness, hardship, survival.*

All these words occur at a higher level of generality than the narrative itself. And they condense the original. But, besides their appearance at a high level of generality, and their ability to condense text, they also share another feature: they are all abstract words. *Poverty*, for example, is an abstract word that gathers up soup, bread, earth floor, and thin walls. All those latter items are represented by concrete words.

**Abstract words** refer to concepts, ideas, and entities which could be said to have essentially mental existence: words like *hope, freedom, power, unfairness, change, authority* refer to such entities.

**Concrete words** are used to refer to objects, phenomena, and beings which exist physically: *bread, stapler, fire, car, daffodil, Mrs. Blink*.

The entity referred to by *daffodil* can be touched; the entity referred to by *unfairness* cannot. "Wait a minute," you say. "*Poverty* is an abstraction, and it can be experienced, felt." Quite true, and so can *hope* and *unfairness* be felt. But their expression in language occurs in two ways, and the difference between abstract and concrete words accounts for the differences between these two ways of expression.

- *Poverty* (not touchable) names *thin soup and hard bread* (touchable.)

- *Thin soup and hard bread* demonstrate *poverty*.

- *Isolation* (not touchable) names *the cottage* (touchable) surrounded by *trees* (touchable).

- *The cottage* surrounded by *trees* demonstrates *isolation*.

The relations between abstract and concrete expression are very complex — much more complex than these standard examples suggests. A complete account of the full ascent from concrete reference to abstract reference would have to include a stage or level where words **generalize** or **typify** large numbers of instances. So

*(all the) people who visit social-service agencies for help*

can be generalized as

*social-service clients (or clientele).*

In Chapter Eight, we will examine the role these typifying words play in the style of writing of some social-science genres. And when we consider some current research and theory about academic writing (Chapter Six), we will see that scholarly expression also favours a process which turns **events** or **actions** into **things**, and the names for these things become generalizing abstractions. So, while

*(all the) people who <u>cultivate</u> plots which <u>provide them with just enough to live on</u>*

can become

*subsistence-plot <u>cultivators</u>,*

the typified action can itself become an abstraction which generalizes many events or actions:

*cultivation of subsistence plots*

or

*subsistence-plot <u>cultivation</u>.*

Both abstractions and typifying general terms come in for some criticism. We will consider these criticisms later, and reflect on the social role such expressions play in the academic community. For now, we should recognize that abstraction is an important feature of academic writing.

## 3.2   Abstraction and generalization as products of reasoning

The examples in section 3.1 above present abstraction and generalization as ways of referring to the world. But they are also products of reasoning. When we generalize, we reason by interpreting specifics to identify common features. Having noticed, for example, similar behaviour in many individuals, we might say, "Through the 1980s, the baby-boomers were the most re-lentless consumers the marketplace has ever seen." When we express an abstraction, we reason by giving a name to the iden-tified feature: "The values and behaviours of baby-boomers were characterized by *materialism*." When we write down those generalizations and abstractions, we offer the products of our reasoning. When in our reading we encounter generalizations and abstractions, we are meeting the products of the writer's reasoning.

The following exercises ask you to develop abstractions from concrete data. They will help you focus on the abstraction *proc-ess*, letting you experience the fact that abstraction is not only a type of reference. Abstraction is also something we *do*, under certain circumstances. The kind of thinking involved in the ab-straction process is prized in scholarly communities.

## exercise

1. Write a passage which describes a room in your home, using concrete words to account for its physical components — its furni-ture, surfaces, dimensions, occupants, and so on. Continue your description by using abstract words to interpret the specifics you have written about. (Remember how the abstractions "poverty" and "isolation" were able to gather up and interpret details about Ti-Jean's house — walls, food, floor, trees outside.)

2. When you have written this passage, take a look at it. Underline the words that refer concretely; circle those that express abstrac-tions. Consider the pattern these words make, the experience they present to the reader. Would the passage make a different impres-sion on the reader if the abstract expressions preceded rather than followed the concrete expressions? If the reader encountered only abstract claims? Only concrete description?

## exercise

Read each of the following paragraphs, and then develop a claim about these statements' general significance:

1. What abstract word or words name the conditions described in the passage? What is the passage about?

2. What do we learn from the specifics in the passage? In replying to this question, write a sentence or two using the abstract word or words which answer Question 1. Use that sentence (or two) to introduce these facts to a reader.

PASSAGE A **"Baboons"**

Among communities of olive baboons of the Serengeti savanna, some male individuals get the shady spots for midday rests and use the highest branches, safest from predators, as perches. Females groom these males, keeping them free of parasites. These males get the most food, and they have easy access to sexual partners. Other males in the group have what food they dig up stolen from them and have their sexual liaisons interrupted by sexually privileged males. And they are overrun with parasites.

Adapted from Robert M. Sapolsky 1988 Lessons of the Serengeti. *The Sciences*, May-June, 38-42.

PASSAGE B **"Brian"**

(Brian is 14; his behaviour at school troubles staff and other students; he has become aggressive at home and at school; he sniffs glue; he is referred to a counselling clinic.)

Brian was escorted each day to and from school either by family or by social services personnel. At school he was given "jobs" in the classroom during breaks. Two evenings weekly he was taken to a voluntary youth club run by some police officers in their spare time, and at weekends he joined a church youth centre for youngsters like himself, for outings and organized games. Once a week he also went to an intermediate treatment centre, and one morning weekly he attended the clinic for group counselling and activities like painting and building models.

Adapted from Denis O'Connor 1987 Glue sniffers with special needs. *British Journal of Education.* 14, 3, 94-97.

## 3.3    Abstraction and the levels of generality

The levels of generality enable both writers and readers to manage complex information. And abstract words build an important, high-level platform in that system. Abstractions enable writers to name and manage details, representing them compactly and meaningfully. Abstractions cooperate with generalizations, which also condense and manage spreading details.

You have now had some direct writing experience in consciously using abstract words to condense detail in summary, to interpret detail in your description of a room in your house, and to interpret facts about baboons and about Brian. The passage that follows will give you direct experience of the role of abstraction in your *reading*.

Without its stages of abstraction, you could say that the passage is just a description of a picture of a woman in a white dress. But you'll find that, because the passage does express abstractions, it is more than that. The high-level abstractions explain what is significant or important about this picture of a woman in a white dress.

PASSAGE 1    **"White dress"**

Art can directly challenge popular ideas about power and status. But it can also appear to reiterate and display those ideas — at the same time exposing some instabilities in popular ideologies. Royal portraiture, for example, in nineteenth-century Europe, displays notions of imperial and economic power intersecting with ideas of status expressed in images of female sexuality which conflict with measures of social standing. Portraits of the period show royal women in gorgeous, costly clothes, the latest in Parisian styles. Franz Xavier Winterhalter (1805-1873), the most popular portrait painter of his time, painted women of the court in sensuous, luxurious outfits, and ravishing poses. In his *Pauline Sandor, Princess Metternich* (1860), the princess' white dress — designed by the foremost couturier of the time — slips from her side-lit shoulder into highlighted ripples and folds. Wrapped in a diaphanous gauze shawl, the princess wears five strands of pearls at her neck, and five strands on each wrist, her jewels and skin sensually brilliant against a dark, wooded background. She is imperial — but also sexual, dressed as seductively, as some contemporary critics complained, as a café habitué occupying the lowest rung of the social ladder.

Adapted from Carol Ockman 1988 Prince of portraitists. *Art in America*, November, 45-49.

Abstractions — art, ideas, ideologies, power, status, female sexuality — explain what is significant about a particular picture of a woman in a white dress. The diagram which follows shows how these abstractions occupy the highest levels of generality, and how the descent to detail is managed at intermediate stages by generalization: a mention of "portraits of royal women" is more general than mention of one picture in particular, "*Pauline Sandor, Princess Metternich*." In the analysis ABSTRACT references appear in capitals, generalizations are underlined, and specific references get neither underlining nor capitals.

FIGURE I

ART · · · · · · · · · · · · · · · IDEAS/IDEOLOGIES
ROYAL PORTRAITURE · · · SOCIAL STATUS, IMPERIAL POWER
portaits of royal women · · · FEMALE SEXUALITY
costly, stylish clothes · · · · 19th-century women
women of the court in gorgeous clothes · · · ravishing poses

Pauline Sandor, Princess Metternich

highlighted white dress, 5 strands of pearls, shoulder, jewels, skin

café habitué

These levels — stretching from the highest abstraction about art and ideology to the lowest detail that counts the strands of pearls — cooperate with each other. The lower levels depend on the higher ones for significance, and the higher levels depend on the lower ones for proof or demonstration.

Moreover, we will find again and again in our investigation of scholarly writing that abstraction is more than a **cognitive** feature — more, that is, than an expression of the product of reasoning. It also performs **social** functions. We have already glimpsed these social functions in "White dress." The abstractions *ideologies*, *social status*, *power*, *female sexuality* justify the passage's claim on readers' attention. There is some benefit for readers in this.

And these aren't just any abstractions. In many disciplines — the social sciences, history, literary studies — at the end of the twentieth century, ideas about power and social hierarchy, ideology and sexuality are high-value items. Invoking these terms, writers offer readers substantial benefits in exchange for their attention. As well, writers show that they are *in the know*: they can work with key terms in the academic community. By displaying certain kinds of knowledge, they show that they are members of the community.

We will be looking at abstraction again in Chapter Four, where abstraction becomes an object of **definition**, and in Chapter Seven, where we will inspect scholarly introductions and observe close-up the working of high-value abstractions in establishing the scholar's right to speak.

## exercise

(1) Have you noticed key terms your instructors favour? What are they? Do instructors in different disciplines seem to favour different abstractions or do they share some?

(2) High-value abstractions characterize scholarly expression. But they appear elsewhere, too, in other discourses. For example, political talk in the western world has long favoured "democracy," and fairly recently "global competitiveness." Can you think of any other abstractions in use in the speech that surrounds you in your daily life?

## 3.4    Heights of abstraction, depths of proof

Many composition textbooks warn against the overuse of abstractions. In view of the social role of abstraction in scholarly writing, we may have to be cautious about taking such advice too much to heart.

Nevertheless, we should be aware of the kind of cognitive demands that abstraction makes on readers. Writing without abstraction can seem irrelevant to the academic reader, but writing that stays too long at the highest levels of information can be hard to read, and even unconvincing.

Had "White dress" clung to "ideology," "art," "power," "status," and lingered in the rarefied atmosphere surrounding such notions, the reader would soon be out of breath — desperate for descent to specifics. Readers perform best when they can contact reasoning on concrete levels.

We can think of this contact as **proof** (especially in the sense of "proof" as "experience"). In "White dress," the lowest levels *develop* the ideas expressed at the highest levels. Details about Winterhalter's picture of this woman *prove* that art can express conflicts in ideologies of power and status. And in those details readers come into contact with the substance of the larger idea; they experience it. For example, if you have written that your living room possesses the abstract quality of *comfort* or of *austerity*, you can put your reader into contact with the claim by showing what made you say this: what do you have in your living room that you interpret as austere or comfortable?

Proof in writing has a lot to do with demonstrating abstractions and generalities at a lower level, thereby making them acceptable and knowable to the reader. When your instructors ask you to prove your assertions, they are asking for this kind of descent to specifics. Or when they respond non-committally to what you feel is a sophisticated account, they may be suffering from the oxygen-deficit of high-altitude information.

Student writers in graduate and upper-division courses seem especially likely to leave their readers on these airless summits. Perhaps their engagement with high-status ideas is so involving that they lose sight of the ground-level conditions that those ideas spring from in the first place. Like their readers, they too can suffer from a kind of fatigue, or altitude sickness. When they spend too much time among the peaks of abstraction, they have a hard time advancing their theses or honours papers towards their research topic.

Altitude sickness may be a syndrome of the academic workplace, an occupational hazard. In later chapters, we will look at some measures for treating it, or learning how to live with it.

Right now we will acknowledge both the necessity and the risk of abstraction.

## exercise

1. Write a sentence expressing the gist of "White dress." Remember the lessons you learned from summarizing passages in Chapter Two: because the summary is shorter than the original, it cannot afford to retain much material from the lowest level. At the same time, however, the summary that only repeats the original's highest level will not accurately represent its focus and development.

Both 2 and 3 below pursue the same kind of analysis as question 1 above. And both ask for summaries. You may want to do the analysis of highs and lows now, and defer the summaries until after the note-taking summarizing technique has been introduced later in this chapter(Sections 3.6 - 3.6.4). Then you can use these passages for practising the note-taking technique.

2. The following passage is from an article which claims that we need to understand managers "as social agents in a particular time and place" and to understand "what aspects of their social being might tend systematically to produce inappropriate corporate strategies as, for example, an inability to change when change is necessary" (434). In other passages, the author uses General Motors, Xerox, and Lockheed as examples of firms which resisted change even as they had in hand evidence not only of the necessity for change but also of the types of changes that would ensure their survival. The passage below occurs later in the article. Analyze it and identify its highs and lows. Look for abstractions, generalizations, and specifics. Use a tree diagram or a map or both to help you discover the structure of this passage. From your analysis, answer these questions:

(a) what is the author's highest, most abstract claim?

(b) What is the author's lowest, most specific reference? How could the passage have descended even lower?

Write a summary of the passage aiming for 15%-20% of the original.

PASSAGE A In this section, I will try to relate the "objective" source of managers' power with some propositions about what the sense of power entails and how it shapes identity. This part of the argument draws heavily on Bourdieu's analysis of the divergent sources of social capital, how and to what ends they are mobilized, and how they are defended (Bourdieu, 1977; 1984).

One of the interesting things about the social power of high-level managers is that it derives from a variety of seemingly disconnected material, historical, geographical, and cultural sources. This very diversity creates a kind of tacit coherence and self-reinforcement, as the manager's experience in different spheres of his life tends to yield the same message. Further, it tends to naturalize the experience and the sense of power: the manager knows that he has it and feels that this is right without having to explain it, to himself or anyone else ("it comes with the territory").

The material sources of a manager's power include class and position, income and wealth. Technically, what makes someone a capitalist is ownership of capital which is used to accumulate more capital. What makes a capitalist a socially powerful agent is *control* over capital and the ability to mobilize the power of money (see Harvey, 1985). Whether or not they own significant portions of their firm, top managers are, in a sense, honorary capitalists: they have the authority to allocate capital via their investment decisions (for a different view of the class status of managers, see Wright, 1985). Though they may not be immune from later sanctions, they have the authority to risk the existence of the firm even if they do not own it, a power summed up in the widely used phrase "to bet the company."

High-level managers also, needless to say, generally have high incomes and are relatively wealthy. The titles attached to their corporate and civic positions, moreover, mark them as powerful agents in the perceptions of others — including other powerful people. The reflection of their status in the eyes of others, particularly as this implies a shared yet unspoken sense of recognition with others of their type, feeds back upon and reinforces the sense of power derived from purely material sources.

Differential access to educational capital (a university education or, better, graduate degrees in business, finance, or technical disciplines, especially from the "right" schools) provides another kind of support that can function in various ways. In some cases, it is the educational capital itself that is mobilized to gain access to economic capital in the first place (as when an MBA from Harvard University provides entree to a managerial position despite the inexperience or humble origins of the person in question). Academic credentials also provide a tacit guarantee of the general suitability of a person for a managerial career — this is, a career as a socially powerful actor — that goes beyond the specific competences formally attested to by the degree itself. That is to say, although the Harvard MBA only formally guarantees that the holder is well versed in the latest management techniques, the aura of the degree confers a broader social acceptability and a tacit marker of the social power of the individual (see Bourdieu, 1984).

Following Bourdieu, we may also expect that economic and educational capital can be mobilized to reinforce one's control of cultural capital expressed in forms (taste, judgment) and mechanisms (collecting, patronage) of cultural consumption and in a particular relationship to cultural production (for example, personal and corporate philanthropy). In turn, privileged access to cultural capital provides another form of validation of the sense of social power derived from economic and educational capital. We can see this fusion of different forms of social capital at work in the participation by corporate leaders (and/or their spouses) in support of their cultural institutions (museums, the opera, the symphony orchestra, etc.), often in their headquarters' cities. The point, however, is not about the control of cultural production but rather the way in which different forms of social capital reinforce each other and provide a coherent substrate to the sense of social power.

One presumably does not need to amass large quantities of statistical data to claim that most high-level managers in the USA are white males (but see *Fortune* 1990;1992). They are also typically American, and rose to their positions in the postwar period of global US economic and military dominance. Race, gender, geography, and historical moment also combine to foster a generalized sense of power.

Here it can also be seen how the position of top managers differs from that of, say, other white American males in being reinforced on all fronts. The white male blue-collar worker may feel himself empowered within family or among his peers. He may feel himself entitled to look down upon women, minorities, or immigrants or upon the Japanese or Germans who, after all, lost the war. But this sense of power is more likely to be contradicted, hence qualified, in other settings, as when he applies for a loan at the bank, for example, or writes to his senator and receives a form letter in response, or when he enters the workplace.

E. Schoenberger 1994 Corporate strategy and corporate strategists: power, identity, and knowledge within the firm. *Environment and Planning* 26, 3, 433-451, 443-44.

(3) Apply the same analysis to the following passage, locating the highest levels, and the lowest, and writing summary which is 15%-20% of the original.

PASSAGE B     For the woman writer whose ethnic community is patriarchal, ethnic and feminist values and identities must inevitably intersect in potentially uneasy, conflicting, or violent ways. In male-centred ethnic societies, the woman usually remains on the margin, invisible, mute, or constrained to limited stereotypical roles of possession — child or mother, domestic worker, or sexual object. Most assertions of female identity or qualities falling outside the subordinate ranks and delineated kinship roles may be read as subversive of male power and, by implication, of one's ethnic community. To be a free woman, such a woman must be at some level a "no name woman," that is, outcast from her ethnic community. Thus, [Maxine Hong] Kingston's aunt, a "no name woman" who carries an illegitimate child, has broken the Chinese patriarchal laws of kinship and descent, has become a non-Chinese, a nonhuman, and drowns herself in the well, an act of retribution for breaking the name of the father, the final patriarchal control over all women. In the intersection of race and gender identity, the woman who represents the urgencies of her gender (her sexuality, her maternality) against a race imperative is in a position to be violently erased. But that is in the traditional master plot of ethnic patriarch as villain and ethnic woman as victim.

Rejecting this race and gender plot (encompassing female in-
fanticide, clitoridectomy, child brides, dowries, brideburning, catalog brides, enforced purdah, suttee — the archetypal patterns of
female oppression and male masterhood),[1] Asian American
women have been busy inventing new plots that are complicated
by race and class issues. One alternative narrative to the representation of woman as a victim to patriarchy is that of the disem-
powering of the central male figure in the Asian kinship nexus by a
racist and classist white American society. Through the eyes of
Asian American daughters, the father's humiliations, losses, and
pathetic struggles against white social authority are both indict-
ments against racism (and therefore an assertion of ethnic protest)
as well as evidence of patriarchal impotence (and therefore a strip-
ping away of ethnic core identity). Jeanne Wakatsuki Houston and
James Houston's 1974 *Farewell to Manzanar* constructs this dou-
ble-edged critique of Asian/American cultures in its portrayal of
the gradual emasculation of the powerful Papa figure. Because
Papa "didn't want to be labelled or grouped by anyone," the
daughter has grown up in an all-white neighborhood. Because he
had terrified her with the threat, "I'm going to sell you to the Chi-
naman," she grows up with "this fear of Oriental faces." "Papa
had been the patriarch," she tells us explicitly. The internment
process changed him to "a man without a country. . . . He was suddenly a man with no rights who looked exactly like the enemy." The
Japanese values that supported his patriarchal role, through the
internment, have become erased; he is now "without a country,"
"the enemy." In the face of the FBI arrest, "all he had left . . . was
his tremendous dignity."[2]

1   Although such a catalog of social phenomena oversimplifies and over-
    generalizes Asian women's status as victims of patriarchy, it does point to
    a history of unequal power relations in Asian societies.

2   Jeanne Wakatsuki Houston and James Houston, *Farewell to Manzanar*
    (New York: Bantam, 1974), 8, 9, 12, 6.

Shirley Geok-Lin Lim 1993 Feminist and ethnic literary theories in Asian
American literature. *Feminist Studies* 19, 3, 571-595, 579-81.

# 3.5    Travelling companions in the scholarly landscape

As a *writer*, you lead your reader up and down the levels of generalization, demonstrating high-level statements with detail and explaining the general principles at work in specific phenomena. You offer evidence of particular cases, and interpret these cases for your reader, showing their relevance.

As a *reader*, you track other writers' movements up and down the ladder of generalization. Some readers do a better job of this than others. Those who are consciously or unconsciously aware of the levels of information in what they are reading are more likely to remember what they have read — and more likely to be able to summarize it accurately and economically.

Being aware of the ups and downs of what we read may be part of a natural or early-learned capacity we all have as receivers of messages. In conversation, for example, we are aware of the pointlessness of utterances that linger at a very low level of reference: we get restless when a speaker just strings details together without showing some higher order of relevance. As experienced conversationalists, we are skilled judges of the organization of messages.

The materials of conversation, however, are usually more accessible and familiar than those of scholarly writing. The content of scholarly writing is often remote from our habitual interests and beliefs — what has been called our "commonsense" experience of the world. Moreover, the scholarly genres can so deeply transform experience that even what **is** familiar looks strange and foreign, and "commonsense" becomes "uncommonsense."

At the same time as we struggle with the burden of new information, or old information transformed beyond recognition, we are faced with arrangements of the levels of generality which are far more elaborate than those we encounter elsewhere. Dragging this burdensome new information with us, we have to make our way across a precipitous landscape that is rugged with hills and valleys.

If you find academic reading difficult, don't be discouraged: we all find it difficult because of its very nature. And the structures of scholarly prose — steep ascents to abstract, airless summits, treacherous descents to unheard-of valleys of detail from which it seems there can be no exit — are hard going for all of us. And we all feel some alarm at the idea of not only having to understand what we read but also having to be able to summarize it to put it to use in our own writing.

Be assured: this is difficult terrain, and any problems you have in traversing it are not unique. But be assured as well that there are useful techniques for getting around in this territory.

## 3.6 Note-taking

Experienced readers have ways of coping with difficult texts and managing new ideas and information so that they are able to use them in their own writing. These techniques are usually forms of note-taking.

Note-taking operates at the boundary between reading and writing. On the one hand, it secures new information, in effect making a record of reading for re-reading. On the other hand, it *transforms* the text that has been read into a form that is eligible for a new life in a new document. With efficient note-taking, the reader is becoming a writer.

Inefficient note-taking gets stuck in record-keeping. It leaves material untransformed, only making way for re-reading. Such note-taking can get stranded on the airless summits, having secured only the highest-level assertions without accounting for their origins and proof.

Or inefficient note-taking can get stuck in those valleys of detail without exit. Often, hard-working students make pages and pages of notes that painstakingly record the details of their reading — details without overview. They find themselves with a massive amount of material on hand.

Or these hard-working students may do their note-taking right in the original, using a yellow marker to highlight important passages. Unfortunately, it is often the whole text that is highlighted in a glare of yellow that obscures the distinction between levels of information, and suggests that every assertion has equal standing.

With "notes" like these, students are understandably anxious at the prospect of beginning to write — and they may find themselves delaying their draft. Their notes are so bulky and comprehensive as to be unmanageable. Their notes provide no overview of the original, no perspective, no leverage. These are inefficient methods of note-taking.

Efficient note-taking, on the other hand, does give the reader/note-taker an overview of the text. It does provide a perspective on the original. And it prepares the reader to write. Efficient note-taking tracks the structure of information, revealing the ups and downs of the path of argument. It makes a map, locating the high points and situating detail. It identifies *gist* and traces *proof*. Once the argument is mapped, even the most unfamiliar terrain becomes more hospitable.

## 3.6.1    *A strategy for efficient note-taking*

Knowing the structure of a text, you can command its content. The method of note-taking proposed here will provide you with means of managing what you read.

1. It provides an overview of the landscape of the text. This overview will help you absorb new information, and it will help you distinguish between crucial high-level material that your summary must retain and low-level material that your summary can omit.

2. It goes towards ensuring accuracy. This method forces readers to recognize *all* the connections and emphases in the original — not just the ones they grasp most readily.

3. It makes reading an *active* process. It puts readers to work, preventing them from being just bystanders or spectators. Having already warmed up during the reading process, readers are ready for the exertions of writing.

4. It avoids the pitfalls of copying.

This strategy for note-taking is a very self-conscious form of reading. So it may seem laborious and mechanical. However, it is only a more methodical version of what capable readers do anyway when they encounter a difficult text that they want to put to use in their own writing. They scribble in the margins; they gloss passages; they write summarizing statements and commentaries in their notebooks. They do all this to get hold of the text firmly so they can use it in their own thinking and writing.

Our reading/note-taking/summarizing will be very methodical — more laborious than real-life practices. But we undertake it to discover the structure of information and to learn that, whatever the difficulty of the text and the writing assignment connected with it, we have a strategy for handling difficulty.

## 3.6.2   *Collapsing a passage*

We will call this reading/note-taking/summarizing strategy "collapsing" because that is what we are going to do: we are going to "collapse" a text into a portable unit that can be carried off for other occasions (your writing assignments). And we are going to collapse it without damaging or disfiguring it.

Our first sample text is a five-paragraph passage from *Reading Television* (1982) by John Fiske and John Hartley. The passage comes from a chapter in which the authors review the results of various "content analyses" of television — results from studies conducted as early as 1954 and from more recent studies. The overall aim of this chapter, which appears early in the book, is to show that simple quantitative surveys which "count" the incidence of certain types of televised images and episodes cannot fully explain the meaning of a sequence of TV transmissions, or of TV as a phenomenon. The authors argue instead for an approach which would account not just for the parts (and their frequency or infrequency), but also for the *relationships among the parts*. The number of white female nurses who show up on TV, for example, is not an informative figure in itself. We must know what other ideas and images these characters are associated with when they do show up.

In the selected passage, Fiske and Hartley analyze the results of inquiries into violence on television. (You will find them referring to "violents": by this they mean figures or characters who perform violent actions.) We aim to *collapse* this passage into a 70-90 word summary — a summary which accurately represents the content and logic of the original. Figure 2 demonstrates our aim graphically.

FIGURE 2

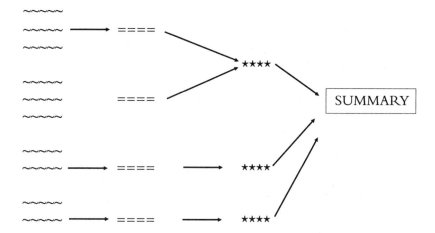

Column 1 is the text we are reading. At the first stage of note-taking, we transform it into the nuggets of information presented in Column 2: these are the **main points** of each paragraph. They are the **gist** of each section. They answer a question you ask yourself as you leave each paragraph: "What do I predict to be necessary in the paragraph for understanding the rest of the passage? That is, what should be kept in mind from this?" *To make sure your note-taking will liberate you from the original, freeing you to use your own words when you actually come to write the summary, make every effort to compose these answers in fragments and phrases. Make every effort to avoid simply copying out sentences of the original.*

To compose Column 3, a further reduction and transformation, we assess each of the Column 2 items. If they operate at too low a level of detail (remember how texts spread out at the lowest level of generality, too space- and time-consuming for summary), we delete them, crossing them out. If they are repetitions of earlier items, we arrange for them to be absorbed into the other items. If items are two elements of the same point, we rewrite to incorporate them with one another, making just one item. If they can be neither deleted, absorbed, nor incorporated, we just carry them forward. The contents of Column 3, the products of this evaluation process, are what we must present in our summary. These are the essentials which the summary must find a way of representing.

Here is the passage about TV violence. You should try summarizing it on your own first. But, for your guidance, we also provide a sample of the collapsing technique applied to this passage, as well as a sample summary. Notice that, just as everybody's diagrams of levels of information in the Chapter Two exercises would not be the same, so too the results of the reading/note-taking/summarizing technique will not be the same.

PASSAGE 2     **"TV Violence"**

In general, all violents are more logical than non-violents; the key to violence with a happy fate is efficiency; unhappy-fated killers and victims are presented as bunglers. Violents are also the most masculine, and the victims the least masculine.

FIGURE I

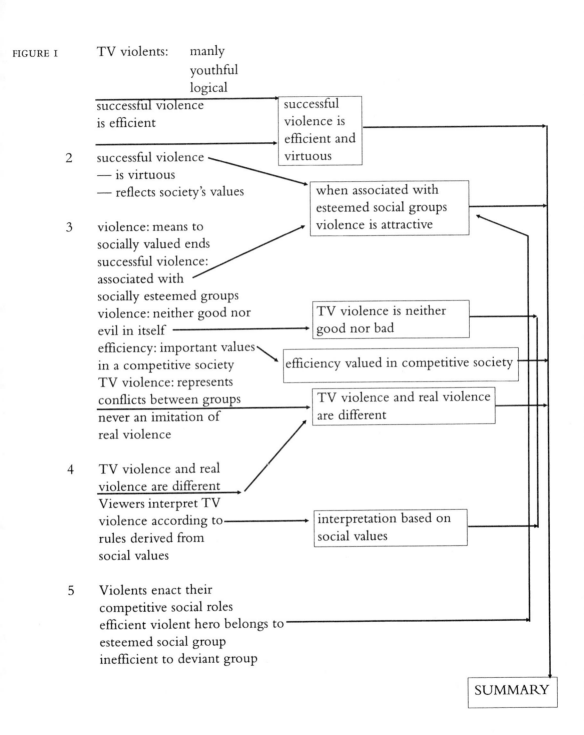

The attractiveness of the hero correlates with his happy fate and efficiency; "violence does not mar, nor non-violence improve, the attractiveness of the hero," comments Gerbner, who goes on to sum up the implications of his findings thus: "Cool efficiency, and, to a lesser extent, manliness and youth, appear to be the chief correlates of success and virtue in a fairly impersonal, self-seeking, and specialized structure of violent action" (1970, p. 78). He concludes that violence is not a matter of simple behaviour, and that television portrayals of it mirror rather than illuminate our society's prejudices. The television message system is, he suggests, a system of "cultural indicators" by which the value structure of society is symbolically represented.

Violence, then, is used in the pursuit of the socially validated end of power, money, and duty, and is *inter*personal although *im*personal: that is, takes place between strangers. So, despite its obvious connection with power or dominance over others, it is not the dominance of one personality over another but of one social role over another social role. It is linked to socio-centrality, in that the victims are likely to belong to less esteemed groups, defined in terms of age, sex, class, and race, and the successful aggressors are likely to be young, white, male, middle-class or unclassifiable. Violence is not in itself seen as good or evil, but when correlated with efficiency it is esteemed, for efficiency is a key socio-central value in a competitive society. Violence on television, then, is not a direct representation of real-life violence. Unlike real violence, its internal rules and constraints govern what it "means" in any particular context to the observer, rather than the combatants themselves. Its significance in a television fiction is that it externalizes people's motives and status, makes visible their unstated relationships, and personalizes impersonal social conflicts between, for example, dominant and subordinate groups, law and anarchy, youth and age. It is never a mere imitation of real behaviour.

In other words, all the evidence of content analysis points us to a crucial distinction between violence in televised drama and real violence, and should make us aware of the inaccuracy of the commonly held belief that these are similar in performance and effect. Television violence is encoded and structured into a governed relationship with the other elements of the drama; this relationship is controlled by rules that are themselves derived from social values, and which are common to all television texts in their particular genre. Our familiarity with the genre makes us react to violence according to its own internal rules, and not as we would to real violence. We know, as we approve of the death of the socially deviant criminal under the hail of socio-central police bullets, that we would not approve in the same way if the equivalent real-life villain were gunned down in front of us. The difference in our reaction is not explained by saying that a death on television is weaker, less perceptually imperative, for the difference is one of kind, not of degree.

It is at this level that violence is seen as a complex system of signs of behaviour, more or less efficient, by which the socio-central hero and deviant villain enact the competitive relationship of their roles. The policeman/detective hero is a sign of socio-centrality; the criminal/victim becomes, then, the social deviant, not only because criminal behaviour is by definition deviant, nor because criminal victim/status correlates with deviant groups — the wrong sex, class, race, or age — but also because, in a competitive society, inefficiency or bungling is deviant. The criminal is distinguished from the hero primarily by his inefficiency and his social group, his morals, methods, and aims are the same.

PASSAGE 3

## Sample summary

Fiske and Hartley argue that television violence — unlike real-life violence — is neither good nor bad; its interpretation depends on what it is associated with. When violent actions are efficient and successful, and associated with esteemed social groups, they are virtuous. When they are performed inefficiently, by members of socially subordinate or deviant groups, they are interpreted as un-

attractive. Fisk and Hartley note that efficiency is a crucial value in a competitive society: television violence is
one means of expressing this social value.

## 3.6.3    *Making do with less*

In transforming the original into a summary, we notice that, as
the authors develop their ideas, they repeat themselves — especially in confirming their main points about the interpretive
connection between social values and the difference between
TV violence and real-life violence. They even signal to the
reader that they are repeating themselves: as they begin to restate their argument and insist on its implications at the beginning of the fourth paragraph, they say "In other words. . . ."

The summary's economy requires that we reduce this repetition. We cannot repeat these main ideas as often as the authors
of the original do. But we do recognize this repetition as an important signal: the repeated points are crucial, and they must
show up in the condensed version of the authors' longer argument.

## 3.6.4    *How the note-taking strategy monitors and manages the summarizing process*

Constructing the gist of each paragraph allows us to check our
own summarizing (reading-into-writing) process.

(a) We can verify that we really understand the connections between each part of the argument (between, for example, the
idea that violence in itself is neutral and the idea that efficiency
is a positive value in a competitive society). If we haven't really
grasped these connections, we are going to have trouble writing
a coherent summary.

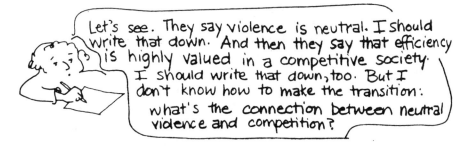

(b) We can verify that we really have accounted for *all parts* of the passage. We can make sure that we haven't been waylaid by some part of it that appeals to us because of our own particular interests or biases.

(c) By collapsing the passage to short fragments expressing *gist*, we ensure that we will be free to express the argument in our own words, and avoid copying. (In Chapter Two we looked at an example of the incoherence produced by copying.)

(d) Collapsing the passage helps us see the argument as a whole and at a glance. This means that we can manipulate and arrange the parts to satisfy the new requirements (mainly brevity) of the new text we are making. For example, in my summary, I abandoned Fiske and Hartley's arrangement of statements and chose to begin the summary with elements that actually occur in the middle of the original passage: the assertions that TV violence is not like real-life violence, and that TV violence in itself is neutral, neither good nor bad.

## 3.6.5 *Working with longer texts*

In the "TV violence" example, we are working with a very short text. With such a short text, it is practical to account for the gist of each paragraph. When you are working with longer passages — articles, chapters, even whole books — this thoroughness may not be practical. Then you may want to define your targets differently — not by paragraphs but perhaps by half pages or by stages of discussion. Often writers will help you with this, dividing their text into labelled sections. Then you can track the argument by constructing the gist of each section. If you find yourself getting lost, however, you can always shift down to paragraph level, registering each step of the discussion.

---

## exercise

---

1. Using the note-taking and summarizing strategies suggested above, write a summary of the following passage. Aim for 15%-20% of the original.

### "Schooling"

Universal free public school systems had been established in the majority of the states and in Upper Canada by 1860. In the United States, over half of the nation's children were receiving formal education, and more students than ever before now had access to levels of schooling previously restricted to an elite few (Cremin, 1961; p. 16). In Canada, under the direction of Egerton Ryerson, the Ontario Schools Act of 1841 had subsidized the existing common school system; by 1872, British Columbia had legislated a public school system modeled on that of Ontario.

Late-19th-century literacy instruction in Canada differed in one crucial respect from its American counterpart. For whereas Canadian schools imported curricula from England, teachers in America were by this time provided with locally developed textbooks, in the tradition of the McGuffey readers. Noah Webster's *American Spelling Book* (1873), the most widely used textbook in United States history, not only promoted American history, geography, and morals, but was itself a model for an indigenous vocabulary and spelling. Textbooks and dictionaries of this period attempted to engender a national literacy and literature free of European "folly, corruption and tyranny," in Webster's words. In Canada, by contrast, classrooms featured icons of colonialism: British flags and pictures of royalty adorned the walls, younger students were initiated to print via the Irish readers, and literature texts opened with Wordsworth's and Tennyson's panegyrics to the Crown. In Canada, the reduction in pauperism and crime associated with illiteracy was seen as requiring the preservation of British culture and a colonial sensibility; in the United States, "custodians of culture" (May, 1959; p. 30) sought to assure economic independence and political participation. The match between these differing societal and educational ideologies and the "civilizing" effects of traditional three Rs and classical education was near-perfect.

The model for this classical education was found in the philosophy, psychology, and social theory of Plato's educational treatise *The Republic*. Platonic psychology subdivided the mind into three faculties: reason, will, and emotion. The child, a "barbarian at the gates of civilization" (Peters, 1965; p. 197) was regarded as a bundle of unruly impulses needing to be brought under the control of the faculty of "right reason" — that is, morally informed rational judgment. Paraphrasing a speech of Ryerson's, the *Journal of Education* declared in 1860 that "a sensual man is a mere animal. Sensuality is the greatest enemy of all human progress" (in Prentice, 1977; p. 29). To that end, rigid discipline and rigorous mental training characterized classical instruction.

Adopting Plato's stress on mimesis and imitation as the basis for development of mind, classical pedagogy stressed rote learning, repetition, drill, copying, and memorization of lengthy passages of poetry and prose. Mental, moral, and spiritual edification were to be had through exposure to, in the words of Matthew Arnold (1864), the "best that has been thought and said in the world." Accordingly, the intermediate and secondary grades adopted a "great books" literacy curriculum which featured the Bible, Greek and Roman classics, and after some debate, acknowledged works of English and American literature; "far more time [was] spent . . . on ancient history and dead languages than upon the affairs of the present or even recent past" (Joncich, 1968; p. 48). In the United

States, public high schools retained a modified classical curriculum, sans Greek, as a "uniform program." This universal implementation of a classical curriculum in secondary schools forced practical studies of law, bookkeeping, and vocational skills outside the public system. In Canada, it was left to industry to initiate vocational education (Johnson, 1964; p. 65).

Curricular material did not vary from grade to grade according to controlled level of difficulty. In practice, this meant that the same literary texts, particularly the Bible, would be studied in greater and greater detail and depth; underlying "truths" were explicated in terms of grammatical rules, rhetorical strategies, moral content, and aesthetic worth. In the elementary grades, students copied passages for "finger-style" penmanship exercise, in preparation for advanced composition study. Thus, stylistic imitation and repetition, guided by explicit rules, dominated writing instruction; students at all levels undertook précis and recitation of exemplary texts.

Following the European model, reading took the form of oral performance to an audience. Individual reading time was limited, and all students progressed at a fixed rate through the text. Both in grade and secondary schools, each student, in turn, would read passages aloud; those not reading were expected to listen attentively to the reader, since the intent of oral reading instruction was not merely to ascertain the reader's ability to decode the text, but to develop powers of effective public oration. Pronunciation, modulation, and clarity of diction were stressed. In the 19th-century classroom, reading was neither a private nor a reflective act, but a rule-bound public performance.

Although texts were meticulously dissected and analyzed, and block parsing was a daily routine, the emphasis was not on mere grammatical correctness. In theory, analysis and repetition subserved the development of sensitivity to the aesthetic and didactic features of the text. Thus, the student's encounter with the text, whether fairy tales or Shakespeare, was to be both aesthetically pleasing and morally instructive — in accordance with the Horatian edict that literature should be "dulce et utile."

In the same way, vocabulary study subserved the ends of moral and literary education. Spelling lists often featured poetic language and Biblical and literary terminology. Precision of meaning and rhetorical effectiveness were to be achieved through the apt selection of words from this cultural lexicon — the range of vocabulary legitimated by "literati" as appropriate for each generic form of literate expression. The overriding sense of conformity and decorum was reflected in the rules that constrained classroom discourse and behaviour. Corresponding to each literate act was a correct bodily "habitus" (see Bourdieu, 1977); reading, writing, and speaking were performed in prescribed physical postures. Moreover, "provincial" speech codes were frowned upon as evidence of rudeness or ignorance; textbooks of this period advised students to cultivate the friendship of children of higher station, so that they might assimilate more cultured and aristocratic speech habits.

Suzanne de Castell and Allan Luke 1986 Models of literacy in North American schools: social and historical conditions and consequences. In *Literacy, Society, and Schooling*, ed. S. de Castell, A. Luke, K. Egan. Cambridge UP, 87-109, 92-94.

2. Questions 2 and 3 in the exercise in Section 3.4 above suggested that you might postpone the summarizing tasks to this point, after the note-taking/summarizing technique had been introduced. If you did postpone the summaries, do them now.

## 3.7 Reported statements

Most academic essays depend on outside sources of information. Everybody knows this. What people beyond the academic community may not be so aware of is the condition we discussed in Chapter Two: that is, that not only students but professional scholars as well depend on "sources." A main characteristic of the genres of professional scholarship is the way one piece of writing openly, explicitly demonstrates its dependence on other pieces of writing. In fact, unless scholars enjoy international renown — unless their names are virtually household words in academic circles — they can scarcely publish a sentence without locating that sentence amongst what other people have written on the topic. The scholar's **position** is one defined in relation to other scholars, rather than a position of independent, stand–alone wisdom.

When the scholarly situation is so definitively characterized by dependence — or interdependence — we can expect that the ways of speaking which serve this situation will represent that dependency in **style** — in characteristic features of writing. And what we expect turns out to be true. So pronounced is the condition of dependence and interdependence that scholarly writing has even developed its own elaborate, rule-governed systems for identifying the sources of statements: documenting systems of footnotes, endnotes, lists of works cited. Even at a glance, you can tell the difference between a work in a popular genre — a self-help book, for example, about changing your career in mid-life, or about finding and nurturing your inner child — and a work in a scholarly genre — a book about postmodernity and romanticism in late twentieth-century education, for example. The self-help book will be free of documentation; the other one will be laden with it.

But footnotes and works-cited lists are not the only features of style that represent the distinctive interdependence of texts in the scholarly genres. There are equally important, although less rule-governed, ways of representing statements as having a source other than the current writer. They are perhaps less conspicuous to outsiders, but, to members of the academic community, they are as crucial as features of documentation. These practices represent words as **not belonging to the present speaker**. Language specialists often refer to such words as "reported speech." Here is the difference between a statement represented as reported speech and one not so represented:

(a) Fiske and Hartley argue that television violence, unlike real-life violence, is neither good nor bad.

(b) Television violence, unlike real-life violence, is neither good nor bad.

In later chapters, we will observe that some other genres also contain reported speech, and we will investigate features which distinguish the scholarly genres' special use of reported speech. Here we acknowledge that academic readers are familiar with the features of style which represent statements as reported speech. They use these features in their own writing; they expect to see them in other people's scholarly writing — including students'. We will note also, in a preliminary way, that reported speech establishes a writer's **position in relation to statements**. **Position** is important in all speech, and especially complicated in scholarly expression, and more than only a matter of reported speech. But, most simply, and for the time being, we can see that the writer of (a) above says,

This statement about television violence is not my statement. It comes from other speakers.

Television violence, unlike real-life violence, is neither good nor bad.

The reporting clause "Fiske and Hartley argue" **positions** the writer of (a) at some distance from the statement.

Professional scholars are used to inscribing their work with indications of their position vis-à-vis the statements they make. These indications are a sign *in writing* of the research process. Students who learn to position themselves vis-à-vis their statements will replicate the sound of scholarly expression. But you may also find some security in writing this way, for it can more properly represent your actual position as a learner. Instead of writing about penal institutions in nineteenth-century Britain, or bureaucracy in the Qing dynasty, or agrarian societies in seventeenth-century France as if you know these things from firsthand experience (which you don't), you can write about them as things you have learned, from identifiable sources. You can write about them as **things people have said**. This is an authentic position for a student writer to take, and one which academic readers will recognize and appreciate.

## 3.7.1    *Making a frame for summary*

Dependent on sources, much of the writing you do will be summary. And practising summary is a good time to practise using some of the signals of reported speech. These signals provide a **frame** for your summary. The frame

(a) introduces your sources openly and directly;

(b) establishes the boundary between different sources of information, showing that you are moving from one source to another;

(c) establishes the boundary between material you have collected from other sources and your own commentary on or evaluation of this material.

## 3.7.2 *Making a frame: introducing the source*

Your reader is eager to meet your sources of information.

So your first step is to introduce your source to your reader in a straightforward way. One form of straightforwardness identifies the source by author and title, and broadly describes what the source does.

PASSAGE 4    Bruno Latour and Steve Woolgar's ◄——— AUTHORS' NAMES: here, both
*Laboratory Life: The Construction* first and last name. Not all
*of Scientific Fact* (1988) is an frame styles use the source
ethnographic account of the author's first name, as you will
routine, day-to-day activities see in examples presented Chapter 7.
at the Salk Institute for Biological
Studies. Latour and Woolgar TITLE: not all frame styles state
reject the distinction between the title of the source. Chapter 7

social and technical activities in science: their study embraces every aspect of scientific activity, and thus establishes the scientific fact as cultural artefact.

will present instances where title is left out.

PASSAGE 5 James Milroy and Lesley Milroy's *Authority in Language: Investigating Language Prescription and Standardization* (1991) summons research, including the authors' own, in sociolinguistics ⬅ and historical linguistics to attack what they call the "complaint tradition," which they associate with the making of Standard English.

BROAD DESCRIPTION OF SOURCE: what kind of writing it is, and/or what its main finding is.

.

After forthright introductions like these, the broad description can be narrowed to adapt it to your essay's topic. Passage 6 shows such narrowing. .

PASSAGE 6 In *Communications* (1962), Raymond Williams analyzes the content of British print and electronic media and describes the relation between content and the profit motive. Among other things, Williams' research reveals a category of publication — mostly women's magazines — that advises readers on how to manage every detail of their domestic and working lives.

NARROWING SIGNAL: shows that the writer will not be accounting for the whole book in what follows. (Without this signal, a reader who knew the original and had found some other part of it most noteworthy might consider this writer to be misrepresenting the original.) Other wordings which can signal this narrowing are "one area of Williams' findings," "one focus of Williams' work. . . ." Maybe you or your instructor can think of other typical wordings for this operation.

## 3·7·3    *Making a frame: keeping in touch*

Broad introductory sources acquaint your readers with your sources. But they should not be left to maintain the acquaintance alone. The further your readers move from that introducing statement, the less certain they will be about the source of information. Say, for example, we rewrite passage 6 without mentioning Williams after the introducing statement, and then go on to summarize in greater detail, still keeping Williams out of the picture. Passage 7 below shows a frame that dissolves too soon.

PASSAGE 7

In *Communications* (1962), Raymond Williams analyzes the content of British print and electronic media and describes the relation between content and the profit motive. There is a category of publication — mostly women's magazines — that advises readers on how to manage every detail of their domestic and working lives. Advice is closely related to shopping information. Readers are shown how they can adjust to problems in their lives by making certain types of purchases which advertising features associate with domestic tranquillity or picturesque romance.

By now the reader can't be sure whether the observations about shopping information and adjustment to problems come from Williams, from another source, or from the essay-writer's own reasoning. And this uncertainty occurs despite the thoroughness of the introducing statement. The introducing statement needs help from other conventional frame elements:

| | |
|---|---|
| *Communications* | focusses on . . . |
| | inquires into . . . |
| | explores . . . |
| | investigates . . . |
| | |
| Williams' study | shows that . . . |
| Williams' research | reveals |

|         |                      |               |
|---------|----------------------|---------------|
|         | goes on to describe ... | notes ..      |
|         | maintains that ...   | explains ...  |
| Williams | claims ...          | considers ... |
|         | observes             | examines ...  |

Rarely do such frame elements need to appear in every sentence: too much framing can sound odd. But the appearance of frame elements at intervals throughout the summarized material will keep your reader directly in touch with your sources. Moreover, the frame helps you establish the boundary between your summary and your own reasoning, showing where the summarizing ends and your own commentary begins. At this point, moving beyond the frame, you begin to compose **critical summary**.

---

## exercise

---

1. Examine the following passages and underline all features — wordings, notations — which frame these writers' summaries of other writers' work, and represent statements as *reported speech*.

PASSAGE A    **"Propaganda"**

[The popular view of propaganda which predicts the presence of an active propagandist] is not the only one rejected in Ellul's comprehensive and pioneering Propaganda: The Formation of Men's Attitudes. He sees the tendency to equate propaganda with "lies" as likely to further the interest of propaganda by concealing its nature as "an enterprise for perverting the significance of events" behind a facade of inassailable "factuality" (Ellul 1973, p. 58). It is in this sense that education, despite its professed belief in the liberating effect of literacy, can be seen as a pre-propagandist process through which facts are interpreted according to the symbols which express a group's collective ideas about its past and its future (Ellul 1973, pp. 108-12). Ellul's account is disturbingly provocative, even though he occasionally slips into a mood of what has been rightly criticized as "Aristotelian Christian pessimism" (Sanzo 1978, p. 205). I shall return later to some of his arguments and examples, but would first like to summarize a section of his book in which he makes a crucial distinction between two types of propaganda in literature.

In his attempt to define categories of propaganda, Ellul (1973, pp. 61-87) makes four distinctions within the general phenomenon. Each of these distinctions embraces a pair of types, the first one of which is associated with popular views of "classic" propaganda. The four distinction he makes are between: 1. political and sociological propaganda; 2. agitation and integration; 3. vertical and horizontal propaganda; 4. rational and irrational propaganda.

A. P. Foulkes 1983 *Literature and Propaganda*. 10.

PASSAGE B **"Consciousness"**

Jaynes [*The Origin of Consciousness in the Breakdown of the Bicameral Mind*] holds that human consciousness, which he defines as our awareness of ourselves as selves, began at a much less distant date than most theories of consciousness presume. According to Jaynes, consciousness began to develop in human history roughly 3000 years ago; by 700 or 800 BC, almost all of the Indo-European world had become conscious. Jaynes claims that consciousness is generated by language, but not by any sort of language. Since human language predates the development of consciousness by at least 50,000 years, Jaynes asks us to consider that there "could have been at one time human beings who did most of the things we do — speak, understand, perceive, solve problems — but who were without "consciousness" (Jaynes, 1986, p. 131). What such preconscious people lacked were the defining elements of consciousness as Jaynes sees it: first, a spatial quality or mindspace in which we "see" ourselves introspecting; second, an "analog I" which functions in consciousness as the agent of this mental kind of seeing (that is, a metaphoric self we automatically construct to move about in mind-space concentrating on one thing or another); third, the capacity to narrate, to fit all events into the past and the future, to read time spatially. Such characteristics allow Jaynes to define consciousness as an "analog of what we call the real world . . . built up with a vocabulary . . . whose terms are all metaphors or analogs of behavior in the physical world" (Jaynes,

1986, p. 132). If consciousness is essentially the operant of this linguistic and metaphoric function, then consciousness must have developed after the human evolution of language.

Laura Mooneyham 1993 The origin of consciousness, gains and losses: Walker Percy vs. Julian Jaynes. *Language and Communication* 13, 3, 169-182, 169.

2. Re-write these passages by eliminating all signs of reported speech. How does the position of the writer appear to change as a result of this change in style?

## 3.8 Writing beyond the frame: critical summary

Having composed an accurate, compact summary of difficult reading, you have done something important. In reconstructing a complex argument, you have created a worthwhile text. By representing the argument in your own terms, you show that you have commanded it, not just repeated it. Your readers will appreciate your achievement, but they are probably also hoping for something more.

Some readers might ask explicitly for the "something more." They will ask you to write a "critique" or a "critical summary" of assigned readings. They may go so far as to direct you towards the critical stance they want you to take: "Consider $x$'s discussion in light of recent developments in $y$ theory." Or your instructors may give no such explicit instruction. Only when you get your work back will you find out about these hidden expectations. For no reason you can make out, you get $B$ instead of $A$. The reader has no complaints about your reconstruction of the source, but, still, something is missing. Or your *B* is accompanied by a comment from the reader complaining that you haven't developed a critical attitude, or you haven't said where *you* stand, or you haven't come up with any "conclusions."

In different disciplines, and even in different courses in the same discipline, this missing part, or shadowy expectation, has different manifestations. But we could say that, in general, it is a requirement for a **critical stance**. Your reader would like to see you evaluate the argument you have reconstructed in your summary. This doesn't mean you have to condemn the argument as mistaken, or praise it as excellent. Nor does it mean you must express an "opinion": "In my opinion these are strange ideas. . . ." After your meticulous reconstruction of complicated reasoning, praise or blame or personal attitudes may seem anti-climactic or clumsy. And, after you have submitted yourself to the authority of the original, respecting every turn and stage in its argument, you may feel you are in no position to criticize.

So what is this "critical stance"? How do you come up with it? Different instructors will offer you different — and sometime obscure — advice on developing what we are calling a critical stance. They will be trying to tell you about a delicate process: detaching ourselves from our own knowledge of something in order to judge the knowledge itself.

TAKING A CRITICAL STANCE

The use of reporting expressions (*claims, suggests, argues. . .*) to frame summary constitutes a **position** for you: these are not your statements; you are at some distance from them. Moving beyond the frame also constitutes a **position**: one where you do claim statements as your own. The following sections suggest ways you can construct a position for yourself, and then offer four samples of critical stances appropriate to the scholarly genres.

## 3.8.1 *Developing a critical stance: inspecting connections and evidence*

Your own experience in constructing a summary of the argument can be one of your first sources of material for developing a critical stance. An argument that looks airtight and irreproachable at first reading can show flaws when you try to reconstruct it. Pieces that seem to slide together easily in the original suddenly won't fit together in the new version you are making. Take note of these difficulties in the summarizing process. They may be evidence of weakness in the original, places where some connections are not entirely solid. So, ask yourself

- are there weak connections in the original?

- are there gaps in the reasoning of the original?

- are there some connections that turn out to be especially difficult to reconstruct?

Just as connections that look sturdy in the original can become flimsy-looking in the reconstruction, so too can evidence that seems convincing and abundant in the original become slight and flimsy-looking on further inspection. So, ask yourself

- what kinds of evidence does the source provide? does it seem sufficient to justify the writer's main claims?

Notice that even if you come up empty-handed when you ask yourself if the evidence is sufficient — "well, yes, it seems OK" — you have still taken a step towards a critical stance when you identify the *kind* of evidence the writer has presented. Your reader will appreciate your observation that, for example, the evidence is "mainly anecdotal," or "wholly quantitative," or "limited to detailed analysis of one instance."

Moreover, you don't need to state these observations as aggressively negative. By simply expressing your awareness of the *kind of proof* or the *kind of argument* the original offers, you move towards a critical stance. Similarly, your discovery of a flimsy connection in the original doesn't have to be inflated into a condemnation. Maybe *you* can beef up that logic with your own reasoning ("although it is not entirely clear from the Connors' account just how social class correlates with retirement choices, we might speculate that . . ."), respecting the original writer's glimpse of the connection and recognizing that even some extremely valuable arguments and insights don't have their whole logic worked out in their original expression.

## 3.8.2    *Developing a critical stance: the other side of the argument*

Once you have immersed yourself in the argument you have analyzed and reassembled in summary, you may find it difficult to get free of it again, difficult to detach yourself from its explanations and arrangements of evidence. One way of keeping your distance is to see the original as *one side* of an argument by constructing the *other side*. Ask yourself

- what views does the original oppose?

Often, the original will outline the argument it opposes; other times, you will have to coax the rival argument out of the margins. In either case, to detach yourself from the domain of the original, ask yourself

- what would someone who held those opposing views say about the argument you have summarized?

For example, people who claim the televised images of violence habituate viewers to real-life brutality would oppose the views expressed in the Fiske and Hartley passage on TV violence. By constructing the competing interpretation of TV-watching, you can situate Fiske and Hartley's argument in relation to other views.

Notice that, by presenting the other side of the argument, you do not commit yourself to opposing the material you have summarized. You may see the original as having convincingly overcome its rival, or as having failed to do so. Or you may make no judgement either way, but simply point out what territory is contested by these competing claims. Each of these three positions can constitute a critical stance.

## 3.8.3 Developing a critical stance: generalizability

By detaching yourself from the original, you get some perspective on it: you see it as part of a larger picture. You estimate your source's contribution to more general issues. To sketch in the larger picture, ask yourself

- what important phenomenon does the argument address? why is this an important phenomenon?

In naming the important phenomenon, you can resort to abstractions of the type we examined earlier in this chapter. (Is the source about ideology, about social control, or gender, or ethnicity, or the social construction of knowledge? Is it about class and power?)

In evaluating the generalizability of the original, you show how it contributes to our knowledge of the world. In explaining that contribution, you can also speculate on the original argument's potential contribution by developing and applying it in areas it does not itself reach. You can also locate it amidst other reasoning, showing how it relates to larger trends.

## 3.9 Summary takes a critical stance: four examples

In passage 8 the summary takes a critical stance by locating the original amongst other writing (other sociological inquiry into science and general trends in scholarship) and in relation to a larger abstraction ("knowledge").

PASSAGE 8      As Latour and Woolgar observe, previous studies of the
               sociology of science have preserved the distinction be-

tween the social and the technical, and have thereby preserved the prestige of science and its aloofness to the outsider's gaze. By ignoring the exclusive boundaries around the practice of science, Latour and Woolgar reduce its mystery and its unassailable status. Their efforts in this regard make *Laboratory Life* a central contribution to reasoning which, at the end of the twentieth century, has pursued the idea that knowledge is something we *make*, not something we discover. Facts are not absolute but socially and historically contingent.

In passage 9, below, the summary takes the original's argument and develops it to generalize about gender roles and "family norms." Reaching beyond the original, the summarizer qualifies her statements with wordings like "his findings can help us understand," "we could speculate. . . ." In Chapter Seven, we will examine such wordings and the role they play in marking the writer's position as going beyond what has been firmly established by others.

PASSAGE 9    Williams limits his study of women's magazines to analyzing the link between feature-article advice and the accompanying advertisements, suggesting that editorial content and profit motive cooperate indirectly. But his findings can also help us understand how gender assigns women a special role in the maintenance of family norms: we could speculate that these publications deliver to readers more than just images of ideal family life. They also instruct the reader in minute behaviours, prescribing exact household practices associated with domestic ideals. The woman who takes these instructions to heart will help her family measure up to the ideal.

Passage 10 objects to an element of the original's argument, finding a weak connection between a main claim about, on the one hand, literacy and language standardization and, on the other hand, associated and undeveloped assumptions about the nature of writing itself.

Milroy and Milroy describe spoken English as more context-sensitive and therefore more variable than written English. Two claims develop from this. The first is that testing in schools tends systematically to favour middle-class children whose spoken dialects coincide with written norms and to discredit those with limited access to written forms. Most current research and theory supports this view. The second claim is less compatible with current theory, although it may be in accord with general, public notions about language. Milroy and Milroy say that writing is itself the source of standardization. Literacy, in their view, triggers natural tendencies towards standardization. While some might contest this claim in itself and see these tendencies as political rather than natural, other associated assumptions about writing are even more open to question. For example, Milroy and Milroy appear to recognize something called "good writing" (51, 52), while it seems unlikely that they would distinguish between "good speaking" and bad, for their argument depends throughout on recognizing functional variety in speech: speech is properly diverse, not standard. At the same time, they dwell on writing's tendency to "ambiguity" (63, 80), owing to its contextual haziness as it spans time and distance. Somehow, standardization helps to eliminate this problem. But it is hard to see why the natural, context-sensitive variety evident in speech is not also a factor in writing — or why it would not also be a factor if it were not for the political forces of standardization.

The next example takes a critical position in relation to a passage you have already read and summarized. It identifies a connection (between social control and the rejection of the spelling book) which the summarizer could not account for. It expresses views which oppose or at least question the original's argument ("Some might argue. . . " expresses this stance without fully committing the summarizer to it). It finally relates this particular argument to very large abstractions: the role of reform in social control, dissent, resistance.

Curtis accounts for curricular and pedagogical reform in Upper Canada by claiming that its proponents aimed to eliminate the need for "'social control'" in the "simple sense" in political rule. It is not entirely clear in the excerpted passage how the rejection of the spelling book contributed to this project, but Curtis' analysis of Ryerson's instructional philosophy does draw attention to the possibilities for a less blatant, less "simple" form of social control than "propaganda," "coercion, terror, or bribery." As Curtis interprets them, Ryerson's reforms manipulated individuals by reaching into the mind and personality, recruiting character to the service of the state. Some might argue, however, that the formation of moral attitudes is in fact a proper purpose of schooling, and beneficial rather than sinister. Modern educational philosophies still look for means to develop moral character, encouraging and rewarding, for example, sharing and cooperation among primary-school students. Moreover, we might question whether there is any educational system that does not try — overtly or implicitly — to recruit the child's personality to the values of the institution or the community or the state.

Nevertheless, Curtis' account of Ryerson's pedagogy does alert us to the role of reform in social control. While reforms can seem to remove forms of injustice and unrest, they may in some cases only be replacing one form of control with another that is less conspicuous and less open to dissent and resistance.

## 3.10 Locating the critical stance

Once you have developed material that extends beyond the frame and provides you with a critical stance, you may wonder where you should put this material.

Chapter Four introduces you to principles that will help you predict your reader's experience of your writing. These principles will also help you make decisions about where to develop your critical position. For the time being you might consider two simple patterns for arranging a critical summary.

(a) Offer your reader your well-framed summary, and then present your evaluation of the material you have summarized. That is, let your source have the floor first, and then take your position.

(b) Compose a beginning paragraph that broadly introduces the content of the material to be summarized, and also alerts the reader to the position you will eventually take. Then present the summary with commentary following.

These are the simplest patterns for critical summary — not the only ones, and not always the best ones. As you get more experience in academic writing, you will find yourself able to make more discriminating judgements that lead to more complex structures, custom-made for each writing situation.

## exercise

Take a critical stance in relation to two passages you have already read and one of which you have already summarized: write an evaluation of the argument Fiske and Hartley present in the TV violence passage (Section 3.6.2) and of de Castell and Luke's analysis of North American educational practice in the nineteenth century (following Section 3.6.5).

# Portrait of a reader

## 4.1   Making arrangements for readers

Some of the exercises in previous chapters have confronted you with decisions about how to arrange your material: how to start, what ideas to put next to each other, how to get from one idea to another, on what point to end. The summarizing technique introduced in Chapter Three is meant to liberate you from the arrangement of the source, so you don't find yourself just listing main points in the order in which they appear in the original and hoping the reader won't notice loose connections between these points. Whether you enjoy that liberty or not may depend on whether you feel you have any grounds for making decisions about arrangement.

This chapter begins to establish criteria for making arrangement decisions. Some of these criteria are conventional: that is, readers respond well to certain patterns of arrangement because they are used to seeing those patterns in certain situations: for example, introductions of a certain length with a certain kind of focus. These formal features that organize prose are important, and, throughout this book, we will be looking into some of the main organizational conventions of the scholarly genres.

But conventional criteria are not the only ones to consult when you make decisions about how to organize your material, how to get from one point to another. Effective writers keep the reader in mind not just as a stickler for form but as a reasoning intelligence who works efficiently under some circumstances, and inefficiently under others. The discussion which follows begins to sketch a portrait of this reader — reckoning his capacity for remembering, concentrating, tying things together. I expect that you will recognize some of the features of this being. As readers, we all share pretty similar capacities for remembering, concentrating, and figuring things out. And you will also find that the work you did in Chapters Two and Three — analyzing levels of generality, situating abstractions, reducing passages to gist — will contribute to your portrait of the reader. Some ways of arranging levels of generality put gist within easy reach and make the reader behave very cooperatively; other arrangements are less likely to encourage cooperation from your reader.

You will discover as well that it is from the organization of prose, its arrangement, that **topic** emerges. The reader we are sketching is able to negotiate topic with the writer. Under certain conditions, the reader is a willing and clever collaborator with the writer in these negotiations. Under other conditions, he is resistant and dull. It is best to think of the **writer** as the one responsible for those conditions.

Sometimes, however, it can be tempting to blame the reader when negotiations break down. Real-life experience tells us that there are some cranky readers in the world — people with a bone to pick, or with some volatile prejudices that are ignited by what they read. Real-life experience also tells us that sometimes writers — and maybe especially student writers — don't get a fair hearing, for a variety of reasons. These bad experiences can construct in writers' minds a distorted picture of The Reader generally. The distorted picture can make writers feel they are not responsible for their readers' reception of what they have written, and, at the same time, it can also stand in the way of writers getting a sympathetic view of their readers at work.

This chapter is devoted to developing that sympathetic view, and this chapter and later ones are devoted to helping writers come to terms with some of the inevitable constraints — both cognitive and social — on reading and writing. But first it might be a good idea to look at the picture of the reader you already have in your mind, before we begin to draw a new picture.

---

## exercise

---

This exercise can help you and your instructor talk about how you interpret your situation as a student writer. It is not the only way of finding out how you picture your reader, but my colleagues and I have found that it can shed light on otherwise shadowy sensations and ideas.

In groups of three or four, discuss your answers to the questions below. Make notes of the answers and your discussion.

1. What do you do when you get a marked essay returned to you? (Interpret this question broadly, mentioning any physical or mental operation you go through in handling that returned essay.)

2. What do you consider typical marking commentary or annotation on essays? What do professors typically say about essays?

Collaborate with other members of your group to compose a 300-400-word discussion paper summarizing your findings, accounting for differences and similarities in your habits and perceptions. Try to construct a connection between your behaviours and feelings upon having a marked essay returned to you and your ideas of professors' typical remarks. (For example, if you typically celebrate the return of an essay, this may be directly related to professors typically expressing delight at the perfections of essays.)

Exchange papers with other groups, or read them aloud to the class. In discussion, try to portray the kind of readers you and your classmates picture as receiving essays. How do these readers read?

## 4.2    Conditions for *topic*: meaning and recall

Although I cannot predict the particular results of the exercise above, I know from experience that writers can have negative opinions about readers' sincerity and open-mindedness. And they can attribute disappointing grades to insincere efforts and closed-mindedness on the part of readers. I would not deny the justice of such opinions. Sometimes academic readers (and other types of readers) are difficult, even hostile beings, owing to the circumstances of the academic context (and other contexts for reading and writing).

But to dwell on difficulty and hostility is to lose sight of other, more helpful characterizations of readers. In this section, we will start to build that helpful characterization — one which can guide your decisions about arranging, drafting, and revising your work. We start at a very basic level, by considering some fundamental conditions of remembering and understanding.

There used to be a party game — a test of memory — played at bridal showers and birthdays. In this game, the party-giver brought in a tray covered with a cloth. Under this cloth were twenty commonplace items: a safety pin, a pencil, a measuring spoon, a packet of matches, or other small articles like these. In turn, each player was permitted a ten- or 15-second glimpse under the cloth. After this quick look, contestants had to write down as many of the items as they could remember. The player who remembered the most won the game.

### A PARTY-GOER REMEMBERS ONLY SIX ITEMS

Despite the commonness and familiarity of the items — everybody recognizes a safety pin or a spoon — *recall* was very difficult (that's why it was a game). It was hard to remember the items because their selection and arrangement was *random* and, hence, not *memorable*. Had the items all been cooking utensils or all articles stocked by, say, a stationery store, the task would have been easier. In that case, the collection would have been arranged according to some higher organizing principle, and that principle would have made recall easier.

We could say that the collection on the tray had no *title* or no *topic*: nothing to correspond to "A Display of Items Used for Meal Preparation" or "An Arrangement of Articles Useful for Clerical Work." The tray collections were not *about* anything. They had no meaning, and, as a result, their "nonsense" was unintelligible and not memorable.

*Meaning* and *intelligibility* depend on a dominating organizing principle. This is true not only in party games but also in communication. High level concepts like "Meal Preparation" and "Clerical Work" dominate lower level assertions, and they make utterances intelligible. They make texts readable. They help us understand what we read, and they help others understand what we have written. They are the basis of the text's *topic*. Topic emerges from the reader's experience of the levels of generality.

## 4.2.1   Aboutness

For an utterance to be communicative, it has to be about something. We know this from our ordinary experience as senders and receivers of messages. When aboutness is missing, we are acutely aware of its absence.

In this speech at the bus stop, reference is clear but meaning is unclear. The listener can easily understand what kinds of things the speaker is referring to and would not deny any of the speaker's claims: he knows best about his sister; an article about insulation could very well have appeared in the newspaper; many people feel an obligation to mow their lawn. But the utterance as a whole, as a text, is unclear and uncommunicative. It is not *about* anything; it has no *meaning*. We find evidence of this meaninglessness in the fact that there is no conceivable *title* for the utterance, no answer to the question "what is this all about?"

The speaker's message is obscure. There is no more reason for these sentences to appear together than for the items on the party-game tray to appear together.

## 4.2.2    *Coherence and the effort after meaning*

The bus-stop speech illustrates in an exaggerated way a feature of human communication: the need for **coherence**. Despite the acceptability of the man's sentences (they are grammatical; they combine familiar words in a plausible way), the speech as a whole is not coherent. So important is this feature of communication that some linguists specialize in studying coherence: the conditions that make a group of sentences a text and, hence, meaningful.

The exaggerated nature of the bus-stop man's incoherence makes that case a simple one: there is no conceivable title for his utterance, no reasonable answer to the question "what's this about?" His listener dismisses his speech as nonsense. We may avoid conversations with people like the bus-stop man, mostly because we don't know what to say in reply. Not knowing what the topic is, we don't know what kinds of comments would count as relevant.

But other cases, where incoherence is less conspicuous or obvious, may actually cause more problems. They cause problems because of another feature of communication recognized by linguists. This phenomenon has been called the *effort after meaning*. In *Cohesion in English* (1976), M.A.K. Halliday and Ruqaiya Hasan describe the effort after meaning (although they do not use this term). They call it the "very general human tendency to assume in the other person an intention to communicate, an assumption which is no doubt of very great value for survival" (54). In other words, listeners and readers will give speakers and writers the benefit of the doubt, and, even when meaning is not at all clear, they will do their best to make sense out of a text.

Making the effort after meaning, listeners or readers try to supply the *topic* for themselves when the text does not make that topic clear. Listeners and readers will try to answer the *aboutness* question for themselves from the materials available, however scant or confusing they may be.

Listeners and readers make the effort after meaning when facing any text. They soon abandon the effort in the most extreme cases of incoherence — like the bus-stop man's speech. But even the slightest hint of *aboutness* or connectedness will encourage the listener or reader to keep trying to discover meaning. The listener or reader will try to figure out the connection between sentences.

Is the principle of *effort after meaning* a consolation for writers? Does it mean they can relax, knowing that their readers will go to great lengths to figure out what they mean? Not really. As we will find out, the effort after meaning is not always a friendly principle.

## 4.2.3 *Ambiguity and the effort after meaning*

Here we will observe the effort after meaning in operation. We can see the "very general human tendency" at work in our own reactions to pairs of sentences.

*Mountain climbing is a costly and time-consuming sport.*
*My neighbour plays hockey at 5 a.m. two mornings a week.*

We respond to the fact that these sentences occur next to each other. Proximity signals that they have something to do with each other, and we make an effort to find out what it is — an effort after meaning. In effect, we try to discover what the writer had in mind that made her put these two sentences one after the other.

In this case, our effort after meaning is likely to be more sustained than that of the bus-stop listener, who would soon abandon the effort in the face of such irreconcilable concepts as tooth extraction and home insulation. Here, we can detect at least a hint of aboutness and connectedness. We can make out a higher level of generality to which both statements belong: "sport." The utterance is *about* sport. But aboutness is still a slight structure here: we ask "*what* about sport?"

Although we have something to go on here — the two sentences share the abstraction "sport" — we don't have much. The writer hasn't given us much guidance. So we speculate. We hypothesize and try to supply a full *topic* in our effort after meaning. "Costliness" and "5 a.m." may have something in common: does the writer mean to say that some sports are simply too difficult to pursue, too inconvenient? Or does she mean to say that hockey, in contrast to climbing, is not costly? Or that hockey players can get their playing over with early in the morning, while mountain-climbers are still out scaling peaks? Which message does the writer mean to convey by putting these two sentences together?

Because we are left to speculate — left on our own with this — we are likely to say that the passage is ambiguous. It lacks a strong topic despite the shared dimension of "sport." In making their effort after meaning, different readers are liable to come up with different conclusions about the utterance's *meaning*, and it is possible that none of these conclusions will match the writer's intention. If the writer assumes that the reader got what she intended when, in fact, the reader has constructed a different topic, and the writer goes ahead on this mistaken assumption, soon reader and writer will be miles apart in their negotiation of meaning. Hard feelings could result from this: the effort after meaning can be unfriendly to writer's goals.

Sometimes ambiguity is not only acceptable but prized — as in literary texts, where it can be a compelling feature. And the "sport" sentemces would be acceptable in conversation, where there is some history surrounding the utterance — an on-going and shared interest, for example, in people's commitment to the sports they choose. Or they might be acceptable where there is some element in the immediate context of the utterance that makes it relevant and coherent — a television report about a big climbing expedition that makes the speaker and the listener both think about how much effort goes into some recreational projects.

Moreover, different genres — each of which serves social contexts that both reader and writer recognize — can display conditions not unlike the sport sentences, where the connection between adjacent sayings, the relevance of one to the other, is not clear on the surface. In reference genres, like encyclopedias, or computer manuals, sentences next to each other can seem to bear only a general relation to one another. Here is an entry from *The Encyclopedia of Aquarium Fish* (David J. Coffey, Pelham, London 1977) for Brachygobius ("bumblebeefish"):

A native of Indian and south-east Asia. Has a yellow body with broad, vertical, dark brown or black bands. It is most at home and spends most of its time close to the bottom of the aquarium. (70)

This is generally *about* the bumblebeefish, but what is the connection between the fish's origin, its appearance, and its favourite spot? Does the author mean to say that, *because* of its dark-striped yellow body, the fish lurks at the bottom? What does the fish's colour have to do with the bottom of the aquarium? Aware of the genre, most readers would not ask such questions. The social use of encyclopedia genres is such that readers bring information requirements with them, and these requirements contribute the meaningfulness which an explicit topic does in other genres.

  I wonder why my bumblebee-fish stays at the bottom. Is it sick?

 Oh. I see. It prefers the bottom. It's not sick.

So the reader's context of understanding makes the sentence "It is most at home ... close to the bottom of the aquarium" **relevant**, and meaningful.

It has been observed that some parts of some academic genres have a list-like structure that seems to answer unstated questions like the bumblebeefish question. John Swales (*Genre Analysis: English in academic and research settings* 1990) has noted this condition in the Method sections of research articles. In Chapter Eight we will see that the Background section of ethnography can also present a coherence structure similar to that of the encyclopedia article. But, for the most part, the academic genres are not like the reference genres in their coherence structures. That is why simply offering extra information about Dickens ("Charles Dickens was born in Portsmouth") in case your reader might be interested, or have a question about Dickens ("Where was he born?"), doesn't work.

I'm making a map of the birthplaces of famous writers. I'll read this English essay to see if I can find out where Dickens was born.

Readers of academic genres expect that each sentence will have an ascertainable and text-controlled (*vs.* context-controlled) connection to the sentences which precede it. This expectation is related to the system of levels — stretching through concrete specifics through generality to abstraction — which we investigated in Chapters Two and Three. Ascents to higher levels establish the relevance of lower-level mentions, constructing the particular coherence of the academic genres. Essays without such ascents can leave the academic reader with an impression of incoherence. (So, if it were to become an academic essay, the bumblebeefish entry would have to construct a higher level of statement — maybe something about *habitat* and its significance.)

---

## exercise

---

Read the following groups of sentences. Monitor your own effort after meaning by asking, for each group, "what is this about?" In each case, you will find one or more very high-level answers — like the abstraction "sport" in the mountain-climbing sentences. Then go further by constructing plausible answers to the question "why has the writer put these sentences together?" — that is, construct plausible topics for each passage. Compare the results of your effort after meaning with those of your classmates. These comparisons will reveal the range of ambiguity in each passage. Fix the passages by controlling the reader's effort after meaning: make topic clear.

PASSAGE A

Demographers observe that countries in which people are well fed, in which infant mortality is low, in which women have access to education are countries in which the birth rate and the rate of increase are the lowest. Physiologists observe that it takes 50,000 calories to produce a baby. They note that if two women are identical in all regards, except that one is better fed than the other, the better-fed one will lose fewer of her periods and will recover sooner after a birth, so she can bear another child.

Adapted from Nathan Keyfitz 1994 Demographic discord. *The Sciences* September/October, 21-27.

PASSAGE B    In the 1780s in New England, women began binding shoes in their homes to increase the earnings of their families. They sewed shoe uppers alone in their own kitchens. These shoe binders had no craft status. They did not organize to demand higher wages.

Adapted from Mary Blewett 1983 Work, gender, and the artisan tradition in New England shoemaking, 1780-1860 *Journal of Social History* 17, 221-48, cited in Ruth M. Alexander 1988 "We are engaged as a band of sisters": Class and domesticity in the Washingtonian Temperance Movement, 1840-1850. *The Journal of American History* 763-85, 769.

PASSAGE C    In 1912, one-third of recruits to the Toronto police force were former policemen, half of them Irish. In 1920, 1930 and 1940 roughly one-quarter of Toronto policemen born in Britain had served on Old Country constabularies. Many Toronto policemen had spent several years in the British or Canadian armed forces, a trend that was most pronounced in the decade after World War I when the public sector was under pressure from the Great War Veterans' Association to hire veterans. The architects of the early twentieth-century Toronto police department, Magistrate Col. George T. Denison and Chief Constable Col. Henry Grasett, had served in their younger days in units mustered against the Fenians. Denison was an ardent imperialist, a recognized expert on cavalry tactics and an advocate of preparedness and cadet training. The first-class constable of 1921 earned roughly $1800 a year following pension deductions. According to Michael Piva's study of real wages and the cost of living in early twentieth-century Toronto, this did not leave the average family man with much of a monthly surplus after paying rent and grocery and fuel bills. During the 1920s, policemen were denied salary increases. In relation to many skilled and most public sector workers, policemen were well paid.

Adapted from M. Greg Marquis 1987 Working men in uniforms: The early twentieth-century Toronto police *Histoire-Sociale — Social History* 20, 20, 259-277.

## 4.3 Sources of incoherence in academic writing

Even experienced writers of academic prose can end up troubling their readers with passages that don't measure up to the coherence patterns typical of scholarly genres. Even professional scholars, writing up the results of extensive research, can find themselves filling huge pockets of detail that begin to take on a life of their own, regardless of the topic they started out with. Student writers can also find themselves in this situation. We will call this condition **disproportion**, and in Section 4.3.1 we will look at its probable effect on the reader, and at ways of correcting it.

In addition, student writers can often find that, even before they begin writing, they have committed themselves in the planning process to a scheme that will make the reader go through exhausting efforts after meaning which, in turn, lead to sensations of incoherence. We will identify this planning problem as originating in **list-like outlines**, and in Section 4.3.2 we will look at ways of making the plan a constructive instrument that helps you ward off incoherence when you start writing.

## 4.3.1 *Disproportion and the reader*

Sometimes those areas of your writing which do not convey a strong sense of topic to the reader come about because of disproportion in your essay. In developing an idea, you descend to lower levels of generality, and you find yourself pursuing details that require a lot of explanation and verification. They take a lot of space. Although you may feel yourself securely on track, your readers may not feel so confident. They may feel abandoned in this long valley of detail, and begin to look for their own way up and out, having given up the hope that you will rescue them and lead them back to a higher level of generality.

Mitsubishi regrouped itself    former samurai    1985: 50 chaebol controlled 552 firms    controlled 80% of GNP

Stranded in the valley of detail, the reader responds to ambiguity by trying to make his own hypotheses about meaning. Constructing topic without direct guidance from the writer, he is liable to make faulty decisions that lead him far away from the essay's intended destination. Or he may simply stop concentrating — the effort after meaning is too demanding.

Passage I illustrates the conditions which trigger these undesirable reactions in the reader.

PASSAGE I

### "Asian corporations"

Corporate growth — the development of multiunit firms — can be explained in terms of business response to the conditions of industrialized markets. According to Chandler (1977), when markets grow, businesses need to develop efficient systems of management to handle increased volume and coordinate multiple activities. Another theory also explains corporate development in industrial economies in terms of the market: as the number of transactions increases in the process of transforming raw materials into market goods, uncertainty increases (Williamson 1977, 1981, 1983, 1985). To reduce uncertainty, businesses grow, internalizing transactions and thereby governing them more reliably. These explanations of corporate development, however, do not fully account for corporate growth in Japan and South Korea, where prevailing organizational structures predate industrialization.

The Japanese economy is dominated by large, powerful, and relatively stable enterprise groups. One type of enterprise group consists of horizontal linkages among a range of large firms; these are intermarket groups spread through different industrial sectors. A second type of enterprise group connects small- and medium-sized firms to a large firm. These networks are normally groups of firms in unrelated businesses that are joined together by central banks or by trading companies. In prewar Japan, these groups were linked by powerful holding companies that were each under the control of a family. The zaibatsu families exerted strict control over the individual firms in their group through a variety of fiscal and managerial methods. During the U.S. occupation, the largest of these holding companies were dissolved, with the member firms of each group becoming independent. After the occupation, however, firms (e.g., Mitsui, Mitsubishi, and Sumitomo) regrouped themselves.

In Japan in the Tokugawa era, from 1603 to 1867, a rising merchant class developed a place for itself in the feudal shogunate. Merchant houses did not challenge the traditional authority structure but subordinated themselves to whatever powers existed. Indeed, a few houses survived the Meiji Restoration smoothly, and one in particular (Mitsui) became a prototype for the zaibatsu. Other zaibatsu arose early in the Meiji era from enterprises that had been previously run for the benefit of the feudal overlords, the daimyo. In the Meiji era, the control of such han enterprises moved to the private sphere where, in the case of Mitsubishi, former samurai became the owners and managers. In all cases of the zaibatsu that began early in the Meiji era, the overall structure was an intermarket group. The member firms were legal corporations, were large multiunit enterprises, and could accumulate capital through corporate means.

In South Korea, the chaebol — large, hierarchically arranged sets of firms — are the dominant business networks. In 1980-81, the government recognized 26 chaebol, which controlled 456 firms. In 1985, there were 50 chaebol that controlled 552 firms. Their rate of growth has been extraordinary. In 1973, the top five chaebol control 8.8% of the GNP, but by 1985 the top four chaebol

controlled 45% of the GNP. In 1984, the top 50 chaebol
controlled about 80% of the GNP. The chaebol are similar to the pre-war zaibatsu in size and organizational
structure. Their structure can be traced to premodern political practices and to pre-World War II Japanese industrial policy: Japan colonized Korea in 1910.

Adapted from Gary G. Hamilton and Nicole Woolsey Biggart 1988
Market, culture, and authority: a comparative analysis of
management and organization in the Far East, *American Journal of
Sociology.* 94, 552–594.

The writer of passage 1 states her topic in the first paragraph.
This is what the reader expects, and it's good to fulfil that expectation. But we soon find that this statement does not hold up
over long stretches of text which follow. Right after the first
paragraph, where the writer has made her high-level claims
about corporate organization and Asian firms, she plunges into
explanations of Japanese corporate linkages, merchant houses in
feudal Japan, (relatively) low-level detail about Mitsubishi,
samurai owners, statistics on growth among the chaebol in
South Korea. These explanations and clusters of detail are huge
compared to the modest size of the high-level claims in the first
paragraph.

Despite a clear topic statement at the beginning, the writer
of an essay with a disproportionate shape like this is letting ambiguity seep in. The reader may or may not interpret the explanatory details as the writer intended.

Maybe this seems unreasonable. After all, the writer *told* her reader what her topic or "thesis" was: why can't he just keep that in mind? Well, he simply can't. He has too much on his mind already, what with central banks, trading companies, samurai, the U.S. occupation, 80% of the South Korean GNP. We have to face the fact that, by the end of the second paragraph, or maybe even sooner, the reader has forgotten the topical claims about the industrial-market *vs.* cultural explanations for corporate organization. These claims having slipped his mind, the reader now makes the effort after meaning on his own, in the midst of what he experiences as incoherence.

Think of the reader making his way through the description of Japanese firms' linkages. All this fits loosely within the high-level categories of "corporate structure" and "Japan," but its exact connection with the topic of alternative explanations for corporate structure is not secured. This is not to say that it *isn't* connected, but that the reader needs to be shown *how* it is connected, or he will soon abandon the initially-stated topic and look for other ones that explain why the writer is saying these things. (Think of the reader with a perpetual question in mind: "Why is she telling me **this now**?")

Left to make their own way through material that does not clearly demonstrate its relevance, readers are liable to hypothesize new topics — answers to the "what-is-this-about?" question. These hypotheses may be correct, but it is more likely that they won't be. The material you have so painstakingly gathered to develop and support your main point will have been wasted. It will be used by the reader to support some other purpose altogether. For example, a reader of the second paragraph in passage 1 may begin to get ideas about the failure of U.S. influence, or about the irresistible domination of powerfully linked firms.

Even when we recognize readers as not just any readers, but instructor-readers who are specialists in the subject, and possibly even familiar with these details, we still have to respect their efforts after meaning. Facing a passage like passage 1, they have to continually construct topic for themselves, without explicit verification that this is the topic or meaning the writer intended. These readers have to express judgements of such writing (a fact we faced in Chapter Two) and without such verification they can be reluctant to judge the work favourably. And, when readers have continually to construct topic for themselves, uncertainty and a kind of fatigue, or an indifference to what comes next can set in. Although marking comments may not say "I got tired and became indifferent," a *B-* or *C* grade when you hoped for *A* can often be attributed to the reader's experience of disproportion — a small, fleeting statement of topic and a huge, enduring expanse of lower-level data.

We could say that the coherence problems of passage 1 are structural. They have to do with the arrangement and organization of the text. Taking this structural perspective, we can illustrate disproportion spatially.

FIGURE I  •••••••••  **topic** (or "thesis")

•••~~~~  partial renewal of **topic** (Japan & enterprise)
~~~~~
~~~~~
~~~~~  all about 20th-century Japanese firms
~~~~~

•~~~~~  a little bit of **topic**
~~~~~
~~~~~  all about pre-industrial Japan
~~~~~
~ ~~ ~~~~~

•••~~~~  partial renewal of **topic** (Japan & Korea)
~~~~~
~~~~~
~~~~~  all about size & growth of *chaebol*
~~~~~

Supporting material — explanation and detail — is massed in such a way as to overshadow by its uninterrupted volume the high-level claims that are intended to establish and confirm *topic*. We will use this spatial interpretation of disproportion to demonstrate an improved structure. The improved structure insures that the reader interprets supporting detail in light of the intended topic.

FIGURE 2

•••••••••              **topic** (or "thesis")
•••••••             **supporting paraphrase of topic**

•••••••••            **renewal of topic** (corporate structure,
•••••••••            Japan, enterprise) with narrowing of topic
•••~~~~             (Japan in this century)
~~~~~
~~~~~
~~~~~               all about 20th-century Japanese firms
~~~~~
•••••••••            renewal of **topic** (explainations of
•••                 corporate structure)

•••••••••            **partial renewal of topic** (commerce in Japan,
•••~~~~             cultural influence)
~~~~~
~~~~~               all about pre-industrial Japan
~~~~~
~~~~~

•••••••••            **renewal of topic** (cultural explanations of
•••                 corporate structure)

•••••••••            renewal of **topic** (Japan and South Korea
•••••••••            culture and corporate structure)
~~~~~
~~~~~
~~~~~               all about size & growth of *chaebol*
~~~~~

•••••••••            **renewal of topic** ( Asian corporate structure
•••••••••            preindustrial culture)

While the first structure abandoned readers to make what they could of supporting details, the revised version **interrupts** the imposing bulk of lower level material to **reinstate** or **reactivate the topic**, and **control** the reader's interpretation of this material. Passage 2 shows how the revision reads. The reinstatements of topic are in **bold**. These are the points at which the writer steps in to manage the reader's effort after meaning.

**"Asian corporations"**

**Corporate growth — the development of multi-unit firms — can be explained in terms of business response to the conditions of industrialized markets.** According to Chandler (1977), when markets grow, businesses need to develop efficient systems of management to handle increased volume and coordinate multiple activities. **Another theory also explains corporate development in industrial economies in terms of the market**: as the number of transactions increases in the process of transforming raw materials into market goods, uncertainty increases (Williamson 1977, 1981, 1983, 1985). To reduce uncertainty, businesses grow, internalizing transactions and thereby governing them more reliably. **These explanations of corporate development, however, do not fully account for corporate growth in Japan and South Korea, where prevailing organizational structures predate industrialization. While the historical conditions of industrialization may explain why North American and European corporations operate the way they do, Japanese and South Korean corporate structure can be better explained as the result of other conditions: cultural factors which favour family links and which have all along adapted corporate management to older, pre-industrial forms of authority.**

**The Japanese economy is dominated by large, powerful, and relatively stable enterprise groups of business units — groups whose structure can be traced to traditional patterns of authority and family connection. Contemporary corporate structures in Japan are distinguished by characteristic systems of family connection that have persisted throughout this century, re-emerging powerfully in the post-war period. Today in Japan,** one type of enterprise group consists of horizontal linkages among a range of large firms; these are intermarket groups spread through different industrial sectors. A second type of enterprise group connects small- and medium-sized firms to a large firm. The networks of large firms are the modern descendants of the pre-World War II zaibatsu — powerful, family-controlled holding companies. These networks are normally groups of firms in unrelated businesses that are joined together by central banks or by trading companies. In prewar Japan, these groups were linked by powerful holding companies that were each under the control of a family. The zaibatsu families exerted strict control over the individual firms in their group through a variety of fiscal and managerial methods. During the U.S. occupation, the largest of these holding companies were dissolved, with the member firms of each group becoming independent. After the occupation, however, firms (e.g., Mitsui, Mitsubishi, and Sumitomo) regrouped themselves. **While market conditions can account for some features of the Japanese corporate structure, these persistent network linkages are better explained by cultural frames which influenced the organization of commerce long before industrialization reached Japan.**

**Commercial growth in Japan arose amidst and adapted to traditional authority in a feudal rather than an industrial culture.** In Japan in the Tokugawa era, from 1603 to 1867, a rising merchant class developed a place for itself in the feudal shogunate. Merchant houses did not challenge the traditional authority structure but subordinated themselves to whatever powers existed. Indeed, a few houses survived the Meiji Restoration smoothly, and one in particular (Mitsui) became a prototype for the zaibatsu. Other zaibatsu arose early in the Meiji era from enterprises that had been previously run for the benefit of the feudal overlords, the daimyo. In the Meiji era, the control of such han enterprises moved to the private sphere where, in the case of Mitsubishi, former samurai became the owners and managers. In all cases of the zaibatsu that began early in the Meiji era, the overall structure was an intermarket group. The member firms were legal corporations, were large multiunit enterprises, and could accumulate capital through corporate means. **In Japan, the corporate framework of industrial society preceded the appearance of expanded industrial markets, and that framework — indigenous and culturally specific — persists today.**

**Like the Japanese economy, the South Korean economy depends on large groupings of firms which are the descendants of traditional forms of authority and commercial cooperation. Today in South Korea,** the chaebol — large, hierarchically arranged sets of firms — are the dominant business networks. In 1980-81, the government recognized 26 chaebol, which controlled 456 firms. In 1985, there were 50 chaebol that controlled 552 firms. Their rate of growth has been extraordinary. In 1973, the top five chaebol control 8.8% of the GNP, but by 1985 the top four chaebol controlled 45% of the GNP. In 1984, the top 50 chaebol controlled about 80% of the GNP. **But this surge of growth — recent and unmistakable — is nevertheless a phenomenon related to older patterns of commercial affiliation.** The chaebol are similar to the pre-war zaibatsu in size and organizational structure. Their structure can be traced to premodern political practices and to pre-World War II Japanese industrial policy which directed Korean development after Japan's colonization of Korea in 1910. **Intermarket linkages among business units coordinated by family affiliation rather than managerial principle are expressions of preindustrial culture as much as they are responses to expanding markets.**

Each reinstatement returns the reader to the abstraction and high levels of generality that make up the topic, and each reinstatement of the topic wards off ambiguity and uncertainty. In the first paragraph, the paraphrase of the topic gives the reader a chance to think about the issue again, in slightly different terms (culture, family, authority, tradition) which anticipate the discussion which follows.

But even this doubling is not enough to ensure that the reader is going to construct the information in the second paragraph along these lines. The restatement of the topic at the beginning of that section tells the reader not only what to keep in mind, but also how the content of the paragraph will relate to the topic. Before the reader even comes across, for example, mention of the Japanese economy's return to pre-war forms after the U.S. occupation, he is told what this return *means* in this argument: deep-rooted corporate dispositions towards traditional, family-based linkages. And, when the reader has finished with the lower-level material on Japanese firms in the twentieth century, he is told how this material relates to the topic: these network linkages are persistent, and they can be traced to cultural conditions that prevailed before industrialization. If the reader has been reasoning this way, this claim will confirm his reading; if he has not been reasoning exactly along these lines, it will get him back on track, ready for the next stage of the discussion.

Compared to the diagram of the first version of "Asian corporations," the second diagram is heavy with topical repetition (••••). Correcting the disproportion between ••••• and ~~~~ results in this repetition. But you may think that the revised version is *too* repetitive? Why is the first expression of the topic, at the beginning, not enough?

The answer lies in the way the reader's brain works — not just your instructor's brain, but everybody's. Your brain, my brain, everybody's brain can concentrate on just so much at one time. Think of the reader's attention span as a desktop that can accommodate about seven items at a time.

If anything more is added, it either **covers up** one of the prior items, concealing it from view,

or, if the reader is efficiently managing his desktop, he may **file an item for later to make room for a new item.**

Then he will concentrate on what is in front of him — having more or less "forgotten" what has been filed or concealed. Unless he is prompted to do so, he will not retrieve the filed item or look for the concealed item. So **it is up to you to reactivate important ideas**, getting them back on the desktop so the reader will concentrate on them. That is what the revised version of "Asian corporations" did: it returned important ideas to the desktop.

An essay in which lower-level material is disproportionately massive, out-weighing high-level topical material, can leave the reader on his own facing a desktop covered with details. Writing out the results of your research in a first draft, you are liable to find yourself making an essay with just such disproportions — fat and sprawling at the bottom and spindly at the top.

But you can get that kind of draft into shape by introducing topical reinstatements that ward off uncertainty and incoherence. While these fatty disproportions may be a characteristic hazard of academic writing, which favours substantial evidence at lower levels of generality, they can be corrected by frequent and regular ascents to higher levels of generality. The following exercise will give you some practice in making deliberate, constructive ascents to topical levels.

## exercise

This exercise resembles one you did in Chapter Three where you interpreted facts in "Brian" and "Baboons" by finding abstractions which expressed their significance. The passages below — "Transfer," "Tests," and "Buffalo jump" — are like "Brian" and "Baboons" in that they are flat: they do not ascend to higher levels of generality and abstraction to claim the relevance of the data presented. From the perspective presented in this chapter, we would say they lack strong topics: although they are generally about, in one case, the mainstreaming of special-needs students, IQ tests in an other case, and the practices of prehistoric hunters in the third case, readers are still left to construct for themselves the significance of this information. Readers do not perform well under these conditions. (Remember the reader who had lost sight of the topic "market-vs.-cultural-explanation-for-corporate-organization" and was lost in the valley of detail about samurai owners and the South Korean GNP.)

Your job now is to provide readers with strong topics that will guide their efforts after meaning by constructing a high-level claim that can function as a reinstated topic as the reader moves through the passage. (You may wish to refer to Figure 2 to remind yourself of a pattern for such reinstatement of topic.) Suggestions for constructing a topic follow each passage.

## "Transfer"

Some children enroled in special schools which address their particular emotional, behavioural, and educational difficulties eventually move back into mainstream schools. The passage which follows describes a sequence of activities entailed in such a move back to the mainstream.

Standard procedures govern the integration of special-needs students into regular classrooms. First, at a regular review meeting in the special school, the child possibly ready for transfer to a mainstream school is identified. A date is set for a second review of the child's progress and suitability for transfer. If the child's parents are not at the meeting, they are informed of the school's intentions; teachers set up a meeting with parents to discuss the possibility of transfer. Teachers plan behaviour and work targets for the pupil. The special-school head or school psychologist selects an appropriate mainstream school, and the class teacher visits the mainstream school, consulting with its special-needs or counselling teams and collecting information on curriculum and textbooks. The class teacher begins a program to prepare the pupil emotionally and psychologically for the transfer. The pupil and class teacher visit the school. The pupil and his or her parents visit the school. Staff at the special school prepare a school report. At the second review meeting, mainstream-school staff, special-school staff and parents decide terms, dates and objectives for the trial period. These objectives are discussed with the pupil. The special school sends a copy of the school report to the new school and a formal letter to the ministry of education. The trial period begins, with a follow-up meeting towards the end of the trial period. At the end of the trial period, the mainstream school prepares a report on the pupil's progress, making recommendations. The pupil transfers permanently to the mainstream school or returns to the special school. A second letter goes to the ministry of education.

To begin the process of building the passage up to higher levels of generality — endowing it, that is, with a topic —

- find a general, possibly abstract NAME or NAMES for the activities it describes; find a word or words which express what larger realm of human activities these activities belong to;

- find a NAME for the purpose of these activities;

- identify the values which would guide those who would recommend and/or perform such activities (what characteristics do these activities share? what does each step in the procedure have in common with other steps?)

- think about whether these activities seem good or bad to you; translate your sense of goodness or badness into terms which specify the valuable or undesirable characteristics of these activities (maybe you will sense a mix of good and bad).

Rewrite the passage in such a way as to give it a strong topic, making paragraph divisions where necessary and keeping in mind that the divisions between paragraphs are especially suitable places to locate your ascents to abstractions and high levels of generality.

PASSAGE B **"Tests"**

Historically, IQ tests have been used as a measure of educational input (with intelligence viewed as the "raw material" for schooling) to sort pupils so they could be efficiently educated according to their future roles in society. Test results could also be used to identify those who would be excluded from schooling. Goddard's 1912 data "proved" that 83 per cent of Jews, 80 per cent of Hungarians, 79 per cent of Italians, and 87 per cent of Russians were "feeble-minded." These data were used to justify low immigration quotas for those groups. Terman's test data "proved" that "[Indians, Mexicans, and Negroes] should be segregated in special classes. . . . They cannot master abstractions, but they can often be made efficient workers." Terman found many inequalities in performance among groups on his IQ test, which was adapted from Binet's work in France. Most seemed to confirm what he already knew: that various groups were inherently unequal in their mental capacities. When girls scored higher than boys in his 1916 version of the Standford-Binet test, he revised the test to correct for this apparent flaw by selecting items to create parity among genders in the scores. Other inequalities — between urban and rural students, students of higher and lower socioeconomic status, native English speakers and immigrants, White and Blacks — did not occasion such revisions.

Adapted from Linda Darling-Hammond 1994 Performance-based assessment and educational equity. *Harvard Educational Review* 64, 1, 5-29.

To develop a strong topical guide for the reader of this passage

- find a general, high-level NAME or NAMES for the motivations of the testers and the results of the testing described here;

- identify the relations between the tests' uses and the test-takers' scores (note that, while the first statements refer principally to education, they also point beyond the school-room, to "roles in society," and the passage goes on to mention "immigration quotas").

Rewrite the passage in such a way as to conduct the reader towards an understanding of the significance of this information: what do we learn about testing, science, and the social order?

PASSAGE C     **"Buffalo jump"**

At ancient buffalo jumps, like the one at Head-Smashed-In, Alberta, pre-historic hunters drove buffalo over cliffs to their death. From the beginnings of this practice, about 5,700 years ago, until about 2,000 years ago, the hunters consumed only the choice cuts of the slaughtered animals and left the rest to rot. Then practices changed. The hunters began dragging much of their kill at Head-

Smashed-In to flat land close by. After drying or roasting the bison flesh on hearths, they crushed the animals' long bones into splinters, boiling the fragments to render bone grease. To boil bones, prehistoric families first had to heat stones in a fire and then drop them into a hide-lined pit filled with water. Good boiling stones were rare at Head-Smashed-In, for the local sandstone crumbled during heating. So band members brought their own stones with them — tons of quartzite and other rocks from more than a mile away. The bone-boiling process was necessary to the production of pemmican. During prehistoric times, the Peigan and other members of the Blackfoot Nation rendered bone grease to stir into mixtures of smashed dried meat and saskatoon berries, making massive 40-kilogram bags of the long-lasting food. The grease not only added to the usable protein in the meat but made the mixture extremely stable. According to one account from the Canadian fur trade, a bag of pemmican was slit open and safely consumed 20 years after it had been prepared. After techniques for producing pemmican developed, later bands began to pitch semipermanent camps in the nearby Oldman River Valley. Having extensive stores of pemmican for the winter, they no longer had to range so far afield for food.

Adapted from Heather Pringle 1988 Boneyard enigma. *Equinox* May-June, 87-104.

To begin to build up this flat, disproportionately low-level passage

- find general NAMES for what it is about; find words which express what larger realm of occurrences these changes and practices belong to;

- identify the main characteristics of the practices and situations described;

- express the significance of these data: what do we learn by finding out about these ancient occurrences?

Rewrite the passage in such a way as to make its topic clear, dividing for paragraphs where necessary.

## 4.3.2   *List-like outlines*

First drafts of academic essays may be naturally prone to the disproportions that lead to incoherence. Having acquired the mass of lower-level materials that typically substantiate scholarly arguments, you want to get it down on paper. The drafting of research results can produce structures that would eventually leave readers feeling uncertain about how all this material fits together. Unrevised, such structures would induce uncertainty in readers, making them ask, "Why is *this* next to *this*? What is all this adding up to?"

This eventual uncertainty on the part of the reader can be traced to common circumstances of drafting. It can also sometimes be traced to conditions at another, earlier stage of the writing process, which is also deeply influenced by the imposing bulk of lower-level evidence that academic writers have to deal with. Just as in the drafting stage, where you may often find yourself hostage to your own voluminous data, so too in the **planning** stage you can find yourself a servant of your own thoroughness. Having collected so much information, you now have to organize its delivery to your reader.

So you begin to *sort*, grouping like items together — mentions of South Korea here, mentions of Japan over there. Like all writers, you are feeling a bit anxious at this stage of the composing process.

So, when you remember what you were taught in school about a proper *outline*, you feel as if you are getting somewhere. You write down

I. Introduction

and you feel a bit better. In need of good feelings at this unsettling stage of composing, you go ahead with what you were taught in Grade 7, or Grade 10:

I. Introduction

II.
    A.
    B.
        1.
        2.
    C.

III.
    A.
        1.
        2.
    B.

IV. Conclusion

What a relief. You have remembered that the first levels have Roman numerals, and the next levels use capital letters, and so on. You also remembered that you can't just have *one* lower level — just *II.A.* followed by *III.* If you go lower at all, you have to go at least two steps. *II.A.* requires *II.B* — minimum.

    This kind of outline can be a useful memory device: it reminds you to mention certain parts of your research. Otherwise you might forget. But this kind of outline also has flaws, and if you rely on it too confidently, these flaws can cause problems when you come to actually writing the essay. For one thing, the outline makes no estimate of the essay's proportions: it can fail entirely to account for the volume of each element. II.B.2 may be hugely disproportionate, smothering the stages of discussion which precede and follow it, overwhelming the reader's mental desktop. If you rely solely on your schoolroom outline, and don't screen the product for disproportion, you can end up with an incoherent essay — despite the outline's orderly and proportionate appearance.

Disproportion is not the only risk you run by relying on this kind of planning. There are other potential problems as well, also to do with incoherence. Strange as it may seem, even the most intricately ordered and labelled outline can fail to generate the **strong topic** you need to keep your reader on track and to ward off uncertainty. (It was the strong topic that was called on repeatedly in the revision of "Asian corporations.") The schoolroom outline can mislead you into thinking that you have a topic, when really all you have is a general name for what you are talking about: "sport," "Japanese firms," "Toronto policemen," "irony in Pride and Prejudice." Establishing and frequently reinstating these general names is good. In fact, it is the least you can do for your readers, and they certainly expect it of you. But it is not nearly enough to control their effort after meaning (as we saw in the first version of "Asian corporations," where the most that could be said for the second paragraph was that it was mainly about Japanese firms in the twentieth century).

To see how a schoolroom outline can fail to generate a strong topic, and can mislead you as to the coherence of your planned essay, we will examine such an outline.

**Literacy in Renaissance Italy**

I. Introduction

II. Literacy in business
     A. Different handwriting for different purposes
     B. Notaries
     C. Numeracy
          1. Ledgers
          2. Abacus schools

III. Domestic literacy
     A. The ricordanze (memoranda)
          1. records of family history and accounts
          2. notation of good advice, mention of local history
     B. The letters of Allessandra Macingli Strozzi to her husband

IV. Literacy and the Church
    A. Church attitudes towards literacy
        1. illiteracy and superstition
        2. literacy and heresy
    B. Censorship
    C. Keeping records of who went to confession

V. Literacy and the state
    A. Bureaucratic communication and control
        1. census
        2. passes and licences
        3. reports
    B. Literacy as a threat to secrecy
    C. Graffiti and political posters

VI. Conclusion

Material for this outline adapted from Peter Burke 1987 The uses of literacy in early modern Italy. In *The Social History of Language*, ed. P. Burke and R. Porter. Cambridge: Cambridge UP. 21-42.

Someone with an outline like this might seem ready to write.

And she may indeed be ready to go — if, that is, she is prepared to recognize and make up for the deficiencies in this plan as she goes along.

    The first deficiency appears with *I. Introduction*. What is she going to *say* in her introduction? Maybe she will write, "There was literacy in many forms in Renaissance Italy. There was literacy in business, at home, in the Church, and in the state." The writer suspects that this will not impress her reader, so she tries for something more compelling: "Literacy has been an important issue in societies throughout modern history, and Renaissance Italy was no exception. People in business used reading and writing. . . ." But what is the "important issue" in that? The writer may struggle with her introduction for a long time — maybe for an hour, maybe all day.

The outline offers no help to the struggling writer: it has, after all, constructed no topic other than the general category "Literacy in Renaissance Italy." And its weakness here is only the first sign of its deficiencies. Say the writer does get going, composing an introduction by default, and heads into section *II. Literacy in Business.* She tells about "different handwriting for different purposes" (why is handwriting significant?), and then the outline directs her to tell about "notaries" — because their handwriting was a certain way? Why are "notaries" next to "handwriting"? This outline, for all its headings and indentations, is only a list of mentions, grouped under general names. Making the outline according to schoolroom rules may have been satisfying, but actually writing the essay is not so satisfying. Having to introduce "notaries" right after "different handwriting," the writer can feel uneasy about her reader's reaction: what will the reader make of this gap? How will she cross it?

Other gaps lurk throughout. Here are some of them:

- Arriving at *III. Domestic Literacy B. The letters of Allessandra Macingli,* the writer finds she has a lot of material on this woman's letters about her children — their first steps, their remarks about their absent father. So she writes out all this accumulated information. But how is the reader going to interpret this material so disproportionately comprehensive that it begins to make a world of its own? The reader may begin to construct his own topic: "Renaissance attitudes towards child development." And, then, how will her reader behave when she has to make the transition from letters about children to Church ideas about superstition? What's the connection? Why are these two subjects next to each other? Only the most strenuous and ingenious effort after meaning could construct a topical bridge between these two sections.

> This looks dangerous.
>
> THIS WAY
>
> letters about children
>
> church concern about superstition
>
> A READER AT THE GAP

- *IV. Literacy and the Church C. Keeping records of who went to confession* comes up against *V. Literacy and the state.* What is the connection? Is the Church *like* the state? Or unlike it? In what way? Is the reader supposed to go on to *V. Literacy and the state* expecting confirmation of what was said about the Church? Or are the state uses of literacy and their consequences revealingly different? Or is "the state" just next on the list, with no meaning intended?

- *V. Literacy and the state B. Literacy as a threat to secrecy* tells about the problems rulers had with leaving evidence behind when they or their officials wrote things down. But then comes *C. Graffiti and political posters.* Posters and graffiti aren't secret at all. What's the point here?

- *VI. Conclusion* — what *is* the conclusion? What is the point of all this?

An experienced writer would be disturbed by all the gaps, disconnections, and discontinuities in this plan for an account of literacy in Renaissance Italy. She would know that her reader was going to react awkwardly — either constructing off-track meanings, or, more likely, finding the effort too much and abandoning it, taking the essay as only a list of things the writer has found out.

A writer might be able to repair these gaps in the drafting process, making connections and developing a strong topic. These repairs could be hard work, involving false starts, new starts, and serious thinking. But eventually the writer might come up with a topic something like this:

> business and family uses of literacy show how calculation and accounting for details in <u>personal</u> affairs were valued. This might suggest that individuals saw themselves increasing their <u>control</u> of their personal lives. <u>But</u>, going beyond the individual and family to Church and state, while we still find literacy serving individual control (reading the Bible privately, writing graffiti), we also find literacy as an instrument of large-scale control of the population (census, records of confession)

This topic answers the "what-is-this-about" question much more powerfully than the pseudo-topic "literacy in Renaissance Italy." Moreover, the topic's complex answer to the aboutness question is a sign of how functional it will be in establishing meaning for both writer and reader.

- It gives the writer important things to say in her introduction, preparing the reader for the argument that follows.

- It can be reinstated at frequent intervals, showing the reader what to concentrate on and how to fit the parts together. It can show, for example, how graffiti relate to census-taking (they are competing effects of literacy: on the one hand expressions of individual dissent and, on the other hand, expressions of state control).

- It can guide the writer in the use of her research results, directing her, for example, to reduce material on children's first steps and emphasize instead how family letters enabled people to keep in touch and informed despite physical separation.

With this strong topic in hand, the writer is in a good position to deliver to the reader a coherent essay. And the reader, instead of facing a loosely assembled list of things the writer knows, will make efficient efforts after meaning: concentrating, remembering, and reasoning productively. Once the strong topic appears on the writing scene, this story about making an essay heads for a happy ending.

This version of composing shows the writer discovering gaps and incoherence in the list-like outline and, heroically, repairing those gaps with a new-born topic. But this is only one way of telling the story of the birth of a topic. Topics do not always show up at just this point when the writer faces facts and realizes her outline is faulty. Different writers and different writing situations can await the fertile moment at different stages in the composing process. Sometimes writers might conceive of their topic when they review their outline and spot disconnection: aware of the gap, they come up with the meaningful connection, the proposition that justifies these two things being said next to each other.

Or sometimes the topic might emerge when the writer is composing her first draft. Trying to get from section *III* to section *IV*, she finds herself stuck for a "transition."

Writers who discover connections while they are drafting might also be the kinds of writers who can do a good job with an only barely coherent first draft. They read over what they have written, predict that their readers are going to feel stranded or confused at some points, and rewrite to establish connections and topic.

Other times, the topic arrives as the essay **plan** is developing. For many writers (including students with a heavy workload), it is not practical to count on writing and rewriting until a strong topic is coaxed out of successive drafts and all gaps and discontinuities are repaired. With a good plan in hand at the start, overworked writers can avoid the kind of time-consuming revisions that call for the whole essay to be reconstructed.

But the traditional form of the schoolroom outline may block the kind of planning that will reveal the routes and connections which themselves constitute a strong, complex topic. The list-like flatness of the schoolroom outline in itself seems likely to generate flat, list-like essays. So you might experiment with other representations of your essay in the planning stage. You might try forms that keep your materials suspended above linear order until you are ready to arrange for their presentation to a reader. For example, you might try just loosely positioning, on a single page, high-level names for sectors of your material:

*community*        *knowledge*

*science*

Then reflect on these materials, elaborating them, and mapping routes between them:

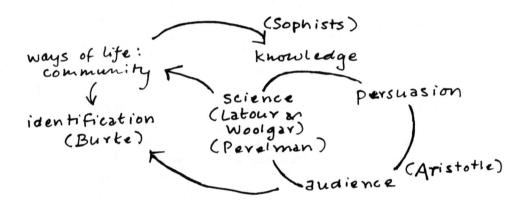

Then contemplate this map (which is in fact your **topic**, although it is not yet in propositional form), and practise different routes you might take: "if I start at 'community' and 'ways of life,' I can go next to 'knowledge' as locally produced and that will let me bring in Perleman's and Latour and Woolgar's descriptions of scientific communities . . ., but then I'm not sure how I'll get to 'persuasion.' Maybe by going right back to 'ways of life' or maybe I should go right from 'community' and 'ways'"

of life to 'persuasion' . . . ." Once you have plotted your route, number its destinations in the order you have decided on.

This technique may help you overcome the pitfalls of the schoolroom outline, and come up with the kind of arguments typical of scholarly writing. But, of course, there are no rules for when and how to construct a topic, only an unavoidable principle: an essay without a strong, complex topic risks incoherence.

## 4.4 Topic as structure and process

In Chapters Two and Three, we investigated the levels of generality, looking at how abstractions, generalities, and details positioned themselves in relation to one another. In your reading, analysis, and summarizing of a passage, you developed your awareness of the multi-level *structures* of prose.

This chapter has been concerned with the *processes* associated with these structures — that is, it has looked at reading and writing on the one hand, and the organization of prose on the other. Readers use texts' abstractions and high-level generalities to manage their comprehension. In planning, drafting, or revising, writers construct high-level, often abstract propositions to control lower-level information and build connections between parts.

In the remainder of this chapter, we will develop our understanding of these structures and processes. First we will revisit the idea of *topic*, to acclaim it as the source of meaningfulness. Then we will go on to add to our portrait of the reader at work, to consider practical issues related to topic — namely where to put topical statements and how to estimate a reader's need for them.

## 4.4.1 *Topic as meaning*

Let us make a strong claim. Let us say that topic is meaning. By interpreting lower-level statements, your topic demonstrates that what you are saying is relevant to larger issues, and it says how it is relevant.

So far, one of our tests for topic has been the aboutness question. Facing an assembly of items or sentences, we ask, "What is this *about?*", thereby screening the collection or passage for connections. The items on the party tray were disconnected: they were not about anything. The bus-stop man's sentences were disconnected: we can't say what he is talking about without repeating each item.

But we also found that, even when we can say what a passage is about, we can't necessarily say what it *means*. Items in a passage could show enough connection to allow us to say the passage was about "sport," or "schooling," or "Toronto policemen," or "shoe-binding," but we still could not make any confident claims as to what the writer *meant*. So, now, to test for topic, we move beyond the question "What is this about?" to "What does this mean?"

In the passage about Toronto policemen (p 122) (which is "about" Toronto police because each sentence mentions something to do with them), we recognize and understand the things the writer is referring to when he mentions that many Toronto policemen had been in the armed forces, and we understand what he is referring to when he mentions the department administrators' military experience. We don't deny this information — even though it may be news to us. But we don't know *why* he mentions these things. We don't know what he *means to say*.

Before we look at circumstances which give rise to meaning, we will reflect briefly on the social measures of information itself. These measures differ in different situations, so that "meaning" can sometimes be derived from context. The simplest case is the question-and-answer situation.

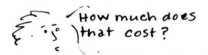 How much does that cost?

 It's $45.98

**B** doesn't have to explain the meaning of the information he offers: that is, he doesn't have to mention any high-level abstraction like, for example, global competitiveness or fiscal policy in post-industrial economies to establish the significance of his remark. Because **A** has asked a question, the relevance of **B's** remark is located in the context of his utterance. Sometimes people anticipate unstated questions.

It's 100% cotton.
Completely washable.

School culture is full of questions and answers. These questions and answers structure much of the interaction in school. Anticipating questions, students pay special kinds of attention to teachers' remarks.

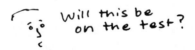

Will this be on the test?

And, in school culture, students get used to being asked questions by people who know the answers:

- Under what conditions did British Columbia enter confederation?

- What <u>three</u> sources of evidence does the author use to support her main point? (Answer in complete sentences.)

Answers to questions don't need to explain their relevance or significance. Their meaning is already established. And, in fact, a questioner who asked to know the relevance of an answer would seem out of line.

What time is it?   It's 3:20   Why are you telling me that?   You ASKED!

Accustomed to question-and-answer discourse, students get used to producing prose whose meaning is located in the surrounding school context. They write passages without prominent topic structures, and these texts are acceptable in the schoolroom.

At university, some of these question-and-answer structures persist — or seem to.

- Describe the main features of the Young Offenders Act.

When a writer does as he is told — answers the question about the Young Offenders Act — and gets his paper back with a **C** or **B-**, he may feel like the person who cooperatively answered the question about the time, and then was confronted with more questions. This seems unfair.

The instructor who asks the exam or essay question probably does have some of the same motives as the teacher who asked about confederation: she wants to see if the student knows this material, and some of her expectations may be satisfied by statements which are all, generally, "about" the Young Offenders Act. But, as an academic reader, she also has other expectations. Even though the writer is still a student, he is writing in genres that derive many of their features from the genres of professional scholarship, where there is no explicit or implicit question from an implied teacher who already knows the answer. Statements demonstrate their relevance not through context but through topic structures that touch the abstractions and high-level generalities we have been looking at.

## 4.4.2    *Topic as guide to interpretation*

In the schoolroom question-and-answer setting for writing, details don't need to be interpreted by the student writer. (While some schoolteachers may be pleased to see high-level interpretations, many high-school students know that interpretation is risky in that it may conflict with textbook generalities that are the basis of testing.) The question is in effect the reader's guide to interpreting statements and the writer's intent. The question establishes and secures meaning.

But when there is no question, the meaning of lower-level statements can be uncertain, as we know from previous examples. Before we investigate the implications of this condition for writers and readers, let's take one more look at just how uncertain meaning can be when a passage is unsecured by a context of interpretation. Here is mention of, say, a situation in a story.

> The table was bare, the floor swept clean. The window
> was open, and a keen breeze crossed the room. The walls
> glimmered in the pale light.

We have no problem figuring out what sorts of entities or conditions these sentences refer to. We all know what *bare tables*, *clean-swept floors* and *open windows* are, although each of us has different mental images of these entities. As for what the passage is about, it seems to be about "a room." Details have been sorted according to this implicit heading.

However, the fact that the passage does not disclose *meaning* — despite plain reference and some "aboutness" — becomes clear when we add alternative sentences at the beginning of the passage. We could say

> The scene was one of desolation and abandonment, of emptiness. The table was bare, the floor swept clean. The window was open, and a keen breeze crossed the room. The walls glimmered in the pale light.

Now *bare table* and *open window* mean desolation, loss, absence. Alternatively, the reader could approach the same sentences with a different statement of topic, a different guide to meaning.

> All clarity and candour, the scene suggested renewal and fresh beginnings. The table was bare, the floor swept clean. The window was open, and a keen breeze crossed the room. The walls glimmered in the pale light.

Now *bare table* and *open window* don't mean "desolation" any more. Now they mean renewal, promise, hope. Although the second, third, and fourth sentences continue to refer to the same entities or circumstances in each case, their meaning differs according to the sentences that introduce them. Those introductory sentences are **topic statements**. The topic statements

- construct a higher level of generality by giving a general and, in this case, abstract name to the details of the passages;

- establish the meaning of the objects and conditions referred to;

- guide the reader's interpretation of the facts mentioned.

The exercise below will give you a chance to see *meaning* developing out of mentions.

---

## exercise

The following passages are like the first bare-room passage in that they make clear enough reference but they do not establish meaning. Provide each passage with two, alternative topic statements to guide the reader's interpretation of the passage's mentions. These alternative topics will guide the reader to different interpretations of the phenomena being referred to. Compare your topic statements with those of your classmates.

PASSAGE A  The PTL Club, an hour-long programme broadcast by the Global Television Network at 7:00 a.m., originates in North Carolina. Viewers of the PTL Club become "partners" by mailing in a monthly contribution of fifteen dollars or more, and have the option of donating a larger "one-time gift" in exchange for a record, book, art print, or other item whose monetary value is less than the contribution. The PTL Club features a resident singing group and maintains its own orchestra.

PASSAGE B  When the Lethbridge Herald was purchased by Thomson Newspaper Ltd., in 1980, the publishers noted the paper's substantial legislative reporting and political commentary. They suggested less political and government coverage and more "women's news," more stories about community events, more coverage of leading citizens, service clubs, chambers of commerce, merchants.

Adapted from Klaus Phle 1988 The buck stops here . . . *content* July-August.

PASSAGE C  In the large convent schools which educated the daughters of the middle and artisan classes of seventeenth-century France, girls who were not at work on their books worked on sewing. Where possible, specialists taught handwork, often in large, well-lit classrooms. Schools which educated girls from the upper classes taught handwork only to a certain level of expertise, highly skilled work being seen as inappropriate for "modest young women of good family." In many pauper schools of France, reading was at best a minor concern, often overlooked altogether. Students worked in silence, sewing, knitting socks, and lacemaking while they listened to spiritual instruction.

Adapted from Elizabeth Rapley 1987 Fénelon revisited: a review of girls' education in seventeenth century France *Histoire Sociale - Social History* 20, 40, 299-318.

## 4.4.3   *Reader meets topic*

The alternative revisions of the bare-room passage all place the topic statement at the beginning. The reader meets the topic before she encounters the facts which develop it. We seem to be taking for granted that this is where topic statements go — on the top, like a hat.

Perhaps we should not feel so assured. Maybe topics are not like hats. Maybe they can be scarves or boots or belts. Before we plan our outfits, we should get a better idea of what occasions we are dressing up for.

Take, for example, the practice of developing a critical position, introduced in Chapter Three. In that section I said that, in writing critical summary, you had options as to where to locate your critical stand. You could show some of it at the beginning, and then arrange for it to reappear from time to time throughout the summary, giving it full attention in the conclusion. Or you could save the evaluation entirely for the conclusion. Each of these choices will have different effects on the reader.

Say you tell at the start the gist of evaluation, expressing yourself at a high level of generality and abstraction: "Although Michaels relies heavily on quantitative methods of content analysis, his survey of print media does help to explain the role of newspapers in generating moral panic in national communities." As you go on to summarize the original, you keep "quantitative methods" and "moral panic" in topical focus, and in your conclusion you show what is limiting about quantitative methods, and you explain the significance of the moral panic phenomenon. In this case, your reader has your evaluation *in mind* throughout, and interprets what you report about the original in light of these claims.

If, on the other hand, you save your critical stand for the end, the reader will experience your summary differently. She will interpret material from the original without being guided by your critical position, maybe getting ideas quite different from the ones you are heading for. The concluding evaluation may come as a surprise.

Sometimes these surprises are effective. They startle the reader into re-thinking material from the centre of the discussion. And it is possible that instructors who are used to reading critical summary are prepared to be surprised. They are used to a reading experience that suddenly shifts perspective, and they like it. And reviews published in scholarly journals often have this surprise structure.

However, critical summaries may be a special case — an academic genre where surprises are conventional. You will remember that the revised version of "Asian corporations" goes to great lengths to *avoid* surprises. The topic is repeatedly reinstated to guide the reader's interpretation of facts. The diagram which illustrated the new structure of the argument showed regular ascents to high-level topic claims.

But the diagram can be misleading if we take it to be only a prescription for *formal* regularity — "Rule 1: Reinstate your topic every 250 words." In fact, in making decisions about positioning your topic statements, you should rely not on such prescriptions but on your judgements of the *reader's experience* of your writing. To make judgements about your reader's experience, you need a reliable concept of this being who reads what you write. Earlier in this chapter, we started to develop such a concept, sketching a portrait of the reader at work. We pictured him at a desk, the top of which represented his attention span, his capacity for concentrating and remembering. We saw how this desktop could accommodate a certain number of items — and no more. If more items arrived, they pushed off or covered up what was already there. In effect, the reader no longer had the concealed or removed items *in mind* .

Now we will add to that portrait of the reader. We will sketch in features that help us make judgements about position and frequency of high-level topic statements.

## 4.4.4    *Keeping the desktop tidy*

The reader's desktop is a finite area. It can't get bigger. In other words, the reader's attention span — or short-term memory — is inelastic. No matter how hard the reader tries (or how urgently you wish he would try), he can only concentrate on a relatively small number of things at a time. This is the way the human brain works. Writers have to learn to live with this inescapable condition of reading comprehension.

This small, inelastic space for paying attention may make the reader seem like a limited being, hardly worth addressing with an interesting essay. Moreover, this limitation does not match other qualities of our own reading experience: we read articles, chapters, books, and we have a sense of remembering a lot more than the handful of items that happened to be the last ones to pass across our mental desktops. We need to add features to the portrait of the reader — features that will account for this circumstance, and represent the reader as a worthy addressee, capable of grasping big ideas, under the right circumstances.

To the picture of the reader and desktop we will add a **management device**. To manage the flow of information and make the most of it, the reader operates a mechanism which detects

(a) those items which can be combined to form a single item, thus leaving room for new items to be concentrated on;

(b) those items which can be put aside on a nearby table as not centrally relevant at this point but liable to be necessary at any moment;

(c) those items which can be neglected, left to fall off the desktop when other material arrives —

— or sent to long-term memory files which house all we know but aren't thinking about right now.

Now that the reader is equipped with an information management device, we will observe the operation of this device under certain reading conditions.

**Case 1. The reader faces an essay without repeated reinstatements of a strong, complex topic.**

(a) He encounters a series of mentions whose relationship to each other is not expressed.

When no clear topic explains the relationship — that is, *interprets* the details — the reader can't operate the management device to combine items into a higher, more compact concept. They take up space that's needed for new items (the reader stalls, doesn't move forward). Or they simply fall off or get covered up by the next information the reader meets (they slip the reader's mind). In other words, the reader finds he can't concentrate on what comes next, or he simply forgets what he has just read.

Or the reader might make the effort after meaning despite the absence of topic.

These speculations — none of which is confirmed by the essay itself — take up space on the desktop, making it harder for the reader to concentrate on new items as they arrive.

(b) When the reader's management device notices that an issue which has been important so far, and worth keeping on the desktop, suddenly withdraws from the text while other issues arrive, the device has to make a decision about what to do with the now overshadowed item.

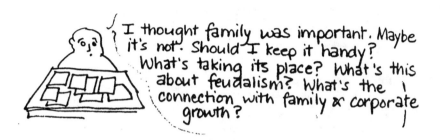

These speculations themselves take up space on the desktop, absorbing valuable processing capacity, deflecting the reader's concentration from new material to problems in managing information itself. The reader has to think about what is going on rather than about what is being said. Either the device will make a default decision, letting the old material drift away randomly, or it will take the risk of investing in the overshadowed issue, keeping it nearby and referring to it from time to time, bringing it back to the desktop to check for its relevance.

Of course, the investment may be unprofitable. The issue may never come up again, yet the reader uses valuable space to entertain it.

(c) Finally, when the management device is not properly instructed by a strong topic, it may make some very inefficient decisions about long-term storage. Encountering a big claim early in an essay, and finding it neither developed nor repeated in subsequent passages, the device may judge that it is not important enough to keep handy. So the claim gets sent to the long-term memory files — that big, elastic capacity that houses the individual's experience and knowledge of the world.

Now the material is not exactly forgotten, but it is no longer in mind. And, stored in long-term files, it is relatively *inaccessible*, compared to items on the desktop and on temporary holding surfaces. If the device has made a mistake, and it turns out that this material *is* needed, the reader has to go and retrieve the item from the long-term files.

The retrieval takes up attention capacity. During the time the reader spends retrieving something from long-term storage (assuming he *can* retrieve it, and hasn't simply forgotten it), the desktop gets dishevelled. When he returns, he finds that things have fallen off, and have to be recalled by re-reading.

List-like essays which string together what the writer has learned, essays without regular ascents to higher levels of generality and interpretive abstractions, essays without strong, reinstated topics — all these kinds of essays fail to trigger the efficient operation of the information-management device. The reader finds it hard to concentrate, remember, reach conclusions. The reader is not likely to appreciate the essay as meaningful.

Maybe this management device seems like a rickety contraption — prone to error, oversensitive to distractions, too liable to break down. Under the conditions of Case 1 — incoherence, missing topics, list-like flatness — the device *is* a fragile, high-strung mechanism. But under other conditions, it is very efficient.

**Case 2. The reader encounters an essay which repeatedly reinstates a strong, complex topic.**

(a) By providing unmistakable guides to interpretation, the topic explicitly instructs the device on how to combine lower-level details into higher-level, space-saving generalities and abstractions. This combining reduces bulk on the desktop without sacrificing information, and leaves the reader room to concentrate on new material.

(b) The topic explicitly instructs the device as to which issues can be temporarily removed from the desktop but should be kept handy for later use. When they are needed, the topic explicitly recalls them, and shows how they relate to the current contents of the desktop.

(c) The topic explicitly instructs the device as to which issues are only peripheral and can be sent to long-term storage, or, if worse comes to worst, even forgotten. These materials won't be needed later, and don't have to take up the reader's limited and valuable resources for paying attention.

Coherent essays with a strong topic structure activate the reader's information-management device with clear instructions. The reader concentrates, remembers, and reasons efficiently. The reader appreciates the essay as meaningful.

## 4.4.5 *Positioning the topic*

With the portrait of the reader more fleshed out, we can return to the question that came up earlier: where should you situate topic statements in your essay? When this question came up before, we had only formal answers: "at the beginning," "every 250 words." Now we have access to better answers — answers based on cognitive rather than formal conditions.

Make your decisions about topic statements according to your judgements about the conditions of the reader's desktop.

- If the desktop is littered with a string of mentions that the reader is liable to dwell on too much or that are simply liable to fall off, reinstate your topic to enable the management device to combine and reduce these details to a compact, meaningful concept.

- If it is time to switch the contents of the desktop from one area of your discussion to another, make sure your reader realizes that the main points of the content that is now yielding to other material have to be kept in mind, kept handy. And tell your reader how the new material relates to the points that are temporarily withdrawing.

- If you have presented information or ideas that are not going to be needed again, make sure you let your reader know that he doesn't have to keep them handy. (Consider eliminating them altogether, to avoid miscuing the management device.) If, on the other hand, you find that later stages of your essay depend on concepts introduced much earlier and probably by now abandoned by the reader, find ways of keeping those concepts topical during the long interval when they are not in immediate use. And when you do bring them back to the centre of the desktop, remember that they have been out-of-use, and the reader needs to be reminded of their significance.

By consulting the portrait of the reader, you will probably find yourself positioning strong topical propositions at paragraph divisions. These are the sites where the management device has to make important decisions about what to do with the contents of a crowded desktop as new information shows up: forget, file, save, keep handy.

And, if you stand back a moment and regard this reader at work, you will probably reckon that it is most efficient to instruct the management device *before* it screens and manipulates information coming its way — before it makes mistakes, before it invests in the wrong concepts, before it gets clogged with details.

In conversation, we can repair uncertainties on the spot.

In reading and writing these opportunities for repair don't occur. (Unless you count on your reader re-reading and re-reading your essay until he constructs your topic and meaning for himself. Don't count on that.)

So, generally speaking, you will motivate more efficient comprehension in your reader if you position your high-level topic claims *out front* — in your introduction and at paragraph boundaries. First provide your reader with the guide to interpretation; then present the information to be interpreted. After you have presented this information, *confirm* its interpretation, to eliminate any uncertainties that may have arisen despite the explicitness of the out-front guide to interpretation.

As well as having some cognitive justification (it contributes to efficient thinking), this arrangement is also conventional in most scholarly genres. In other words, it is a recognized way of doing things. But, even while we accept this arrangement, we should keep two conditions in mind.

First, while the positioning of the topic statement *before* the lower-level material it interprets offers benefits to the *reader*, it is not necessarily a natural position for the *writer*. Sometimes the big topic statement is the last, rather than the first, thing the writer comes up with. So drafts can have fairly slight topic statements — paragraphs beginning like this, for example:

> Another interesting thing to note about the definition of bargaining units in marine industries is the inclusion of shoreworkers. Early in this century east-coast fishery interests. . . .

Even professional scholars have to rework their drafts to improve their topic statements to get more substantial material up front for readers' guidance — something more than just "what comes next is interesting." Often that material is already there somewhere in the paragraph, maybe at the end, maybe here and there. Revision gathers and positions that information so it can instruct the reader's management device and enable him to maintain an orderly desktop.

Second, the typical high-to-low-and-back-to-high structures of scholarly expression are open to some criticism. Perhaps you have already felt them as constraining or oppressive, tending to contain your writing in forms that can't quite accommodate your reasoning or experience. Some analyses of the scholarly genres go further, suggesting that this is more than a personal predicament. These analyses maintain that the conventions of scholarly prose have developed in such a way as to permit the expression of only *certain types of knowledge* — knowledge which, roughly speaking, *can* be captured in the complex, abstract and generalizing propositions of topical statements. Such propositions exert what to some is an unjustifiable or undesirable **control** over the reader's experience. Scholarly styles force writers and readers to definitive or conclusive stances, and disallow uncertainty or indeterminacy. At the same time, some commentators on scholarly style see political implications in these circumstances, arguing that the forms of knowledge constructed by the scholarly genres have traditionally served central, mainstream or élite interests, and disallowed the perspectives and interests of others, which do not fit under available abstractions. In later chapters, we will reflect further on these criticisms of the scholarly genres and on proposals for change or challenge to scholarly expression.

## 4.4.6    *Think-aloud protocols — catching the reader in the act*

People studying readers' behaviours try to find out about reading comprehension: how do readers get messages from texts? What kind of writing makes the message obscure? What kind makes it clear?

You can probably imagine that this kind of research is not easy. If we want to find out about how people obey traffic signals, we can station ourselves at an intersection and watch cars speeding up, slowing down, stopping and then going again. But how can we watch people read?

To catch readers in the act, researchers have devised ways of measuring minute physical signs of reading, like eye-movement. And other measures try to get at comprehension itself, as a *fait accompli*, by asking readers questions about what they have read, or asking them to perform other tasks to do with their reading.

Another technique for researching the reading process is the think-aloud protocol. The think-aloud protocol asks subjects to report the ideas that are going through their heads as they perform a task — like writing an essay or reading one. Think-aloud reports are like eyewitness testimony of events researchers can't witness themselves. Here is a fragment of a think-aloud protocol, cited in a research article (Yvonne Waern 1988 Thoughts on text in context: Applying the think-aloud method to text processing. *Text* 8, 4, 327-350):

TEXT:

Many people considered him to be an example of the exinanition of classical thought, but he was, in fact, a subtle and thoroughly philosophical thinker in the best classical tradition.

COMMENT:

1. Exinanition? Queer word
2. Well, exinanition, that is really disturbing
3. Ex, that means out or out of
4. Inan, I don't know at all what that means
5. It kind of destroys the whole text
6. So it must be something which is the opposite to being a thoroughly philosophical thinker since it says:
7. He was, in fact, a thoroughly philosophical thinker
8. What you stumble on is the word, kind of, and you want to get its meaning from other things,

9. but this is the only thing it is possible to get out of this,
   I think. (Waern 342)

Think-aloud protocols can be useful for writers as well as researchers. The more writers know about readers' experience of
their prose, the better composing decisions they will make, and
the less they will have to rely on rules and formalities. So if a
writer got the kind of response cited above from a reader, she
would learn that the word "exinanition" caused her reader
problems, taking up processing energy. Notice that the subject
doesn't say the word is *wrong*. He doesn't say one of the typical
marking expressions — "wrong word" or "faulty diction." He
simply reports what is going through his head as he comes to an
understanding of what he is reading. With this kind of report
available, a writer could decide what revisions might benefit the
reader.

The exercise which follows introduces you to a classroom
version of the think-aloud protocol — a technique you can use
to get and give feedback on drafts.

## exercise

With another student in your class, exchange drafts of essays you
are working on. Read your fellow student's draft to him or her, reporting your thoughts as you go. Have your fellow student do the
same for you.

Here is a guide for reporting your reading experience.

(1) Whenever something makes you stop — whether it be sentence
structure, a particular word, even spelling — report the stoppage.
If you are sure you can identify the particular word or words that
make you stop, do so, but don't try to name an error. That is, instead of saying

say

Remember, you are *not marking the essay*. You are not invoking rules. You are only *reporting your experiences as a reader*. (Besides, people are very often wrong when they say something is "ungrammatical.")

(2) When you have trouble in the spaces between sentences, report this trouble.

I'm not sure of the connection between these sentences. I'm wondering if you mean that this is a cause of this. I'm not sure.

(3) Report the condition of your mental desktop and the operation of the management device.

This paragraph is long. I'm not sure what the point is. Are you saying that shoreworkers were unionized on a more radical basis than fishers were? Is this important? I go on and then I'm not sure if this is what I'm supposed to be thinking...

OK. I think this is a new section. But I feel I'm already forgetting what you've just been talking about. I wonder if I should re-read the previous section. Maybe I missed something.

(4) Give a running commentary on your process of constructing meaning.

OK. From this first paragraph, I get the idea that I should concentrate on how shoreworkers were included in bargaining units. It's very political, and has to do with race and gender.

Now I should keep both these ideas in mind. They're both important, and you're going to be explaining the relation between them.

This is still about shoreworkers and gender.

This is good. This is really interesting. I can already see how you could relate shore workers' bargaining to processors' cartels.

(5) Use Chapter Three's "collapsing" technique for summary to show the writer how you are constructing gist.

So the gist of this paragraph is that cartels have been the usual explanation for this kind of bargaining, and it's a good explanation, but it doesn't account for everything. That's the idea I should be leaving this paragraph with.

# 5

# Definition and Comparison

## 5.1    Traditions of Definition

Definition has had a long history in writing instruction. Many composition textbooks and courses include lessons on definition, thereby perpetuating a tradition stretching back to classical times. For centuries, students have been composing definitions of terms like "courage" or "friendship," imitating forms recommended since antiquity.

Like workers in other academic fields, specialists in composition have questioned traditions. Most recently (if we take the perspective of centuries), they have questioned purely formalist exercises: activities, that is, whose success is measured according to rules about form rather than estimates of function. In an era which emphasizes *process* over *product*, definition has tended to drift out of focus. And genre theory itself, the theoretical basis of this book, can put definition exercises in an unflattering light.

Genre theory insists that writing is accountable to the context it serves, rather than to formal rules. So we cannot know if a piece of writing is good or not good, or what goals a writer should have in a piece of writing, until we know what context — what socially defined situation — the writing will represent and serve. When we cannot measure a text against its social function, we are liable to develop rules and regulations for its composition. We are liable to get a schoolroom genre: one that provides a means of controlling students' time, or mainly serves testing purposes (did they follow the rules?). We might wonder if definition is in fact only a schoolroom genre.

To find out, we ask, "Do people write definitions in real life?" When you ask a professor, "What are you working on?" he is not likely to answer "a definition." He will reply with one of the names of the genres used in the academic community — article, book, paper, proposal, review, and so on. (We applied this test to "summary" in Chapter Two, and found that, for professional scholars, summary was a contributing form, and, for students, it can be a stand-alone genre.) If professional scholars don't write definitions, should students spend their time practising definition?

Although students may get along very well without deliberate practice in definition, they may also benefit from such practice. First, definition does appear in the writings of professional scholars — as a contribution to their production of one of the genres they are likely to say they are working on. Below, we will see why this is so, how definition cooperates with other features of academic writing.

Second, the shape and style of sentences that define — their grammar — represents and serves scholarly situations, and the larger cultural role of these situations. M.A.K. Halliday and James Martin have argued convincingly that the aims and values of science (and we would include the social sciences) are configured in features of sentence style which enable the production of certain kinds of texts. As it happens, these features are ones triggered by the activity of defining. So, even though definition as a composing practice has classical ancestors, and many venerable ancestors in the classrooms that carried on the classical tradition, it still turns out to be relevant to current functions of modern science. Practice in composing formal definition will cultivate in your writing grammatical structures which characterize scholarly expression.

Before beginning that practice, we will first consider the idea of "definition" itself, putting dictionaries in their place, and then reflect on the relation between definition and some matters that have occupied our attention — abstraction and the levels of generality.

## 5.1.1 *Definitions and dictionaries*

People rely on dictionaries — either practically, by looking words up, or theoretically, by comforting themselves that, should any problem of meaning arise, a dictionary could settle it. Often associated with this reliance is an idea that dictionaries are responsible for meaning: they make meaning, or they make words mean what they do.

Actually, this idea is backwards. Writers of dictionaries only describe what the meaning of a word already is. Or, better said, they describe *how people use a word*. So some language specialists don't talk about definition at all. Rather, they say that the "meaning" of a word is the set of circumstances under which it can be efficiently used. So, it would be inefficient for someone to use the word "chair" when he wanted someone else to hand in an essay.

This seems to be one of the circumstances where it is not efficient to use the word "chair."

If we adjust our view of dictionaries, and see them as following rather than preceding use, we see that the community of speakers who use the word is the source of its meaning. These speakers (and writers), through their interactions and routine activities, develop and negotiate word meanings — the conditions under which a word can be efficiently used. If we go further, along lines established by current reasoning about the social order, we must acknowledge that "community" should be "communities": within the larger aggregate "society," people get together in different groups, following different routines. These shared routines are sustained by shared interpretations of the world — and shared habits in the use of certain words, including the shared habits of specialist communities. No dictionary can report all these possible communities of speakers and the tacit agreements they have amongst themselves as to the appropriate use of certain words. So, while no dictionary would provide a definition of "chair" that justifies "Your chairs are due next week," a community of language users made up of woodwork teachers and their students could very well find the use of the word "chair" in this sentence appropriate and efficient under the circumstances.

Once we accept that, first, dictionaries only describe uses of words rather than establish definitions, and that, second, those recorded uses are only the most general kind, we can see that there is still work to be done — terms to be captured and refined in the account of their possible uses. (We see also that assignment based on definition does not inevitably call for a dictionary.)

Before looking at some instances of definition, and the structure of the formal sentence definition, we will consider why defining plays a role in scholarly expression.

## 5.1.2    Definition and abstraction

We have seen how an efficiency of reasoning is translated into prose: we have seen how an abstract term at a high level of generality can interpret and condense scattered detail. So this observer reasons to an abstract level ("privilege" and "hierarchy") in interpreting available information.

As a writer, the observer offers these abstract interpretations of specific data to the reader:

PASSAGE I    The hierarchical social structure of some primate groups confers on certain group members excessive privilege, while it deprives others of even the most basic social and physical amenities. Among the olive baboons of the Ser-rengetti savanna, some male individuals get the shady spots....

Without the high-level, interpretive abstractions "hierarchical social structure" and "privilege," the report of olive baboon behaviours is liable to be merely a list, fulfilling only the minimum conditions of topic (generally about baboons, but *what* about baboons?). The reader will make efforts after meaning, trying to construct what the writer has not, and hoping to have his attempt confirmed. Or he will abandon the effort, processing and storing information randomly, forgetting most of what he reads as items slip off his mental desktop.

When you come up with interpretive abstractions, you are making sense of what you have observed. When you offer them to your reader, foregrounding them at the beginning of paragraphs, repeating them at transitional points, you construct meaning for your reader and instruct his information-management device as to the best use of the information you present.

But you can do more. You can get hold of those high-level names for things and make them work harder for you, directing your reader into complex and convincing arguments. When abstractions are defined, they exert even more control over surrounding text and the reader's reception of the text. So "hierarchical social structure" could be defined as

> a system which distributes resources unevenly, creating asymmetries and, thus, relative status. From relative status, power flows.

With this definition in mind as a high-level guide to statements about olive baboons, the reader will find those statements even more readily interpretable and meaningful.

We also know that abstractions, whatever their benefit to reasoning, are also the site of scholars' most esteemed performances. Working with prestigious terms, academics earn recognition. Accordingly, display of control over an important abstraction is an admired accomplishment. Definition is a principal technique for such display.

And it is good to keep in mind that even terms which are extensively used in a scholarly community (and therefore seemingly well understood and not in need of definition) can be effectively redefined and explicated. So, for example, "the welfare model of justice" in criminology, or "patriarchy," in women's studies, literary studies, or some areas of the social sciences, can be re-examined to bring to light the ideas and assumptions which they have come to stand for. From research and observation, my colleagues and I have found that academic readers respond positively to a careful and insightful definition of a widely used term which represents core reasoning in a discipline.

## 5.1.3    *Abstractions defined: four examples*

In the passages which follow, you will see abstraction working hard, going beyond naming. Each passage dwells on a high-level name that represents the essential features of lower-level cases. Each passage not only introduces the name for the phenomenon on which it focusses, but also defines the phenomenon. Read the passages to see how these definitions develop.

**"Cybernetics"**

Cybernetics is the science of maintaining order in a system, whether that system is natural or artificial. Since all
things in the world have a tendency to become entropic,
disorderly, their random deviations from order must be
corrected continually. This is accomplished by using information about the behaviour of the system to produce
different, more regular behaviour. By such means the system is kept on course. The term cybernetics comes from
a Greek word meaning steersman, and it carries the sense
of stability, of constant, correct functioning. Illness is entropic, irregular, an error in the living system, while healing is cybernetic, restoring the body to its original state,
correcting the error. Natural selection is also cybernetic,
disallowing genetic mutations which deviate from the
norm in undesirable ways. Wiener regarded a human society as a self-regulating system kept orderly by the cybernetic mechanism of its laws. Cybernetics enforces consis-
tency. It permits change, but the change must be orderly
and abide by the rules. It is a universal principle of control, and can be applied to all kinds of organization, just
as Shannon's theorems applied to communication of all
kinds. It does not matter whether the system is electrical,
chemical, mechanical, biological, or economic.

Jeremy Campbell 1982 *Grammatical Man*. New York: Simon and
Schuster. 22-23

**"Salutation"**

Salutations are verbal and physical gestures by which individuals acknowledge one another at the beginnings and
conclusions of encounters. They are conventional systems
of greeting and leave-taking that express social bonds and
accord, however temporary or tentative those bonds and
accord might be. The handshake, for example, marks the
boundaries of social encounters in communities where

the absence of physical or verbal recognition can be interpreted as a sign of hostility. Mutual performance of this hand ritual assures individuals of their acceptance or membership in a group. Or the performance may only appear to make such assurances, masking actual hostility, indifference, or competing interests. The handshake seems to signify a suspension of hierarchical relationships: it expresses symbolically a social equality. This symbolic expression may take place despite one participant actually having the "upper hand" in the relationship.

Other forms of salutation in face-to-face encounters depend on verbal expression, accompanied by conventional facial expression: smiling, one participant in a social encounter may initiate the exchange by offering a ritual inquiry into the welfare of another participant. Like the handshake, the inquiry and its response comply with formulaic, culture-specific patterns: in North America, an individual who responds to a ritual inquiry with detail about kin and household will be seen as failing to observe the conventions of salutation.

Handshaking, ritual inquiries and response, and other forms of salutation are signs of the cooperation and mutuality that promote human association and enable productive transactions. Depending on conventional procedures, salutation shows that, whatever else may divide individuals and their interests, they are at least united in their shared knowledge of this ritual and can cooperate in its performance. Salutation supports and reflects larger cultural systems of social coherence which incorporate individuals into groups, recruiting the single actor into community purposes.

PASSAGE 4

## "Ethnostatus distinctions"

Ethnostatus distinctions are those distinctions which an individual or population makes concerning themselves, and the significant others in their lives, in which the factors of legal status and cultural affinity play a varying role. Ethnostatus distinctions can also develop as a product of ascription to a particular cultural group or legal category by individuals or agencies external to the community. In the western Canadian subarctic, government legislation and policy implementation at both the federal and provincial levels have probably played the most prominent role in the development and maintenance of such distinctions. The product of these distinctions is the development of separate ethnostatus identities which may shift and surface from time to time in different socio-political contexts or situations. In this sense, the concept of ethnostatus precludes the identification of "ethnic" groups as defined in the anthropological literature.

Barth, in his classic essay on "ethnic groups and boundaries," argued that membership in a particular ethnic group effectively governed all behaviour in virtually every social situation, and further "that it cannot be disregarded and temporarily set aside by other definitions of the situation" (1969:17). As I shall demonstrate, ethnostatus distinctions rarely produce "ethnic groups" in this sense, since, according to my conception, the identities formulated tend to govern behaviour only in certain contexts and can be readily set aside or altered as the situation dictates. Further, it is evident that a concentration on boundaries between ethnic groups, as Barth suggests, would not prove fruitful in understanding ethnostatus distinctions precisely because such boundaries are too amorphic. While ethnostatus distinctions have the potential of forming ethnic groups, the existence of such groups must be demonstrated and cannot be presupposed.

In a similar vein, ethnostatus groups are not the equivalent of "factions," as defined in the literature. Nicholas (1965:27-29) has presented five characteristics which define "factions": they are political groups; they are conflict oriented; they are not corporate groups; members are recruited by a leader; and recruitment occurs according to a variety of criteria, such as religion and kinship. As Nicholas (1966:52) notes, factions are primarily involved in political activity, "the organized conflict over public power." As I shall demonstrate, ethnostatus distinctions by-and-large do not reflect groups organized by a leader to achieve a political goal, and certainly there is no active recruitment.

James B. Waldram 1987 Ethnostatus distinctions in the western Canadian subarctic: implications for inter-ethnic and inter-personal relations *Culture* 7,1, 29-37, 31.

PASSAGE 5     **"Issues management"**

In the last 20 years, business organizations have been increasingly held accountable for their corporate performance in a variety of arenas (Wood, 1991). Firms have been confronted by an organized, activist, and concerned set of stakeholders (Ansoff, 1975; Freeman, 1984) clamoring for improved corporate performance on a wide range of social and political issues, from clean air and nutritional labelling to equal employment opportunities. Many corporations have developed internal procedures and created formal staff functions to respond to the barrage of demands they face (Brown 1979; Chase, 1977, 1984; Ewing, 1987; Marcus & Irion, 1987; Post, Murray, Dickie, & Mahon, 1982; Wartick & Rude, 1986).

The process of addressing such issues has been labelled "issues management" (Chase, 1977, 1984; Jones, 1983; Wartick & Rude, 1986). This process is conceptualized as a firm's identifying, analyzing, and responding to social and political concerns that can significantly affect it (Jones, 1983; Wartick & Rude, 1986). Ideally, issues management acts as an early warning system (Ansoff, 1980) through which firms anticipate the demands of or constraints imposed by various actors in their external environment, including legislatures, regulatory agencies, public interest groups, and the media. In practice, however, issues management comprises both anticipatory responses and responses to crises when firms have been unable to anticipate and avert them.

We distinguish issues management from the broader "strategic issues management" referred to by Dutton and her colleagues (Dutton & Duncan, 1987; Dutton & Jackson, 1988). Those authors defined strategic issues as those perceived as having an effect on organizational objectives. We focused on corporate responses to social and political issues or economic issues with the potential to generate a social or political response. Strategic issues management includes purely competitive issues as well. However, these distinctions are fuzzy at best since issues identification requires interpretation by organizational decision makers (Daft & Weick, 1984; Dutton & Jackson, 1988; Jackson & Dutton, 1988; Rands, 1993; Thomas & McDaniel, 1990) and "the meaning of an issue is not inherent in the environmental events" (Dutton & Jackson, 1987:77). The same issue may evoke a marketing response from one firm and a public relations response from another firm.

Daniel W. Greening and Barbara Gray 1994 Testing a model of organizational response to social and political issues. *Academy of Management Journal* 37, 3, 467-498, 467-468.

These definitions have different information profiles. "Cybernetics," which comes from a book designed for the non-specialist reader, presents its subject as mainly new to the reader. "Salutation," an example composed for this occasion, takes phenomena familiar to the reader and reorganizes them as elements of a larger abstraction, making them in a sense unfamiliar in the interests of analysis of these everyday occurrences. (In Chapter Eight we will look more closely at this process of defamiliarization in the interests of inquiry and analysis.) "Ethnostatus distinctions" and "Issues management" come from scholarly publications where they focus lengthy presentations of the results of the writers' research. Readers are constructed as specialists aware of the matters involved, but open to being reminded of them and having subtle but important distinctions pointed out. Both "Ethnostatus distinctions" and "Issues management" invite other voices from the scholarly community to contribute to the definition.

The passages develop their definitions in a variety of ways, using strategies we will look into later in this chapter. But each has in common one feature in particular: a core statement which defines the phenomenon as an equivalence, saying in effect

**x = y**
*Cybernetics **is** the science of maintaining order in a system. . . .*
*Salutations **are** verbal and physical gestures. . . .*

Ethnostatus distinctions **are** those distinctions which an individual or population makes concerning themselves, and the significant others in their lives. . . .

In "Issues management," the core statement is postponed until some instances have been recorded (demands for "clean air and nutritional labelling") and then it arrives something like this:

issues management **is** a firm's identifying, analyzing, and responding to social and political concerns that can significantly affect it

The equivalence form of these core statements coaxes out particular grammatical structures. The subject of the verb is short, the complement much longer (for reasons we will see below). The subject is an abstraction, and both subject and complement tend to immobilize events or actions: so, while, on some occasions,

**A** salutes **B**
in
salutation,

both **A** and **B** are gone and the action stopped in a noun. While on some occasions

*A* manages issues
in
**issues management,**

*A* is gone and the action stopped in a noun. While some technician or scientist or even some device may work to **maintain** order in a system, they all disappear when "maintain" takes a nominal (or *noun*) slot in the complement: "the science of *maintaining* order. . . " And, while particular people may distinguish themselves from others in certain ways, they are separated from this action when "distinguish" turns into noun **distinctions**. It has been argued that such transformations are characteristic of the expression of western scholarship — an argument we will examine more closely in the next chapter. For now, we will note that the procedure of defining one *thing* in terms of another *thing* triggers an academic-sounding sentence.

Writers tend to position these core statements of equivalence near the beginning of their definition. These statements become the footing on which the rest of the definition is constructed.

Once these footings are established, writers develop the definition. They may "double" the core definition, as in passages 3 and 4, adding more of the features which distinguish the phenomenon. Or, as in passage 2, they may mention the conditions which explain the fact of the phenomenon's existence. If the writer thinks the information will be useful to developing his claims, he may linger at the word itself: "The term cybernetics comes from a Greek word meaning steersman, and it carries the sense of stability, of constant, correct functioning." The writer can also compare the phenomenon with similar ones, pointing out the differences: ethnostatus distinctions create groups that in some ways can resemble "ethnic groups" and "factions" (which have been defined by other writers), but in other important ways differ from them. "Issues management" is distinguished from "strategic issues management." The writer may also put the phenomenon into context, showing its operation in the larger system of which it is part: salutations are part of systems of social coherence; issues management is part of social changes ("[i]n the last 20 years") which have led to firms being held accountable for their performance; cybernetics plays its role in the universe itself (the biggest system of all).

And each passage uses examples to develop the definition: handshakes, healing, nutritional labelling, social differentiation in the western Canadian subarctic. Passage 4 shows most clearly the role of definition and its supporting examples in academic writing. The writer tell us that he has specific evidence to confirm the claims he is making as he defines ethnostatus distinctions: "As I shall demonstrate. . . ." Although he presents the definition before the examples that support it, we might very well assume that, in real life, the evidence came first, and the name which interpreted the evidence, along with the definition which refined it, came after. In his article, the definition is an information-management device, on the one hand interpreting scattered data from his research, and on the other hand offering the reader a clear focus for a complex argument.

So, finally, the cluster of data, the interpretive name, and the definition are reciprocating elements:

DATA → ABSTRACTION interprets data by naming the phenomenon

DEFINITION explains the phenomenon and the data, which become examples that develop the definition

## exercise

The second exercise in Section 3.2 in Chapter 3 asked you to find an abstract word to name the conditions described in "Brian." Focus on the abstract noun you came up with. Define it, integrating specifics about Brian as examples which develop the definition.

## 5.2    Techniques for developing definition

Material for the definition will come from your research, from your experience of the world, and from your own reasoning. There are no rules which dictate exactly what a definition should look like, but figure 1 below shows how a fully developed definition can have three focal nodes.

FIGURE I

FOCUS on the phenomenon itself,
isolated for scrutiny:
> formal definition
> reflection on the word itself
> comparison
> division

## DEFINITION

FOCUS on the "career"
of the phenomenon:
> examples
> account of variation
> associations

FOCUS on the phenomenon's
situation in a larger context:
> role in system
> cause and effect
> frequency

In the sections which follow, we will look at how writers can fulfil each of the nodes and their parts, keeping in mind the fact that essay writers who use definition are under no obligation to track through every station on the map. These locations represent not rules but strategies. The writer uses only that material which convincingly and efficiently supports an argument. And, while sometimes the structure of the definition is the structure of the whole essay, at other times, the definition is only a part of the essay's structure, an attentive moment where assumptions and distinctions are established.

## 5.2.1 Focus on the phenomenon itself: formal sentence definition

When the definition focusses on the phenomenon itself, it isolates the entity for scrutiny, separating it from the accidents, mix-ups, and blurry boundaries of real life. So we could say that the focus is ideal. If I claim that

Daycare is the institutional provision of care-taking services to young children, these services including feeding, supervision, shelter, and instruction.

I am ignoring cases where it is hard to distinguish between baby-sitting and daycare, where children are not exactly fed but feed themselves (or refuse to eat), where care is provided on so informal a basis it might not be called "institutional" at all. I am providing an ideal, formal definition of daycare, offering a statement of equivalence. On one side is the phenomenon —

**daycare**

— and on the other side is the definition:

**the institutional provision of care-taking services to young children, including feeding, supervision, shelter, and instruction.**

The defining side of the statement first *enlarges* our view by identifying the larger class to which daycare belongs —

**the institutional provision of care-taking services**

— and then *narrows* our view again by identifying the features which differentiate daycare from other members of this class (from, for example, health care, corrections, education):

**. . . to young children, these services including feeding, supervision, shelter, and instruction.**

The following definition shows the same pattern of *enlargement to classify* and *reduction to differentiate*. This is the classical pattern of formal sentence definition. Passage 7 also shows one of the development options open to the writer: following formal definition, the writer can "double" the definition by saying what the phenomenon *does*.

PASSAGE 7  Broadcasting is a system of social control which, through the transmission of electronic signals, normalizes the diverse experiences of individuals. Broadcasting interprets events and life conditions in ways which confirm society's ideological centre.

In passage 7, the definition first *expands* our focus by identifying the *class* to which broadcasting belongs (systems of social control), and then *differentiates* it from other members of the class (laws or customs, for example). Moreover, passage 7 shows that formal definition can be in itself a step in an argument. Someone else could have defined broadcasting differently — as a result of having interpreted data differently, or of having different data to interpret.

PASSAGE 8  Broadcasting is a system of communication which, through the transmission of electronic signals, illuminates public and private life alike. By linking widespread communities through a shared network of information, broadcasting ensures that citizens in democratic societies recognize common and crucial features of their experience, and enables them to respond to those features as issues.

Clearly, definitions 7 and 8 would serve different arguments. This disparity won't surprise you if you remember that definition is the development of the *interpretive name* the writer assigns to a cluster of data. We know we have to offer our readers these interpretive names to guide their use of the information we present: the data don't speak for themselves. So the definition is bound to be an expression of the reasoning and insight which led us to assign the name in the first place.

For example, if I interpret the conditions of Brian's experience as "therapeutic supervision," and I go on to define that phenomenon, my definition will reflect the reasoning by which I produced the name — reasoning which detected in Brian's case the features of constraint, surveillance, and correction of deviance.

Therapeutic supervision is a form of social restraint which targets an individual as deviant and then, through management and monitoring of the individual's daily experience, seeks to adjust his behaviour to conform to a recognized norm.

The formal definition, with its characteristic classification and differentiation, has an authoritative and "scientific" sound. But these definitions are only proposals — plausible ones, but open to dispute nevertheless. From another point of view, or later on, when more evidence is in, Brian and broadcasting could be defined differently. (Someone else might see Brian's case as hopeful, and define "therapeutic supervision" as "moral guidance.")

In other words, the writer *stipulates* the definition for the purposes of the current discussion, in the service of a particular set of data. The definition has to be a plausible application of the word or words defined. To say

Therapeutic supervision is the celebration of the individual spirit in communion with the natural world

would be implausible. But, at the same time, the definition should not simply reiterate an all-purpose, dictionary definition.

Webster's defines supervision as "a critical watching or direction."

Because they are only descriptions of the most general guides for the use of a word, dictionary definitions will not have the reciprocating relationship with the data and their interpretation that the stipulated definition has. In an essay, dictionary definitions are apt to sit by themselves, never invited into the core of the discussion.

The following exercise asks you to practise writing formal definition. The exercise is artificial in that it does not arrange for the process by which a writer analyzes and interprets data with a high-level name, and then defines that term. Here you will just be assigned the term. Nevertheless, the exercise will give you the chance to try classifying and differentiating.

## exercise

Write formal definitions of the following terms:

- dissent
- retirement
- nationalism
- literacy.

Or choose a term which names a phenomenon you are studying in another course (*narrative*, for example, or *substance abuse*). After you have composed your formal definition, you may feel like adding more, saying what *literacy* or *retirement* or *nationalism* does. Go ahead. Say more.

## 5.2.2 *Focus on the phenomenon itself: word, division, comparison*

To establish the sense of the phenomenon you wish to convey, you can direct your reader to pay attention to the word itself.

PASSAGE 10
Earlier uses of the term "broadcasting" referred to sowing by scattering seeds over a broad area. Modern, electronic broadcasting suggests the same wide scattering: broadcasting focusses not on unique, individual receptors, but on large expanses of population.

PASSAGE 11
As the term suggests, therapeutic supervision combines surveillance with calculated practices designed to correct behaviour that has been diagnosed as pathological.

In addition to directing your reader's attention to the word itself, you can analyze the phenomenon, dividing it into parts.

The two main elements of broadcasting are (1) the technical apparatus which create, transmit, and receive the electronic signal, and (2) the editorial processes which gather and transform information for conversion to electronic signals. As we will see, the characteristics of the editorial process were, for a long time, dependent on the features and capacities of the technical apparatus. Recently, however, innovations in editorial process have begun to influence the design and development of technical apparatus.

PASSAGE 13 In a program of therapeutic supervision, the chief actors are the clinician and the subject who has been targeted for correction. But the relationship between these actors is determined by other elements of the program: the institutional settings which host therapeutic supervision, and the body of knowledge which directs the clinician to interpret the subject's behaviour and respond to it in systematic ways.

Besides focussing on the word itself, and analyzing the phenomenon into parts, you can also direct your reader's understanding of the phenomenon by comparing it to its near neighbours.

PASSAGE 14 Like broadcasting, the print media, particularly daily newspapers, disseminate information to a wide audience. And the reader, like the viewer or listener, always has the option of calling a halt to the process: the reader can put down the newspaper; the viewer can turn off the TV and the listener can turn off the radio. But broadcasting differs from the transmission of information by means of print in the degree of control it exercises over the individual's reception of information. While the reader can select the articles or advertisements he will read, the order in which he will read them, and the pace at which he will absorb information, the viewer has less control: once he begins to watch, he receives information in the order and at the pace the broadcaster has determined.

Like the healing techniques of modern medicine, the techniques of therapeutic supervision address individuals' problems and afflictions with recognized expertise. But, unlike the practice of medicine, therapeutic supervision regards the subject's whole character, not just his affliction. The deviation — from health, from normalcy — is seen as logically entwined with the individual's conduct of his daily life, and every aspect of his daily life becomes an object of expert analysis, interpretation, and adjustment.

Each of these strategies — attention to the word, analysis into parts, comparison — can develop the definition's focus on the phenomenon. But you should handle such strategies with caution: if "attention to the word" contributes little or nothing to the main claims of your argument, then this entry will be only a distraction for readers, cluttering their mental desktops. Similarly, your comparisons and analyses into parts are meant not simply to fulfil the requirements of definition but to advance your interpretation of data — the interpretation that led you to identify this phenomenon in the first place. Like any essay, the essay based on definition has to be coherent. The reader should not be left with irrelevant comparisons or analyses on his mental desktop, taking up limited resources and confusing the filing system.

---

## exercise

---

Test these three strategies — focus on the word, analysis into parts, comparison — for their capacity to develop your definition of

- dissent
- retirement
- nationalism
- literacy

or the term you have selected from your studies in another course. When you find the strategies that can contribute to your argument, write out an expanded version of your original definition.

## 5.2.3 *Focus on the "career" of the phenomenon*

This phase of definition releases the phenomenon from its isolation in an ideal domain and, relocating it in the world, investigates its career there: its forms of occurrence, the local conditions of its occurrence. In many academic writing situations, this phase generates the main bulk of the text, for it is the phase that introduces examples: specific instances of the phenomenon. As we saw earlier, the specific data which lead to the interpretive abstraction are, in the process of definition, converted into examples. You know from your experience in summarizing academic prose that the lower-level information that reports specific cases takes up a lot of space. You can expect that your essay structured according to descriptive definition will also spread out when you present actual instances of the phenomenon.

- The essay which bases itself on a definition of "broadcasting" would turn to presenting data which led the writer to identify the phenomenon and its essential features: statistical evidence, for example, which counted the frequency of certain "events and life conditions"; description and analysis of specific transmissions to show "normalization" towards an "ideological centre."

- The essay which bases itself on a definition of "therapeutic supervision" would turn to Brian and other cases like his. The accounts of Brian and other cases would consistently confirm the essential features of the phenomenon as the definition presented them: surveillance, constraint, interpretation of daily conduct, prescription of adjustment measures.

Looking at the individual cases, you will also be in a position to observe and report the range of variation among specific instances: all cases will not conform in the same way to the ideal. And, once you have relocated the phenomenon in the real world, you may find that you have a chance to observe its associations with nearby phenomena. The cases of "therapeutic supervision," for example, may tend to occur in conjunction with poverty (people lower on the socio-economic scale may tend more often to be targets of this practice), or formal schooling (the school cooperates in the program of supervision), or systems of professional accreditation which license the clinician (not just anybody can step in to control Brian's life and correct his ways).

The exercise which follows asks you to exemplify the phenomenon you have defined. In most writing situations, you would be working in the other direction — constructing a definition from a cluster of instances, rather than constructing examples to support a definition. But I assume you got your definition from some form of specific experience — your knowledge of anti-abortionists' practice of dissent, for example, or your knowledge of the retirement of one of your co-workers. Now you can retrieve that original source to compose examples of the phenomenon you are defining.

---

### exercise
---

Provide examples which support your definition of

- dissent
- retirement
- nationalism
- literacy

or the term you have selected from your studies in another course. Present the examples in such a way as to confirm the essential features identified by the definition.

## 5.2.4    *Focus on the phenomenon's situation in a larger context*

A third phase of definition accounts for the phenomenon's role in the system of which it is part. Sometimes the surrounding system which the writer identifies is conspicuous, one most people would notice as that which assigns the phenomenon its role and its operation. Medical diagnosis, for example, is part of the larger system of medical treatment, or health care.

But other times the writer's way of putting the phenomenon in context is noticeably interpretive: plausible but not inevitable. Just as the definition itself is a proposal — one way of organizing and interpreting data — so too is the contextualizing of the phenomenon. In Passages 16 and 17 below, *centralization* and *professional expertise* are plausible contexts in which to situate broadcasting and therapeutic supervision, and they are compatible with earlier entries in the definition. But they are not the only conceivable contexts for these phenomena.

PASSAGE 16

Modern broadcasting contributes to the functioning of centralized societies. As commercial and government authorities locate themselves beyond neighbourhoods and communities, local resources are no longer adequate to explain individuals' roles in the marketplace or their obligations and privileges as citizens. Broadcasting is one of the mechanisms that replace the traditional, face-to-face interactions which formerly oriented people in public life.

PASSAGE 17

The practice of therapeutic supervision is part of a larger occurrence — that of professional expertise in post-industrial societies with strong institutional sectors. These forms of expertise depend on well-defined inventories of knowledge (such as, for example, counselling psychology) which the expert acquires and then confirms by applying them in specific cases. Both the knowledge and its application depend on institutional settings — to house and disseminate the knowledge by creating experts and to provide occasions for the application of knowledge to programs like therapeutic supervision which permit experts to observe and adjust the behaviour of non-expert individuals.

Putting the phenomenon in context, the writer reveals its significance in a bigger picture: the conditions which cause its appearance, the effects which it contributes. The bigger picture can also reveal the phenomenon's *history*, its emergence or disappearance according to the forces and tendencies which shape contexts.

Like other phases of definition, context depends on the writer's original interpretation of the data. If the writer had analyzed Brian's case or certain television transmissions differently, she would have located therapeutic supervision and broadcasting in different contexts: healing practices, for example, or marketing.

Definition arranges data into meaningful patterns, but it does not fix them forever into those patterns. The data are still there, living lives of their own, open to new interpretations, ready to be regrouped into new sets, awaiting new perspectives from observers who approach them from a different avenue of inquiry. These revisions and innovations and re-definitions are features of scholarly activity.

---

## exercise

Put into context

- dissent
- retirement
- nationalism
- literacy

or the term you have chosen from your studies, explaining the role of the phenomenon in the larger system of which it is part. Contextualize the phenomenon in such a way as to confirm your earlier entries in the definition.

# 5.3 Comparison

In their core statements of equivalence and in their development, definitions reproduce the sound of scholarly expression:

styles which characterize the research genres. These styles embody and serve the reasoning and research practices which scholars typically engage in. Similarly, **comparison** — the sustained activity of finding resemblances and differences — also appears to reproduce, under certain circumstances, scholarly style.

Yet comparison, like definition, also has a schoolroom history. Many generations of children educated in the western tradition have been asked, repeatedly, to "compare and contrast" objects of their learning. So commonplace is this cultural practice that it has been open to satire. Nearly a century ago, J.M. Barrie could make a successful joke about this schoolroom habit. Here he tells about Wendy trying to instruct her younger brothers after they have joined Peter Pan's Lost Boys and are in danger of forgetting the parents they left behind. She tests them by "setting them examination papers . . ., as like as possible to the ones she used to do at school":

> "(A) Write an essay of not less than 40 words on How I
> Spent my last Holidays, or The Characters of Father and
> Mother Compared. Only one of these to be attempted."

Aware of the difference between schoolroom contexts for writing and the contexts of academic writing, we might suspect that comparison is only a make-work project, or only a fixture of the traditional schoolroom, and not relevant to scholarly situations.

Professional scholars, however, do compare things, and the process of comparison is often used to produce new knowledge. In Chapter Three, for example, you read and summarized an excerpt which described and interpreted nineteenth-century education in North America. The beginning of this excerpt compared Canadian and American ideologies. That passage is presented here again, with its typical comparative phrasing printed in **bold**.

PASSAGE 18    Late-19th-century literacy instruction in Canada
**differed in one crucial respect from** its American
counterpart. For **whereas Canadian schools** imported
curricula from England, **teachers in America** were by

this time provided with locally developed textbooks, in the tradition of the McGuffey readers. Noah Webster's *American Spelling Book* (1873), the most widely used textbook in United States history, not only promoted American history, geography, and morals, but was itself a model for an indigenous vocabulary and spelling. Textbooks and dictionaries of this period attempted to engender a national literacy and literature free of European "folly, corruption and tyranny," in Webster's words. **In Canada, by contrast,** classrooms featured icons of colonialism: British flags and pictures of royalty adorned the walls, younger students were initiated to print via the Irish readers, and literature texts opened with Wordsworth's and Tennyson's panegyrics to the Crown. **In Canada,** the reduction in pauperism and crime associated with illiteracy was seen as requiring the preservation British culture and a colonial sensibility; **in the United States,** "custodians of culture" (May, 1959; p.30) sought to assure economic independence and political participation. **The match** between these **differing** societal and educational ideologies and the "civilizing" effects of traditional three Rs and classical education was near-perfect.

The wordings "differed," "whereas," "by contrast," and "differing," along with the sentence structures they trigger, keep the reader's mental desktop prepared for comparison. In addition, clauses thematize the two elements of the comparison: "Canadian schools," "teachers in America," "[i]n Canada," "in the United States."

Other genres besides the scholarly ones and the schoolroom ones use sustained comparative structures. A consumer report, for example, might sustain a detailed, point-by-point comparison of two makes of home-entertainment products, or two or more holiday destinations. These comparisons enable people to make choices. So, in a sense, readers bring their own *topics* with them —

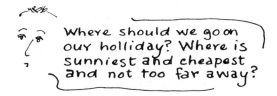

— and even list-like, point-form comparison can be meaningful and coherent to readers in the situations embodied in these genres.

While academic readers can probably be counted on to bring to their reading an attitude of being generally interested, they do not have the consumer's immediate, personal questions in mind. Nor are they as satisfied as the teacher (or Wendy) might be with comparison for the sake of comparison, or for the sake of inspecting the state of students' knowledge of a topic. In other words, comparison in itself and by itself may not satisfy your readers.

Excerpt 18 above on North American education shows comparison occurring not by itself, but in the company of *abstraction*. The comparison conducted in this excerpt holds itself together — that is, justifies itself as relevant and coherent — by means of abstractions: "literacy instruction," "national literacy and literature," "colonialism," "colonial sensibility," "societal and educational ideologies." These are the concepts that interpret and manage details like British flags and Noah Webster's American Spelling Book.

Comparison is one technique for satisfying the conditions evoked by the scholarly genres. It produces knowledge by setting up a particular relationship amongst low-level data — that of similarity and/or difference — and it interprets this relationship by means of abstractions important to the scholarly disciplines.

## 5.3.1   *Arranging comparisons*

Valued abstractions provide the interpretive materials for establishing the relevance of the comparison of Canadian and American schooling in the nineteenth century. But most comparisons are longer than passage 18 excerpted above. And, in that length, readers can be exposed to hazards peculiar to comparison. We will investigate some of these hazards, and remedies for them.

Let's call the entities to be compared **A** and **B**, and let's say there are basically two structures for the writer to choose between in presenting a comparison.

FIGURE 2

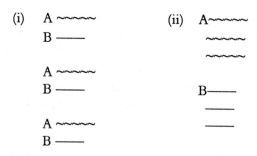

Now let's consider these structures from the reader's point of view.

If the writer chooses (i), alternating between **A** and **B** , he keeps both entities on the reader's mental desktop throughout: the reader is not in danger of forgetting about **A** while **B** is discussed as long as both occupy each paragraph or other small unit of text. This seems to be a benefit. And this structure is often favoured in report-writing and other forms of technical communication, where readers come to the document with a topical question in mind: they know what they have to find out. Schoolroom comparisons may also favour the alternating, **A-B-A-B** structure.

But the alternating structure appears, on the whole, not to be favoured in the scholarly genres. Scholarly writers and readers may find that the overall coherence patterns of the scholarly genres are challenged by the alternating structure, which, by fluctuating between **A** and **B**, makes it hard for the reader to construct a whole picture of either $A$ or $B$. While the *writer* may have a grasp of $A$ or $B$ as a whole, the entity may not come together easily for the *reader*.

If the writer chooses (ii), discussing $A$ then $B$, he avoids this fragmentation. But he faces another coherence problem. The *A-then-B* structure could fracture down the middle, splitting along the fault lines that separate $A$ from $B$. While readers advance through $B$, they are on their own in interpreting $B$ in light of $A$. By the time readers are immersed in $B$ , they have, for all practical purposes, forgotten what the writer said about $A$ .

This is about B. Should I be relating it to something about A? Is it similar or different in this respect? Does it matter?

However, despite the inherent divisiveness of the *A-then-B* structure, you can still turn the essay into a coherent whole, and repair the fault lines. You can overcome inherent divisiveness by applying what you have learned about *topic statements* and their power to guide the reader's interpretation of facts and mentions.

Topic statements are the claims at higher, often abstract levels of generality which represent the significance of lower-level information. In Chapter Four, where disproportion had left the reader constructing her own topics from long stretches of detail about Asian firms and samurai owners and the South Korean GNP, we saw how revision corrected this disproportion by reinstating topical material at intervals throughout the passage. The same strategy, in a slightly more complex form, can also repair the fault line in the *A-then-B* comparison. Your first draft may look something like figure 2 above, but it can be revised for delivery to the reader to look something like figure 3 below. Figure 3 shows main claims about $A$ as , and supported by lower-level material ~~~. These main claims about A, once established, are then carried forward and positioned with oooo —— the topical claims about B . These topical claims about B are supported by lower-level information ===.

FIGURE 3

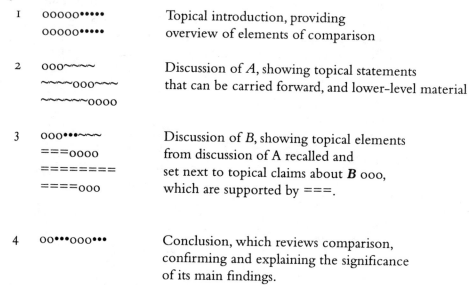

| | | |
|---|---|---|
| 1 | ooooo•••••<br>ooooo••••• | Topical introduction, providing<br>overview of elements of comparison |
| 2 | ooo~~~<br>~~~~ooo~~~<br>~~~~~~oooo | Discussion of *A*, showing topical statements<br>that can be carried forward, and lower-level material |
| 3 | ooo•••~~~<br>===oooo<br>========<br>====ooo | Discussion of *B*, showing topical elements<br>from discussion of A recalled and<br>set next to topical claims about **B** ooo,<br>which are supported by ===. |
| 4 | oo•••ooo••• | Conclusion, which reviews comparison,<br>confirming and explaining the significance<br>of its main findings. |

In this structure, readers are never left on their own to speculate on the reasons for certain features of the two entities being mentioned. Readers' information-management devices are consistently instructed — and reminded — as to what is important and what has to be kept in mind. The first section prepares them for the main issues that will be treated in subsequent sections; the second unit controls what use readers make of material about *A* and packages that material in convenient, portable bundles that can be carried forward to the discussion of B. In the third section, topic statements ••• guide the reader's interpretation and management of information about *B* , and provide efficient points of comparison for the statements about *A* that have been carried forward.

Since we are discussing a condition that occurs over long stretches of text, it's hard to demonstrate with an excerpt short enough to fit into this corner of the chapter. But passage 19 below offers a glimpse of sustained comparison at work. It is a passage from an article comparing two accounts of human consciousness. In Chapter Three, in passage b of the exercise following 3.7.3, you read the beginning of this writer's summary of Julian Jaynes' *The Origin of Consciousness in the Breakdown of the Bicameral Mind.* One-and-a-half pages later, the writer begins her summary of Walker Percy's *The Message in the Bottle.* Passage 19 shows her concluding her summary of Jaynes with a high-level topical claim, rich in abstraction, and then using that abstraction as a bridge to her summary of Percy. Comparative wordings "Percy, too" and "like Jaynes" guide the reader's interpretation of lower-level material towards perceptions of similarity on these abstract grounds.

PASSAGE 22

For Jaynes, then, the history of language as a movement from concrete terms to metaphorical ones is also the history of the development of human consciousness.

Percy, too, understands consciousness as a product of language. In his *The Message in the Bottle,* Percy describes how his obsession to understand the human existential and linguistic predicament returned him repeatedly to the figure of Helen Keller as a child, joining in her mind the cold liquid pouring on her one hand with the letters signed to her by Annie Sullivan on her other, joining them and knowing that water is "water": "For a long time I had believed and I still believe that if one had an inkling of what happened in the well-house in Alabama in the space of a few minutes, one would know more about the *phenomenon* of language and about man himself than is contained in all the works of behaviorists, linguists, and German philosophers" (Percy, 1975, pp. 35-36). What has happened, according to Percy's recasting of the American linguist Pierce, is the delta phenomenon: an irreducible triad of self, object, and sign, a metaphysical leap into symbol-mongering. Curiously, like Jaynes, Percy seems to believe that language does not immediately lead to self-consciousness. Helen, like the unfallen Adam in the garden, spends her first day with language in an exuberant round of naming: only several weeks later do abstract and metaphorical thoughts begin. In *The Story of my Life,* Helen recalls how puzzled she was by the word "love." Miss Sullivan tells Helen that "love" is in her heart, and though Helen is aware for the first time of her own heartbeats, she cannot read her teacher's meaning: "her words puzzled me very much because I did not then understand anything unless I touched it." But two days later, when Helen is laboring at a sorting exercise with different shaped beads, Miss Sullivan touches her forehead and spells "Think" — "In a flash I knew that the word was the name of the process that was going on in my head. This was my first conscious perception of an abstract idea." A moment later, and Helen has come to an understanding of that first abstraction that had eluded her, "love": "the beautiful truth burst upon my mind — I felt that there were invisible lines stretched between my spirit and the spirits of others" (Keller, 1954, pp. 30-31).

Laura Mooneyham 1993 The origin of consciousness, gains and losses: Walker Percy *vs.* Julian Jaynes *Language and Communication* 13, 3, 169-182,171.

## exercise

Following the A-then-B model, write a comparison of the two types of families described by the data below. Compose an introductory paragraph that names the essential issues to be considered, and the connections between them: abstraction will probably arise to fulfil this condition. Write one section on one type of family, and then another section on the other type of family. (In doing so, feel free to develop lower-level material that demonstrates the generalizations provided in the data. Consult your own experience and observations of family life.) In the section on the second type of family, remind the reader of the relevant point of comparison from the description of the first type of family. (Practise using the words and phrases that draw attention to comparisons: "whereas," "like," "unlike," " in contrast," and so on.) Compose a concluding paragraph that confirms the main points of the comparison and speculates on the significance of these matters.

## "Two kinds of families"

| | |
|---|---|
| • parents reason with child, pointing out positive consequences of his or her behaviour for other people | • parents use highly forceful discipline |
| • parents explain reasons for rules and prohibitions | • parents deprive children of rights and privileges; use frequent or severe physical punishment |
| • parents provide guidance and control reflecting at least minimal standards of behaviour | • parents are critical and rejecting |
| • parents are models of positive behaviour | • coercion is dominant mode of relating among family members |
| • children are repeatedly led to help others (e.g. taking toys to hospitalized children) | |
| • result : child sees other people as benevolent and trustworthy; develops feeling of responsibility for other people's welfare; feels self-esteem | • result : child is more aggressive, child regards aggression as normal and even necessary for defending himself and influencing others |

Adapted from Ervin Staub 1988 The evolution of caring and non-aggressive persons and societies. *Journal of Social Issues* 44, 2, 81-100.

## 5.3.2 Comparison and summary

In Chapters Two and Three we saw that summary is an important activity for professional scholars. It is not only students who represent the work of other writers.

In their summarizing, scholars seldom represent the work of just one other writer. More often, they position themselves amidst several sources (sometimes amidst ten or fifteen, or more, as we will see in Chapter Seven). This representation of several sources is a typical scholarly action which, accordingly, develops its own characteristic style — one recognizable to your readers as serving a familiar scholarly routine.

In this routine, writers represent the gist of writer *A*'s argument, then move on to writer *B*'s, then writer *C*'s, and so on. The sounds of this movement — its typical grammar — resemble the sounds of comparison, for good reason. Just as the writer comparing two types of families, or two educational systems, must sustain the relevance of entity *A* while *B* is being discussed, so too the summarizer has to maintain a thread of connectedness between writer *A*'s contribution and writer *B*'s. (This is not easy. Graduate students struggle with the conventional section of M.A. and Ph.D. theses called the "literature review," where the writer takes a position, ideally, amidst *all other* research relevant to her topic. This section has a stubborn tendency to list-like flatness which leaves the reader to construct the relevance of one section to the next.) So a writer positioning herself amidst established ideas about the standardization of language, in order to pursue a question related to this topic, will by summarizing the work of two sources in effect *compare* them.

PASSAGE 20

Whereas Milroy and Milroy (1985) see the standardization of written language as an inevitable product of literate and technologically advanced societies, Bourdieu (1991) opposes such explanations. He argues that language standardization is not merely an instrument of efficiency but, rather, a system for distinguishing and ranking speakers according to a perceived norm.

A characteristic sound of scholarly expression is this movement between and amongst sources. The more dense and repeated this sound of summary/comparison, the more the writer displays her command of work in her field.

Students can benefit from cultivating the styles that permit writers to move from one source to another, so the next exercise gives you a chance to practice this form of expression. It may also replicate assignments you have worked on in other courses, where you are asked to discuss the work of two (or more) other writers. If you think of these assignments in terms of *summary* (using the skills you have acquired in capturing and representing the gist of someone else's work) and *comparison* (keeping in mind the special challenges comparison poses to coherence, and the role of abstraction in maintaining relevance), you will have a strategy for handling these assignments. You may notice too that comparison can redirect summary: you construct the *gist* of writer **A** in light of the gist of writer **B**, adjusting each to accommodate the other.

---

## exercise

---

In previous chapters you read and summarized two passages about nineteenth-century education: "Vocal music," in the exercise following Section 2.5.4 in Chapter Two, and "Schooling," in the exercise following Section 3.6.5 in Chapter Three. Now write a com-*parison-summary* of those two passages. You may find that, in order to establish common ground between these two texts (beyond just "nineteenth-century education"), you have to adjust the focus of the summaries you have already written.

## 5.3.3    Comparison and definition

Unlike comparison in other genres, such as consumer information or technical reports, comparison in the scholarly genres depends on abstraction. We could say that abstraction is the grounds for comparison, the basis for explaining the relevance of **A** to **B**.

|   |   |
|---|---|
| **A**: 19th-century U.S. schools | **B**: 19th-century Canadian schools |
| political ideologies of education: nationalist & colonial | |

Or we could say that abstraction is the shelter under which **A** and **B** cohabit, the roof over their heads.

<u>political ideologies of education: nationalist and colonial</u>

**A**: 19th-century U.S. schools     **B**: 19th-century Canadian schools

In the first part of this chapter, we investigated the explaining power that flows from abstraction when it is developed by definition. The defined abstraction provides a more complex, more thorough set of instructions for the reader's interpretation of lower-level information. The following exercise gives you a chance to practise combining the force of definition with the productive energies of comparison.

## exercise

Two chunks of information follow. Find one abstract term which interprets both. On the basis of the information available, and from your own knowledge of the world, write a definition (two or three sentences) of the abstract term. Use this definition to structure a comparison of the two sets of data.

PASSAGE A   Results of a study by Cecil Helman, a medical sociologist: It is widely believed by lay people that colds are caused by careless exposure of the extremities to chill and damp. Fevers, on the other hand, are thought to be the work of harmful entities ("bugs") that wreak their effects regardless of how the victim has conducted himself or herself. Fevers elicit more concern than colds do. Moreover, these beliefs influence individuals' decisions about whether to seek medical treatment. People visit their doctors about fevers but not about colds.

Adapted from Stephen Shapin 1990 Revolutionary biology. *The Sciences* November/December, 45-59, 49.

SAMPLE B    In the nineteenth century, people considered mentally ill were insane — patently different — and they were put into mental hospitals. The leading causes of mental illness were tertiary syphilis and schizophrenia. At the turn of the century, Sigmund Freud decided that people did not have to be exclusively either crazy or sane, but that a normal person, like himself or people he knew, could be partly crazy. These "normal" people, who were still in touch with reality, exhibited only isolated symptoms of irrationality — phobias, compulsions, and other conditions which were now named "neuroses." Some thirty years later Wilhelm Reich decided that one does not have to display any mental symptoms to be mentally ill, that one can suffer from "character disorders," which can limit the productivity or pleasure in life of even asymptomatic people. More recently, psychosomatic disorders have come to medical and public attention: some people with no symptoms of mental illness have *physical* conditions with psychic roots — peptic ulcers, ulcerative colitis, migraine headache, allergies, and the like.

Adapted from Willard Gaylin 1993 Faulty diagnosis. Harper's October, 57-64, 60.

## 5.3.4    *Last note on comparison*

Comparison of *A* and *B* suggests symmetry: equal time for the two entities. But there may be occasions when such symmetry is not practical. You may have much less material on *A* than *B*. Or, if you are summarizing, *A* may be just a short article, and *B* a whole book, with a more complex and extensive argument than *A*. Or only one small part of book-length *B* may be relevant to article *A*.

In these cases, you should feel free to design an asymmetrical comparison:

FIGURE 4

A

A

B

B

And you should feel free to introduce a third element to comparison even if you have neither time nor space nor need to develop fully your summary or treatment of the third element.

FIGURE 5

A

A

B

B

C

C

There is no equal-time rule for comparison and its elements, no test beyond the reader's satisfaction. And the reader is more likely to be satisfied by a comparison that consistently demonstrates the relevance of lower-level information to larger issues than by a formally symmetrical structure.

# 6

## Academic styles

### 6.1     Ideas about "good" English

Remembering schoolroom experiences, many people regard English teachers as dedicated to monitoring language and detecting error. On social occasions, people sometimes shy away from English teachers, for fear that their speech will be scrutinized. Or, before they enter into conversation, they apologize:

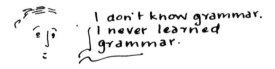

Perhaps there are English teachers who do police people's speech even when they are off-duty, and who deserve to be shunned at get-togethers. But, this possibility aside, what is more important is that popular perceptions of English teachers are only one expression of our culture's ideas about language. The system that perpetuates these ideas recruits a lot of people — more than just English teachers.

One place you can see people serving this system is in letters to the editor which deplore the deterioration of the language. The letter writers remember a time when English was better (usually when they were young), and lament decline in "standards." Often, they blame today's teachers for not living up to the traditional role of English teachers. These letter-writers are servants of the idea that some English is *good*, and some English is *bad*. Accordingly, speakers can also be judged as good or bad users of their own language — disciplined, correct and careful, or slovenly, mistaken and careless.

Besides these self-appointed correctionists, other sectors reinforce such ideas about language. People referred to as "business leaders" complain that their employees, educated under today's lax standards, can't write proper sentences. Campaigners for educational reform want "grammar." Composition textbooks often include pages called "marking symbol guides" which can list as many as 50 or 60 possible "errors," suggesting that writing is a mine-field of potentially explosive mistakenness. Style-checkers in word-processing programs adopt the inventory of error from marking-symbol guides, and register alarm at certain forms of expression. In this system of ideas about language, we could also locate the Plain Language Movement, which seeks to correct legal and bureaucratic uses of language to a standard of readability.

This system of ideas assumes a *unitary* notion of language: that is, it refers to a single, best form wherever there are various forms to choose from. So it has been criticized for its political content: typically, the forms cherished by correctionists happen to be those coinciding with the speech of the educated middle class, while the lamented forms are found in the speech of less privileged classes. In other words, it is not the forms *per se* which are better or worse. Rather, it is the social class with which they are associated that renders them esteemed or deviant. This is an important analysis, with powerful implications. It is also much more complex than my three-sentence summary of it suggests.

For our purposes, studying scholarly writing, the pervasiveness of this ideology of correctness has two relevant aspects. First, people in our culture, and particularly those exposed to advanced education, are used to the idea of "correctness." As they were corrected as students themselves, they go on to correct others. Sometimes, encountering a sentence of student writing which is not what they would have written themselves, or which occurs where the essay as a whole is not living up to their expectations, they will annotate it as "ungrammatical," when the sentence is in fact "grammatical" according to any legitimate description of English. Such annotations can be confusing for students, and make them doubt that they know their own language.

MY problem is grammar. I don't know grammar. I need help with grammar. That's my problem.

Moreover, to support the correction industry, an inventory of rules has developed, and these rules often have little relation to practical uses of the language. In the inventory are rules, or pseudo-rules, about features like passive voice (don't use it), and about sentences beginning with *and* or *it* or *there* (don't write them). These rules are misleading, but widely applied. Even style-checkers in computer software know these rules, and apply them. Since correctness has its most intense career in the classroom, students are apt to be most vulnerable to these rules. (If you use English as a second — or third — language, you may be even more subject to the experience of correction.) You are a product of the correction traditions cultivated in the classroom; so am I. The best we can do is to be aware of their effect on us and on the people who put remarks on student writing.

A second aspect of the ideology of correctness is perhaps more relevant to the study of scholarly writing. A unitary notion of language is at odds with genre theory. Ideas about "good" English — and "good" writing — overlook the way language adapts itself to serve the life of the social order, which is diverse and, in its diversity, includes the academic community with its own peculiar routines and values. Genre theory, on the other hand, predicts not one form of speech but many, and predicts that the differences are meaningful. It predicts that generalized rules for expression which are insensitive to difference or even to the practical workings of readers' capacities for understanding will produce what Pierre Bourdieu calls "semi-artificial" speech — language made in the schoolroom, under circumstances of constant correction. So even students who have been thoroughly taught rules that produce the schoolroom essay can still have problems writing academic essays.

---

### exercise

Review the accounts of your experience in having marked essays returned to you (Chapter 4 Section 4.1). Can you explain your experience in terms of the analysis of ideas about "good" English?

## 6.2 Words on the mental desktop

Genre theory predicts the *diversity* of forms of expression, and the social values encoded in *different* ways of speaking or writing. At the same time, studies of reading comprehension — such as those which informed the portrait of readers and their mental desktops in Chapter Four — reveal some *common* conditions for understanding. In this chapter, we will look at some distinguishing features of scholarly style — features which arise from the typical routines of scholarly activity. But, at the same time, we will evaluate these features for their potential for causing problems for readers. Throughout, we will try to negotiate between these two sets of demands: **social** demands, which respect the distinctive values and expectations of academic communities, and **cognitive** demands, which respect readers' common (and limited) capacities for processing complex information. In this section, we will begin to consider cognitive conditions relevant to style. The next section begins to tackle some of the social conditions relevant to evaluating style.

On our first visits to the reader's mental desktop, we found that the writer's way of arranging information determines what the reader is going to be able to do with that information. An essay which fails to instruct the reader as to the priority of certain items will leave the reader making distracting searches through long-term memory to retrieve items he had taken to be marginal, and dispensable. Or he may be led to hold on to other items only to find that they are minor players in the argument, and a bad investment for processing energies. These are poor working conditions for the reader.

But before the reader ever gets to that level of processing, where the overall structure of the argument is at stake, he has to go through more local levels of processing. He has to, first, decode words, and, second, sort out sentence structure. Both these processes make claims on the same mental resources that the reader applies to concepts and information. And they make *prior* claims. In other words, if the reader has to think twice about what words mean, he will have to use valuable processing energy to decode those words. That means he will have fewer resources left for understanding the argument. If the reader encounters a long, syntactically complex sentence whose core subject and verb are buried in a pattern of dependencies and qualifications, he will have to use valuable processing energy to make out the structure of the sentence. Both these expenditures of energy come *before* the reader's processing of the argument itself. After all, if the reader has not understood the words and untangled the sentences, he is in no position to command the argument.

"If in an epistemological figure characteristics of objectivity and systematicity are present then it may be defined as a science, on the other hand where these criteria are absent, as is the case in Foucault's view in respect of the human sciences, we may only speak of a positive configuration of knowledge being present."

So far, our portrait of the reader has shown him at his mental desk, concentrating on some ideas by keeping them on the desktop, putting some ideas aside but keeping them handy for later use, and sending other ideas to longer-term storage. Now we show him with other material crossing his desktop: words and their references, sentences and their structures. This material takes up space on the mental desktop — space we have already measured and found to be limited and liable to congestion. If the new material — vocabulary and syntax — is demanding, there will be scarcely any room left for ideas and information. "Reading" becomes a process of grinding through the local features of the text, never catching a glimpse of its global structure, its meaning.

These are poor working conditions for the reader. And he will perform poorly, missing the point, getting discouraged. We could presume that no writer would willingly let his reader's working conditions deteriorate to this point.

## 6.3    Scholarly wordings

Scholarly writing is often ridiculed in the popular media. Like the speech of people who have not internalized schoolroom rules of usage, it is deplored by those who believe in "good" writing. Most scholarly expression goes on out of earshot of the rest of the world — in scholarly journals and at scholarly conferences. But when the sounds of scholarship do leak into more public settings, they come in for some criticism, and laughter. So, when a curriculum document reaches the attention of the popular press, those wordings which are traceable to otherwise secluded research domains make people indignant, and amused. An example of "edu-babble" is cited, for entertainment:

> A certain minimum fluency is required before students are able to reflect critically on their own language use. Attention to language forms and conventions should therefore increase gradually as language skill develops and should arise specifically out of the reading and writing being done. Students are more likely to achieve good punctuation and spelling and surface correctness through extensive practice in reading and writing rather than conscious attempts to apply rules out of context.

Then it is rewritten in "plain language":

> Students are more likely to learn correct language uses, punctuation, and spelling by reading and writing than by learning rules in isolation. (*Ottawa Citizen*, reprinted in *The Vancouver Province*, Tuesday, July 5, 1994, A14)

Whatever the defects of the original or the virtues of the rewrite, the rewrite gets rid of material like "certain minimum fluency is required," "attention to language forms and conventions," and "through extensive practice in reading and writing rather than through conscious attempts to apply rules out of context." Such expressions bear the marks of scholarly prose. Actions and attributes are turned into things ($x$ pays attention to $y$ = "attention to" $y$; $x$ attempts to apply $y$ to $z$ = "attempts to apply" $y$ to $z$; $x$ is fluent = "fluency"). And agents of actions and possessors of attributes disappear (who pays attention or attempts to apply? who is fluent? who requires fluency?).

In getting rid of these features, and achieving a "plain language" standard, the rewrite might be said to restore "common sense" to the original. At the same time, it seems to reduce the conceptual complexity of the original: this is, at root, an ordinary idea, a simple one.

I suggest that the original is not in itself bad, nor that the reaction is mistaken. Rather, there has been a genre violation — or several genre violations. The writers of the original perhaps transferred the sounds and styles of scholarly research too directly to a non-research document. And the readers who objected and the rewriters who responded to these objections failed to take account of the fact that the curriculum document was addressed — at least partly — to professionals: teachers and educational administrators. In other words, the **situation** which the document served did not include readers of the *Ottawa Citizen* or the indignant politicians whose consternation was reported.

This example illuminates the conflict between what Halliday and Martin (*Writing Science: Literacy and Discursive Power* 1993) have called the "common sense" of, roughly speaking, our everyday experience of the world and the "uncommon sense" of the learned domains of research. From a distance, it seems tempting to vouch for common sense, and deny uncommon sense as unnatural, deliberately deceiving, or possibly pretentious. People use "common sense" as a term of approval, so its opposite may be something we should disapprove of.

Yet "common sense" has also been the source of some questionable ideas: that whales are fish (to use one of Halliday and Martin's examples), or less innocent ideas, such as that women are inferior to men, and naturally dominated by them, or that children benefit from stern discipline, or that rivers are a good place to get rid of industrial waste. What we take to be common sense is sometimes penetrating insight into the heart of the matter. But sometimes common sense is only unexamined assumptions which, left unexamined, perpetuate conditions that benefit some people and disadvantage others — or benefit no one in the long run. These assumptions are so widely held — that is, so **common** — that they appear self-evident.

Research activities seek to expose some of those assumptions for examination. This process of examination is represented and maintained in the distinctive language of the scholarly genres. So, while in a commonsense world, we all understand the work *think*, and use it in various situations —

When did we get gas?
Hmm. Let me think.

— cognitive scientists who want to find out about how people think would distinguish amongst these situations, seeing that one is a matter of remembering, another is a matter of calculating an answer to a particular question, and the third is a more complex procedure. For the third case, they might (and have) come up with a specialized term: "nonspecific goal strategy in problem solving." Rarely would we hear this term outside scholarly circles — or, indeed, outside the even smaller circle of the discipline of cognitive science.

Some people complain about this kind of wording. They suggest that it is an unnecessarily complicated way of speaking. Why not just say "thinking"? They suggest that, by choosing the specialist term, writers exclude commonsense people and isolate or elevate scholars to a false distinction made of elaborate language. And some suggest that this kind of wording is not only pretentious and exclusionary, but also hard to read. We will examine the grounds for these complaints.

## 6.3.1     *Is scholarly writing unnecessarily complicated?*

Later sections of this chapter will offer broader perspectives on this question, looking at how the structure of a noun phrase like "nonspecific goal strategy in problem solving" cooperates with other features of scholarly genres to produce the discourse which typifies and maintains research activities. In the meantime, we should perhaps grant that, at times, scholars might be advised to say "thinking" instead of "nonspecific goal strategy in problem solving."

But we can make this concession to critics of scholarly style only in light of other considerations. In efforts to reorganize commonsense knowledge of the world into uncommonsense, researchers analyze issues and entities into smaller parts, differentiating those parts into segments which may be scarcely visible to the untrained observer. Those segments — produced by research activity — then become objects of study, and the names for the objects of study are necessary to reporting the results of study: necessary, that is, to constructing uncommonsense knowledge of the world.

So, our opinion of the wording "nonspecific goal strategy in problem solving" may come down to our opinion of research activity itself. Are its products useful?

This is a big question, one inflated to even greater size by our culture's ambivalence towards "science." On the one hand, we invest heavily — materially and socially — in professional research. Tax and corporate dollars support scholars' activities; "experts" and "scientists" are highly regarded and called in as authorities on a wide variety of matters, from family life to outer space. But, on the other hand, we not only ridicule expert language but also question both our investment in "pure" research (that without any immediately foreseeable use) *and* the applications of research in new technologies and practices: we often complain that they have spoiled cherished aspects of our traditional ways of life.

Our ultimate judgements about the complications of scholarly language generally would have to take into account this ambivalence. But, more immediately, we might say that, if the procedures which appear to depend on wordings like "nonspecific goal strategy in problem solving" have good results, then the wording is not "unnecessarily complicated." And one of these results might be a clearer picture of how people reason — how certain kinds of schoolroom problem-questions (*if A is travelling at 50 kph and B is going 56 kph in the opposite direction . . .*) may trigger in children reasoning different from that which the teacher anticipates, or how a doctor's diagnostic questioning may trigger replies that obscure rather than illuminate a patient's condition.

## 6.3.2   *Is scholarly style exclusionary and élitist?*

Scholarly style does exclude many readers. Even within the larger academic community, readers who are members of one discipline can be excluded from the ongoing discourses of other disciplines. Genre theory would predict that this will be so: the more highly defined and particular the **situations** which language serves, the more distinctive will that language be, and the more inscrutable to people unfamiliar with those situations. So we might also predict that any social group — skateboarders or pilots or childcare workers — will develop and maintain speech styles which serve and represent the routines which organize their activities. And these styles will, to a greater or lesser degree, exclude people who don't belong to the group.

But to say that that which excludes is *exclusionary* (and to say this is to take a step towards scholarly style, which prefers a name for an attribute ["exclusionary"] over a verb ["excludes"]) is to suggest something more than just group boundaries. It suggests the operation of **power** — as do claims about élitism. If the effects of scholarly style are consistently to the advantage of those who use it and to the disadvantage of others, then critiques of scholarly ways of speaking need to be taken seriously. This is a big issue, too, and one which we will examine in Chapter 8.

## 6.3.3   *Is scholarly style hard to read?*

This question is also a difficult one, but one which we are in a better position to answer here.

Criticism of scholarly expression has sometimes focussed on what has been called its heavily **nominal** style. This characterization refers to its preference for nouns over verbs, and the way that preference results in big noun phrases like the one that we have been using as our example: "nonspecific goal strategy in problem solving" is longer than "thinking." This difference is visible to the naked eye, and needs no special grammatical analysis to reveal it. Once nouns are preferred over verbs, noun phrases bear a particularly heavy load, carrying content that would otherwise have been distributed throughout the sentence. These concentrated loads appear likely to challenge readers on two fronts: (1) the syntactic density of noun "strings"; (2) the potential ambiguity of these strings. We will examine each of these conditions.

*Syntactic density.* In English, the noun phrase is capable of expanding by picking up other sentence elements. In the series which follows, you will see noun phrases growing by absorbing material from other parts of the sentence.

(i) The noun phrase absorbs an adjective.
>**This behaviour** is criminal.
>**This criminal behaviour** . . . .

(ii) The noun phrase absorbs another noun.
>**The reports** record offences.
>**The offence reports** . . . .

(iii) The noun phrase absorbs a predicate — verb and adverb.
>**Some strategies** work forward
>**Some forward–working strategies** . . . .

(iv) The noun phrase absorbs a predicate — verb and noun (object).
>**Strategies** solve problems . . . .
>**Problem–solving strategies** . . . .

There are some limits to what the noun phrase can absorb, but these examples don't even approach those limits. They exemplify some of the simplest noun–phrase expansions.

You can see that the capacity of the noun phrase provides one of the normal economies of English. By installing, in (iii), "work forward" in the noun phrase, the writer leaves the rest of the sentence free to carry other information:

Forward–working strategies enable the problem solver to explore the problem space to see what moves are possible.

Speakers of English use the capacity of the noun phrase all the time to achieve economies of expression. Instead of saying

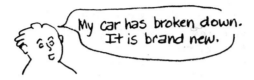

the speaker can economize, presenting the same information in fewer words:

Yet, while this appears to be the "same information," the choice between the two versions is not entirely free. If the speaker were to continue reporting his predicament, the second version would tend to lead to development of the "break-down" topic,

My brand-new car has broken down. I was going along and heard this BUMP-BUMP.

whereas the first version would tend to pave the way for development of the "brand-new" topic:

My car has broken down. It's
brand new. I just got it
last month.


We will see that topic-development traditions in scholarly writing have also influenced scholarly writers' typical choices in structuring noun phrases.

In reflecting on the noun phrase's capacity to absorb material from other parts of the sentence (thereby tending to overshadow the sentence verb), let us first take a **cognitive** approach: what does the heavy noun phrase mean to readers' working conditions? How does the decoding of a long noun phrase impose on reader's limited resources for paying attention?

Most research in this area suggests that readers, as they make their way through sentences, predict the upcoming syntactic category. So, if readers encounter

the . . .

they predict, as most likely but not inevitable, that a **noun** will come next: a word like "goal," for example.

the goal. . . .

(Of course, readers don't need to know the names for syntactic categories. They just need the ordinary knowledge of English that enables people to put together phrases like "the goal," or "the barn," or "the stove," and avoid phrases like "the because," or "barn the.")

If their expectations are disappointed, and they find not a noun but an adjective, "nonspecific," for example —

the nonspecific . . .

— they recover easily, and now predict a noun, since adjectives following determiners like "the" have a high probability of being followed by a noun:

| the | nonspecific | goal ... |
|-----|-------------|----------|
| det | adj | nominal head |
| | noun phrase | |

This seems to complete the noun phrase, and readers are ready for a verb — the goal *is* something, or *does* something. They predict a verb. But what if they encounter another noun?

the nonspecific goal strategy ...

Now they revise their hypothesis about the sentence and its structure: "goal" is not the head of the noun phrase, but only another modifier. (Notice that we have not yet approached the structural limits of the noun phrase. Somebody could write "the nonspecific goal strategy research innovation project.")

Analysis of this predictive procedure first isolates noun strings — that is, nouns modified by other nouns — as the most dense site of such failed-then-revised-hypotheses sequences. Then it proposes that these recursive predictions burden readers' attention capacity. We could see this burden as a micro version of the larger efforts after meaning we explored in Chapter Four, when we inspected that state of readers' mental desktops as they worked to construct the relevance of lower-level information to higher-level concepts. In that chapter, we figured out ways to relieve readers of such burdens. It seems that the same principles should apply to readers' first contact with text: its local wordings.

## exercise

These are noun phrases taken from published articles in a variety of scholarly disciplines. Analyze them along the lines of the analysis of "the nonspecific goal strategy," above: what hypotheses would readers make and then revise as they made their way through these noun phrases?

- labour supply decision-making
- voluntary employee turnover
- issues management structures
- other-race face recognition
- eating pathology scores

So far, our evaluation of the syntactic density of noun phrases has been **cognitive** only: we have been estimating readers' reasoning behaviour as they encounter long noun strings. But readers are more than cognitive beings. They are also social beings. And research shows that, while noun strings may cause trouble for some readers, they are no problem for other readers. Are some readers dull and others brilliant?

In fact, the difference lies in readers' different experience of the world. Readers' social milieux and the background knowledge they have acquired play a big part in their understanding of what they read. In measuring people's comprehension of texts that are difficult in the senses we have been looking at, researchers find that some readers don't understand them and some readers understand them well. It all depends on readers' previous contact with the subject treated by the text. For readers accustomed to the topic, a noun phrase like "labour supply decision-making" is no more difficult than, say, "sewing." (The article from which I took that long noun phrase is about women sewing at home, on a piece-work basis.) Some researchers have suggested that, once a long noun string is an established term in a discourse community, members of that community will process it as a clump.

Let's reassemble the reader as a **socio-cognitive** being, and ask the question again: is scholarly style hard to read? Yes, it is — for some people. Students new to a discipline, for example, may find the nominal style of scholarly writing difficult to read. Perhaps students can benefit from first seeing the scholarly noun phrase as a structure which absorbs other sentence parts, and then methodically unpacking that noun phrase, understanding why it is causing them trouble but not letting it get the upper hand. Later sections of this chapter will provide some opportunities to practise this technique. As *readers*, students can overcome these obstacles once they understand the structure of the obstacle, and where the footholds and handholds are.

As *writers*, students can be wary of all-purpose rules for plain writing that call for verbs instead of nouns, and deplore noun "strings." Their readers will not necessarily have trouble with a heavily nominal style. But writers can also keep in mind the cognitive load imposed by noun strings. There may be times when unpacking a big noun phrase will offer relief to the reader, especially when the noun phrase is not referring to the kind of recurrent, dominant topic entities that "labour supply decision-making" and "nonspecific goal strategy in problem-solving" refer to. So there may be times when passage 2, below, is preferable to passage 1 (where the target noun phrase is underlined):

PASSAGE 1    A recent comparative study of multi-family housing development and maintenance costs based on 1986 construction experience showed that three-storey buildings ultimately provided cheaper housing than high-rises.

PASSAGE 2    A study recently compared costs of developing and maintaining multiple-family housing. It was based on 1986 construction experience, and it showed that three-storey buildings ultimately provided cheaper housing than high-rises.

*Ambiguity.* We have seen that noun phrases are hospitable to other sentence elements: they will take in just about anything. As these bits and pieces are accommodated in the noun phrase, other elements are left behind. When parts get left behind, ambiguity can result. Sometimes the effort required from the reader to resolve the ambiguity is so negligible it is scarcely measurable. The underlined noun phrases in passage 3, which appeared in a daily newspaper, make demands on readers that they meet virtually automatically.

PASSAGE 3    The body, discovered in the basement of a concrete building, was identified as the remains of a newspaper woman who had lived in the neighbourhood in the late 1960s.

"A concrete building" means that the building was made of concrete. But "a newspaper woman" doesn't mean that the woman was made of newspaper. It means that the woman wrote articles for a newspaper. The noun phrases don't make these distinctions (the distinctions are lost when the noun phrase absorbs those other elements). So readers make these distinctions by consulting their knowledge of the world (no women are made of newspaper). And readers make the distinctions easily, without significant processing demands.

Other noun phrases can be slightly more distracting. Passage 4 comes from a news report about social conditions in the United States.

PASSAGE 4     Homeless experts say that the problem will only get worse as the summer goes on.

*What is a "homeless expert"?*

A more likely interpretation soon supersedes the less likely one.

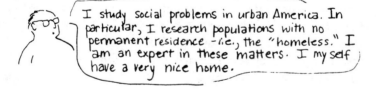

Readers resolve the ambiguity in the noun phrase by consulting their knowledge of the world. This doesn't take long, but it does consume mental resources that might be put to better use under better working conditions.

Other noun phrases can be more stubbornly ambiguous. The following example cannot be resolved by simply consulting our knowledge of the world:

police arrest information

Does this refer to information that police use when they arrest people? Or information police compile when they arrest people? Or does it refer to information about police arresting people? Without surrounding context (or maybe even with it), this noun phrase remains ambiguous. And the underlined noun phrase in the next example (passage 5), repeated from a student essay, could sit for a long time on the reader's mental desktop, while he tried to decode it:

PASSAGE 5     The protagonist suffers from externally imposed reference systems.

*What are "externally imposed reference systems"?* Consulting his knowledge of the world, the reader is liable to remain perplexed. If it turns out that (5) is an important claim in the writer's argument, the reader is going to be at a disadvantage when he tries to construct the writer's meaning. When the writer revised, and unpacked the noun phrase to improve the reader's working conditions, "reference systems" was abandoned. It turned out that, while this term was simple and meaningful for the *writer*, there were other ways of stating the point that made it more accessible to the *reader*.

PASSAGE 6     The protagonist finds her identity imposed on her from
outside. She is the person others see her to be, and their
vision of her is formed by the values and attitudes of the
community.

Finally, when style is heavily nominal — that is, when information is concentrated in expanding noun phrases — an accompanying feature appears, which can also contribute to ambiguity. This feature, which we have encountered before, we will call **agentlessness**. The doers of actions slip away when the actions are turned from nouns to verbs. So, while verb *attend* requires (in active voice) that the doers of the action be identified —

Forty-five property owners and six tenants attended the meeting.

— noun *attendance* allows these agents of the action to withdraw from the sentence:

Attendance was high.

Agentless writing has been condemned as both ambiguous and deceptive, an instrument of concealment. Leaving charges of deception aside for the moment, we must concede that heavy nominals which eliminate agents are liable to be ambiguous. For example, in "labour supply decision-making" **who** decides? (and about what?) Someone who has not read the article from which this phrase was taken might be surprised to learn that the decision-makers were Bangladeshi women in London who chose to do piece work at home rather than look for jobs in garment factories.

The ambiguity and syntactic density of a heavily nominal style are both potential troublemakers for readers and writers. Yet scholarly style risks these troubles: this way of speaking must provide some benefits, some important service to scholarly situations. In the next section we will observe these benefits and services.

Two exercises conclude this section. In the first, you can practise unpacking a heavily nominal passage — something you may want to do when revising writing of your own that risks congesting your reader's mental desktop.

The second exercise presents a passage from non-academic writing that exhibits many of the features we have been talking about as typical of scholarly writing. It is a description of a management position in the private sector. You will be asked to assess its cognitive and social profile: how does its grammar call on reader's reasoning capacities and their knowledge of the world? At the same time, it demonstrates a condition often overlooked by criticisms of scholarly writing: that the boundaries around scholarly expression and research communities are permeable, and the language of scholarship can seep out into surrounding communities. While "labour supply decision-making" may seem like an entirely specialist term, peculiar to academic circles, a term like "dysfunctional family" may once have seemed so too, yet is currently in constant use in the public media and in private conversation. Heavily concentrated in scholarly communities, research language also finds its way into other circles, apparently useful to our culture's (or our cultures') ways and routines.

## exercise

The passage below contains a lot of heavy noun phrases. Screen the passage's style, detecting those segments that impose unnecessary burdens on the reader. Rewrite by unpacking noun phrases, spreading their elements out into other parts of the sentence and other sentences.

### Sample:

Incarceration-based measures are the most common in national prison-use assessment.

### Re-write:

Some measures are based on the frequency with which criminals are incarcerated. These rates are the measure most commonly used to assess the way nations use prisons.

The Australian basic-wage Royal Commission of 1920, seeking working-class standard-of-living criteria, was chaired by a widely-read and respected living-wage champion, husband of a controversial family-planning advocate. Despite the liberal-reform inclinations of the Commission's chair and its nearly 40% recommended basic-wage increase, one of the main legacies of the Commission was the unquestioned equation of the "family" wage with the male-provider wage.

Adapted from Kerreen M. Reiger 1989 "Clean and comfortable and respectable": Working-class aspirations and the Australian 1920 Royal Commission on the Basic Wage. *History Workshop* 27, 86-105.

---

# exercise

The advertisement below appeared in the Career Opportunities section of a national newspaper. Other advertisements in this section included descriptions of positions available in engineering, private- and public-sector administration, personnel and sales management.

Screen the style of this text for features we have identified as belonging to scholarly expression: that is, nouns that represent actions or events, and in doing so lose agents (doers) and objects (done to). What questions might someone ask about who does what to whom? Evaluate this passage for its potential ambiguity and syntactic density. Speculate on why these ways of speaking which seem characteristic of research genres turn up here, in a business genre.

## SENIOR CONSULTANT

### Automotive marketing

Blackburn/Polk Vehicle Information Services (BPVIS) is Canada's leading supplier of motor vehicle and marketing information services to the automotive industry and its allied businesses. We are looking for a Senior Consultant to work with our clients to market our full range of products and services.

We require an individual with the following skill set:

- knowledge of the automotive market and its information requirements
- general understanding of geo-demographics and market research
- general knowledge of direct marketing.

Our services for the automotive industry include market performance evaluation and benchmarking, network planning and location analysis, customer profiling studies, and support services for direct communication and customer retention programs.

The successful candidate will have strong presentation and interpersonal skills and be self-motivated.

Compensation is performance related and is commensurate with experience. Please apply in confidence to _____.

# 6.4 Sentence style and textual coherence

Here are four scholarly passages which can arouse questions:

PASSAGE 7

What appears increasingly clear is that educational attainment is not synonymous with skill requirements in the workplace, and that a single years-of-schooling measure cannot serve as an adequate proxy for the variety of working capacities required by an industrialised society.

Keith Burgess 1994 British employers and education policy, 1935-45: A decade of 'missed opportunities'? *Business History* 36, 3, 29-61, 31.

*Who gets educated? Who requires skills? Who measures what? Who works? Who has — or lacks — capacities?*

PASSAGE 8

During this period [1880-1920] a latent nativist, anti-immigrant tendency in American society and politics grew rapidly, in response to economic problems, urban growth and changes in the nature and scale of immigration.

Mark Ellis and Panikos Panayi 1994 German minorities in World War I: A comparative study of Britain and the U.S.A. *Ethnic and Racial Studies* 17, 2, 238-259, 239.

*Who tended? Who responded? Who had problems? Who moved to cities? Who immigrated?*

PASSAGE 9    The insertion of a Fourth World of indigenous populations who have a distinct vision of their place in a world
that until recently has ignored them (Graburn 1976) cul-
tivates an awareness of the political potential of submerged nationalities that are emerging once again in the
postmodern world. This belated recognition of submerged ethnicities comes in the wake of the demise of
the Second World, which no longer provides the paradig-
matic base for analyses, as the structures of capitalism, so-
cialism, and imperialism are undermined.

June Nash 1994 Global integration and subsistence insecurity.
American Anthropologist 96, 1, 7-30, 8.

*Who inserts a Fourth World? Who is aware? Who belatedly recognizes?*
*Who analyzes? What nationalities and ethnicities are these? Who or*
*what submerged them?*

PASSAGE 10   Our study advances and tests a model incorporating both
institutional and resource explanations for why firms
adopt certain structural modifications, namely, issues management structures. The study . . . provides a model to account for variation in the development of issues management structures across firms.

Daniel W. Greening and Barbara Gray 1994 Testing a model of
organizational response to social and political issues *Academy of
Management Journal* 37, 3, 467-498, 469.

*Who explains? Who modifies what? Who manages? What are the is-
sues and what does it mean to manage them? Who develops structures?*

In context, these passages might not raise so many questions.
But, on the other hand, you may have even more questions than
I have listed. So let us ask one more, overarching question: if
these passages have the potential to arouse so much uncertainty,
why do scholars write this way?

These samples — all heavily nominal — seem to confirm
views that scholarly writing is difficult. But they all appeared in

very respectable journals. This style must in some way benefit scholarly writers and readers, and serve scholarly situations.

Halliday and Martin argue that this "language of the expert" gives priority to **taxonomy**: that is, to schemes for classifying and ordering phenomena. Such schemes depend on names for things. So, in passage 10, the action *modify* (*x*'s modified *y*'s) becomes noun *modification* so it can fit into a scheme of related phenomena, and take an **attribute** — "structural" — which will distinguish it from other "modifications." The *action* or *event* stabilized as a noun can then be worked into an arrangement with other named phenomena, "institutions" and "resources." These arrangements, Halliday and Martin argue, are designed to reveal relations of **cause**. (This is evident in passage 10, where the authors explicitly ask "why?") In this ordering search for causes, the grammar of research genres ends up with heavy nominalizations.

This is a good account of the grammar of scholarship. But we could perhaps develop this account further, along lines laid out earlier in this book. In Chapter Four we talked about **coherence** — about the patterns by which parts fit together and demonstrate their **relevance**. We observed that not all genres have the same coherence patterns, and that the scholarly genres typically maintain coherence by repeated instatements of high-level, abstract topic entities. Other genres, like newspaper reports, thank-you notes, or computer manuals, don't do this.

With these conditions in mind, we can begin to see the role of heavily nominalized expression in supporting these recursive hierarchies of prose. If, over several paragraphs, I were to write about a number of cases where employers preferred to train young employees on the job and tended not to hire people with secondary-school diplomas, I could compress these many cases into "skill requirements in the workplace" and "educational attainment" and specify the relation between them: "not synonymous." These expressions eliminate the employers who hired and taught and the workers and students learned or failed to learn. But they also provide an ascent to the high level of abstraction that will hold this section of the discussion together, and then serve as tokens for this section as the argument develops over ten or twenty pages. These abstract terms — the nominal versions of actions and events — can be reinstated at each of those points when the academic reader's desktop needs instructions on managing information. While the details on particular firms and industries and school curriculum can be filed away, the high-level terms should be kept handy.

So, as the article on German minorities (passage 8) proceeds, particular historical episodes of persecution can be assumed under "nativist, anti-immigrant tendency" (and, in the process we learn more about what "nativist, anti-immigrant tendency" meant in America between 1880 and 1920, and the term becomes fuller, richer). In the article on subsistence economies (passage 9), "awareness" and "belated recognition" become names for the author's stories (from 30 years of fieldwork experience) of her own changing understanding of the relation between "submerged ethnicities" and established but now inadequate ways of analyzing those communities anthropologically. In the article on issues management (passage 10), "variation in the development of issues management structures across firms" is the name that holds together extensive data of 451 firms in three industries, "issues management structures" recurring repeatedly.

Scholarly writers need a concentrated expression they can reinstate to bind together parts of their discussion and to control extensive stretches of lower-level information. These expressions are like elevated platforms from which the extent of the argument can be captured in a glance. There is not much standing-room on these platforms, so, when the arguments are complex, the expression can be complex. In the article on Bangladeshi garment workers, "labour supply decision-making" has to capture at once the article's distinctions as a contribution to analysis of labour markets. The author examines labour as offered by workers rather than required by firms — hence "labour *supply*." And she examines the conditions which determine the decisions people make about work in an immigrant community where husbands' wishes about the wives' work may not coincide with the women's wishes, and where both sets of choices are hemmed in by racial attitudes in the surrounding community. "Labour supply decision-making" is her complex topic, the platform from which expanses of statistical and interview data can be viewed.

These viewing platforms are situated throughout the scholarly essay, often working to incorporate *summary* of other writers' statements. Here, in an article on "voluntary employee turnover" (people quitting their jobs), "employee turnover" is ground shared by the other writers and the current authors, while "job alternatives" (if I quit will I be able to get another job? will it be a good one?) and "job satisfaction" (am I happy in my work? do I get along with my boss? will I be promoted?) themselves compress information.

PASSAGE 11    In a major conceptual advance from previous research directions, Hulin and colleagues (1985) recognized that job alternatives and satisfaction could have substantially different effects on employee turnover across various populations. For example, job alternatives but not job satisfaction might have a substantial and direct effect on turnover among marginal and temporary employees (often described as the secondary labor market). In contrast, both alternatives and job satisfaction might have significant effects on turnover among permanent and full-time employees.

Thomas W. Lee and Terence R. Mitchell 1994 An alternative
approach: The unfolding model of voluntary employee turnover.
*Academy of Management Review* 19, 1, 51-89, 54.

Nominal expressions also tend to appear as writers end one section of argument and move on to the next stage. Here, the writer concerned with subsistence economies concludes a three-part account of the "world crises" affecting the "submerged ethnicities." She uses three expressions which nominalize verbs (and remove their agents) to compress the preceding discussion and make it portable, able to be carried forward compactly to the next section:

PASSAGE 12    These world trends of integration of economies, dependence on finance capital, and erosion of subsistence security have profound consequences for the societies we study, whether they are located in core industrial countries or in developing areas. I shall illustrate their implications in three case studies of integration into the global economy where I have carried out fieldwork. (Nash 13, underlining added)

Unlike most other genres, scholarly genres must live up to demanding coherence requirements, hinged on abstraction and spread through deep descents to specifics and sharp ascents to generality. We could say that these large patterns at text level — characteristic **macrostructures** — determine smaller patterns at sentence level — **microstructures**. The grammar of the research genres is a product of their conceptual organization.

We asked what benefits come from expressions which many measures would estimate as cognitively costly: hard to read. These seem to be the benefits — cognitive cost at the level of sentence and phrase for a profit at the level of textual coherence. Finally, everything fits together. (In the next section we will speculate on some of the *social* benefits flowing from heavy nominalization.)

Yet the model of the reader's mental desktop warns us that those sentence-level costs can be high — to readers who give up, and writers who can't get through to exhausted readers. So sometimes (and maybe not often enough) you will find an academic writer stopping to unpack a passage, and relieve some of the congestion on the desktop.

PASSAGE 13

Pleck suggests that Afro-American women worked more as a reaction to their greater long-term potential for income inadequacy than to immediate economic deprivation. It was as if they were taking out insurance against future problems.

James A. Geschwender 1992 Ethgender, women's waged labor, and economic mobility. *Social Problems* 39, 1, 1-16, 7.

Sensing perhaps that "immediate economic deprivation" (being poor? not having enough money?) and "long-term potential for income inadequacy" (worry about not having enough money later?) are unnecessarily complicated ways of speaking, the author rephrases these expressions in everyday language. Since the nominal expressions are not part of a major topic cluster, this is probably a good move for the writer to make on the reader's behalf.

Writers can reduce cognitive costs to the reader. But what can readers do when they face imposing clumps of nominals? Rather than give up, they can unpack those clumps for themselves, finding the everyday wordings that would represent the ideas at stake, and trying to think of examples of what the writer is talking about.

---

## exercise

Take passages 7 to 10 pp. 236-237 and write them out for yourself. Try to answer the questions posed about these passages. Question passage 14 p.240 similarly, and answer the questions you come up with. In each case try to construct concrete examples of what the writers are talking about.

---

## exercise

Examine an essay you have written recently. Does it have heavily nominalized passages of the kind we have been looking at? Exchange the results of your investigation with classmates who have looked for nominalization in their own writing. If your writings lack these features, discuss their absence: is it just as well? Or is their absence a sign of some structural weakness? (Remember how these noun clumps play an important role in the overall coherence of scholarly arguments.) If your writings do show these nominalizing tendencies, discuss their presence: are you glad of them? Are they performing as they should? Or could some passages be unpacked to improve the reader's working conditions without damaging the topical coherence of the essay?

## 6.5 Prestige abstractions and their rhetorical power

"Voluntary employee turnover" and "issues management structures" are good examples of the nominalizing tendency of scholarly writing. Both of these come from a business journal, and seem characteristic of the way topical abstractions are formulated in the business discipline and in other disciplines, too. They compact a vast array of events and conditions, and hold them steady for scrutiny.

But they have rhetorical force, too, as well as cognitive or conceptual force. They engage readers' interests as Big Issues, matters of concern, and persuade them to pay attention. Even at a glance, we can see that, from the management point of view, these expressions point to serious problems. If you are running a company, and people quit when you prefer them to keep working, you want to know why, and what to do about it. If you are a manager in an industry that arouses environmental concerns, you want to know how to cope with bad publicity. So, while managers themselves may not directly consult these articles for help with their problems, the scholars who teach business courses and research business situations will recognize their relevance. "Voluntary employee turnover" and "issues management structures" are Big Issues.

In other disciplines, where the connection between research and real-world interests is not quite so visible, topical abstractions may have a more diffuse rhetorical, or persuasive, appeal. In the article on London garment workers, for example, the first discussion section is titled "Racism and the construction of community" — Big Issues by anybody's standard. The immediate argument is connected to these prestige abstractions through generalization that sums up the statistical and interview data the author has collected:

PASSAGE 14
> In the face of persistent racial antagonism which regularly spills over into physical harassment and violence, the community remains a source of strength, safety and solidarity for its members. It can only continue to play this role if it is constantly and actively reaffirmed and reconstituted.
>
> Naila Kabeer 1994 The structure of 'revealed' preference: Race, community and female labour supply in the London clothing industry. *Development and Change* 25, 307-331, 326.

The persuasive power of prestige abstractions can compel attention to phenomena we might otherwise overlook. So an article reporting debates about the orthography of Haitian Creole — about how the spelling of this language should go — introduces important abstractions in its title: "The 'real' Haitian Creole: Ideology, metalinguistics, and orthographic choice" (Bambi B. Schieffelin and Rachelle Charlier Doucet 1994 *American Ethnologist* 21, 1, 176-200). Then it immediately invokes other compelling abstractions — "competing nationalist discourses" and "language ideology" — on its first page. Through these abstractions, a discussion of decisions about the rules for spelling in Haiti acquires rhetorical force. These are Big Issues.

You may have noticed that certain abstractions get a lot of use: *ideology* is one of these, *race, gender, class, community* are others. The *social construction* of this or that is also currently prestigious. Abstractions can also be somewhat discipline-specific ("social control" was at one time Big in criminology; "discourse community" has enjoyed prestige in composition and rhetoric studies; "dialogism" has been major in literary studies; "empowerment" had such a heyday in education that it surged into general conversation). But others, like the ones listed above, appear to be shared by neighbouring disciplines. They have prestige value and persuasive force in a range academic communities.

In their prestige, abstractions have a certain life-span. Prestige abstractions rise in prominence in response to social and political conditions within and beyond academic communities. And they decline accordingly. It is hard now to foresee a time when *race* and *gender* will not be Big Issues, or when *community* will not give research rhetorical force, but there was a time when they did not have the prestige they have now.

---

## exercise

The two paragraphs below are the introduction to a report of a group of teenage girls and their way of reading teen romances. It appears in a collection of essays called *The Politics of the Textbook*. Identify the prestige abstractions which make the topic important and which give the author's research rhetorical force.

An important theme in this volume is the central role played by written texts in ongoing ideological struggles for students' hearts and minds. School texts have often been a mode of social control through the "selective tradition" contained within their pages, which elevates the stories of powerful groups to the level of canon.[1] However, students are not some tabula rasa upon which the text inscribes their social identities. Rather, students approach texts from the position of their previously acquired gender, class, racial, ethnic, age, and sexual identities, which mesh with the words on the page. While texts may solidify students' social identities, there is also the potential for unsettling them through oppositional readings. The reading practices of actual students indicate that interpretation is characterized by variety and unpredictability rather than by certainty. Books are, as Foucault[2] observes, a mode of discourse whose authority and meaning is shaped and constrained within a field of discourse of use and negotiation. The knowledge and resistances that readers bring to reading also shape textual meaning, as Fetterly[3] and Morely[4] argue. Reading can become an act of opposition to dominant curriculum arrangements by students who feel oppressed and powerless. The text as a source of multiple, often contradictory meanings is especially apparent in today's popular teen romance novels, which exemplify how young women readers come to grips with the world and also refashion it.

In this chapter, I discuss how middle- and working-class young women, ages twelve through fifteen from adverse racial and ethnic backgrounds, construct their femininity while reading adolescent romance fiction in school. I analyze how the political climate of both the larger society and the classroom shape and constrain meaning production. I also consider the ways in which romance-novel reading relates to readers' future expectations as women. I begin by providing a context for romance fiction in schools by reference to recent events within American society and their relation to the romance publishing industry.

1  See Linda K. Christian-Smith, "Gender, Popular Culture and Curriculum," *Curriculum* 17 (1987): 365-406; Wendy Saul, "Excluded Work from the Selective Tradition," paper presented at the American Educational Research Association's Annual Meeting, April 1988; and

Joel Taxel, "Reclaiming the Voice of Resistance: The Fiction of Mildred Taylor," in this volume.

2   Michel Foucault, *The Archeology of Knowledge* (New York: Pantheon Books, 1972).

3   Judith Fetterly, *The Resisting Reader* (Bloomington, Ind.: Indiana University Press, 1978).

4   Dave Morely, "Texts, Readers and Subjects," in Stuart Hall, Dorothy Hobson, Andrew Lowe, and Paul Willis, eds., *Culture, Media and Language* (London: Hutchinson, 1980), pp. 163-73.

Linda K. Christian-Smith 1991 Readers, texts, and contexts: Adolescent romance fiction in schools. In *The Politics of the Textbook*, ed. Michael W. Apple and Linda K. Christian. New York: Routledge. 191-212, 191.

## exercise

Examine essays you and your classmates have written recently, in this course or others. Do your titles and topics invoke Big Issues? What prestige abstractions do you use —or could you use — to give your research rhetorical force?

## 6.6   Messages about the argument

Heavy nominalization and prestige abstractions distinguish the scholarly genres from other types of writing. Both can appear in other genres (an exercise above showed agentless nominalizations appearing in an employment advertisement; abstraction can show up in that genre too, when employers ask, for example, for "commitment" from potential employees). But they do not operate in the same way they do in the scholarly genres, where they consistently enforce the peculiar coherence of scholarly writing and attach individual research contributions to Big Issues that academic communities adopt and nurture.

The features we will inspect in this section — messages about the argument — also distinguish the academic genres.

PASSAGE 15 ... the study of gender issues generally in rural areas remains relatively neglected (Little 1991).

This paper is an attempt to begin to redress the balance by concentrating on the gender divisions apparent in the material collected by the Rural Church Project, and aims also to highlight the need for further specific study of gender and the rural church. After a brief discussion of the history of staffing in the Church of England, we consider recent published studies on gender roles in the Church and our own material from the Rural Church project survey on the staffing of parishes in five dioceses. We then turn to rural parishioners and consider the influence of gender on church attendance and religious belief, together with attitudes towards women priests. Our conclusion is an attempt to reconcile the very different pictures of the rural church which emerge from the information on staffing on the one hand and attendance, belief and attitudes to women priests on the other.

Susanne Seymour 1994 Gender, church and people in rural areas. *Area* 26, 1, 45-56, 45.

This passage, from a geography journal, exhibits several features we will investigate: it refers to itself ("This paper"); it refers to the author ("We"), but in a limited way, as we will see; it forecasts the argument to follow; it situates itself in relation to what other studies have said — or not said.

To sharpen your sense of these features as distinctive, call to mind other genres, familiar from everyday life. Would you find a newspaper report or a thank-you note referring to itself?

This report provides information on yesterday's protest at the legislature.

This thank-you note expresses gratitude for two gifts received last week.

Probably not, although instances of some other genres (very formal business letters, for example, or legal documents) can refer to themselves. Would you find a newspaper report or thank-you note referring to the author in this (limited) sense?

| | |
|---|---|
| I/we present a series of quotations from participants at the protest. | I/we describe the gift in favourable terms. |

Probably not, although the thank-you-note writer may refer to himself in other senses ("I have been very busy at school and look forward to the holidays"). Would you find a newspaper report or thank-you note forecasting its discussion?

| | |
|---|---|
| These quotations will be followed by quotations from political figures responding to the protest. | Following the description of the gift, brief news about the recipient's family will be presented. |

Probably not. And it is hard to construct a situation where either of these everyday genres would situate the current utterance in relation to what others have said, or not said. ("Little information about this event has been published, since it only happened yesterday." "No one has so far expressed gratitude for this gift in writing.") In Chapter Seven, we will look at this last feature, which situates the utterance in relation to other utterances. In the meantime, we will examine the other features which distinguish the cited passage from, at least, newspaper reports and thank-you notes.

## 6.6.1    *The argument refers to itself*

The underlined wordings in the following passages each refer to the text being written/read. What patterns do you detect in these moments when the article mentions itself?

PASSAGE 16     Over the following pages we aim to challenge this view and demonstrate that restrictive practices of this type have been nowhere near as common or serious as some have argued.

Nick Tiratsoo and Jim Tomlinson 1994 Restrictive practices on the shopfloor in Britain, 1946-60: Myth and reality. *Business History* 36, 2, 65-84, 65. (underlining added)

PASSAGE 17    This study explores the possible cognitive bases for Justice Jackson's conundrum, by closely relating what happens in legal advocates' minds while composing to what happens in court readers' minds as they grapple with a case decision. The study directly compares, for the first time, the thought processes of professional appellate attorneys as they researched, composed and revised a brief for litigation with the subsequent thought process of two independent appellate court readers, charged with pronouncing a decision. Through this comparison of advocates' with decision-makers' "on-line" processes, the purpose of the study is to explore alternative theories for why appellate advocates experience difficulties in forming successful rhetorical strategies for their briefs. In particular, the comparison permits one to explore empirically why these advocates may fail to perceive accurately the effects of their chosen strategies upon judges and court staff readers.

James F. Stratman 1994 Investigating persuasive processes in legal discourse in real time: Cognitive biases and rhetorical strategy in appeal court briefs. *Discourse Processes* 17, 1-57, 1-2. (underlining added)

PASSAGE 18    Two main hypotheses are addressed in this study: (1) that unidentified and untreated learning difficulties may be related to teenage girls becoming pregnant, deciding to raise their children, and dropping out of school, and (2) that teenage pregnancies may *not* characteristically be "unintended."

Helen Rauch-Elnekave 1994 Teenage motherhood: Its relationship to unidentified learning problems. *Adolescence* 29, 113, 91–103, 92. (underlining added, italic emphasis in original)

From this small sample, we might note that these references tend to occur when the writers are making big claims (and promises). Or that the arguments refer to themselves at moments when the writers forecast what is to come. We might also note that in the second and third samples the writers might have used "I" or "we": "I directly compare. . ."; "I address two main hypotheses. . . ."

Are these entities — "paper," "study," "analysis" — stand-ins for the writer? Surrogates in a situation that disallows "I"? Not exactly, for passage 16) shows that the first person "we" can accompany reference to the thing being written/read. And we see in the next section (6.6.2) that, contrary to many people's ideas about prohibitions against "I" in formal academic writing, the first person occurs frequently in published scholarship. Yet we will also see that the scholarly genres' use of references to the thing being written/read is a clue to the limitations those genres impose on "I"/ "we."

---

## exercise

Inspect essays you have written recently or are currently drafting: do you find expressions which refer to the essay itself? If such expressions are missing, try adding them at appropriate points. (Remember how we have just seen such wordings appear at points where writers make major claims or promises.) How do you feel about saying, "This study focusses on three explanations for. . ."? Would you feel better saying "This paper. . ." or "This essay. . ."?

---

We know that your readers, in their professional lives, are accustomed to seeing articles refer to themselves, and that these references are one of the distinctive features of the scholarly genres. Whether all professors see them as appropriate to student versions of the scholarly genres I cannot say. But what we can learn from these samples is that reference to the thing being written/read often coincides with the expression of a major claim, and/or with a forecast of the order of the up-coming discussion. So we can speculate that such references will be a helpful signal to your readers (accustomed as they are to the sounds of the scholarly genres) to pay close attention.

## 6.6.2    The "discursive I"

Sometimes students ask their teachers if they want them to use "I," or to avoid it. This question is often accompanied by a question as to whether the teachers are interested in the students' "own opinions." (I hope the "opinion" question was answered by Section 3.8 in Chapter Three, on taking a critical position.) In the long history of the teaching of writing, "I" and "opinion" have got connected.

Although "I" occurs in the scholarly genres with nowhere near the frequency that it does in daily conversation (where it is a favoured sentence-opener), it is by no means absent from published scholarship. And, in conventional, mainstream scholarship, it would be hard to connect "I" with the ordinary sense of "opinion," in light of the constraints under which it occurs. We will now examine these constraints.

Here are some occurrences of "I" in published scholarship. See if you can infer the constraints which control the use of "I." (Analysis follows, but try to make this out for yourself before looking at the analysis.)

PASSAGE 19    Lesbian theory and feminism, I want to suggest, are at risk of falling into a similar unhappy marriage in which "the one" is feminism. (558)

★ ★ ★

I intend to begin this section by expanding on the argument against reducing the institution of heterosexuality to (a part of) the institution of male dominance. (573)

Cheshire Calhoun 1994 Separating lesbian theory from feminist theory. *Ethics* 104, 558-581.

PASSAGE 20    Let me conclude by returning to the title of this paper.
              (Kabir 329)

PASSAGE 21    ...I shall focus upon expectations and evaluations regard-
              ing the participation of married women, with husband
              present, in the waged labor force. I begin with a discus-
              sion of the "cult of domesticity," explore ethnic vari-
              ations in commitments to the cult, examine the causes
              and consequences of its decline in influence, and evaluate
              the consequences for ethnic groups of difference in rates
              at which married women work for wages. I close with a
              consideration of policy implications. (Geschwender 1)

PASSAGE 22    This article has two purposes. The first is to show that
              ability grouping in secondary schools does not always
              have the same effect, and therefore it is worth seeking
              ways of using it more effectively than commonly occurs.
              A brief review of earlier studies, and a reinterpretation of
              the conclusions of an earlier synthesis, provide the sup-
              port for this claim. The second goal is to explore in-
              stances of relatively successful uses of ability grouping, in
              the sense that high-quality instruction fosters significant
              learning among students assigned to low-ability classes.
              What characterizes such classes? To address this question,
              I draw on evidence from earlier studies by other authors,
              and I provide two new illustrations taken from a larger
              study of eighth- and ninth-grade English classes in 25
              midwestern schools. Although these examples are far
              from conclusive, common elements emerge that, taken
              together, may help to characterize effective instruction in
              low-ability classes in secondary schools.

              Adam Gamoran 1993 Alternative uses of ability grouping in
              secondary schools: Can we bring high-quality instruction to
              low-ability classes? *American Journal of Education* 102, 1-22, 1.

PASSAGE 23    The author decided to investigate the academic achieve-
              ment levels of the teenage mothers with whom she was
              working after being told repeatedly that their favorite
              subject in school was math — an unexpected and per-

plexing finding because girls are generally reported to feel they are not good at, and thus dislike, math (Parsons, Adler, & Kaczala, 1982). (Rauch-Elnekave 97)

On the one hand, the "I" of the writer in these passages seems to hover on the vanishing point. In virtually every case, the "I" construction could be eliminated without depleting content. It could simply disappear ("Lesbian theory and feminist theory are at risk of..."), or be replaced by one of the text-referring words like "study" ("this section begins"), and one sample, (23), mixes such words ("article," "review") with instances of "I." One — (23) — has actually transformed the first-person "I" into third-person "the author"/"she."

So we might look at the typical habitat of "I" — what does it occur with? Then we notice that all the verbs that have first-person subjects refer to some **discourse** action:

- I want to suggest

- I intend to begin

- I shall focus

- I begin with a discussion ..., explore ..., examine ..., evaluate ..., evaluate ..., evaluate ..., evaluate ....

- I close

- I draw on evidence

- I provide

- Let me conclude

Analysts who specialize in the study of the research genres would distinguish among these verbs, finding different categories of discourse action. But, for our purposes, it is enough to note their general similarity: they all describe the speaker in his or her capacity as a writer/researcher. Let us call the "I" of the scholarly genres the "discursive I" — not a mother, or a neighbour of Gatsby, or an anxious person or a disappointed one, or a socially privileged one, or someone about to have houseguests, or someone publishing his first article or his fiftieth, or a white person, or a person of colour, but a writer/researcher.

As a writer in the scholarly genres, you *can* refer to yourself, pointing yourself out to your reader. But your identity is limited.

Attitudes to these limitations run to extremes. So many students have told me that their teachers and professors have instructed them not to use "I" that I think there must still be some *I*-avoidance afoot. Perhaps this can be explained by the limitations on "I" when it occurs in scholarship. Those who would disallow "I" translate the limits into a blanket prohibition.

Taking a different view, some scholars criticize the research genres for the limits they put on "I." Conventions which limit writers to the "discursive I" erase elements of identity that are, in fact, relevant to research and its results. Such criticisms propose that who we are, as social and political beings, influences what we choose to study, how we gather information, and how we interpret that information. The "discursive I" obscures those influences and limits not only the surface expression of scholarship but its deeper character as well. In Chapter Eight we will consider the larger arguments to which such reflections contribute.

## exercise

Passage 20 above — "Let me conclude. . . " — resists elimination of the first person. Can you think of any way of putting this differently? What aspect of the expression makes any change difficult? From this example, can you infer any general features of the "discursive I"?

## exercise

What do you think of passage 23's "The author decided. . . ."? Does it help you to know that this paper was written by a psychologist? Can you devise any other way of writing this passage — without using "I"?

---

## exercise

Inspect essays you have written recently or are currently composing: how do you represent yourself when you write an academic paper? Are you happy with this representation? Would your friends and family recognize you? What options do you feel you have? Do the options vary according to the discipline you are working in?

## 6.6.3    *Forecasts and emphasis*

Like references to the text itself, the "discursive I" of scholarly writing often occurs along with forecasts: statements about how the argument will be organized, what readers can expect.

PASSAGE 24

First, I will summarize prior research indicating that instruction is typically inferior in low-ability classes. Second, I will briefly show that new data from a study of midwestern secondary schools mainly conform to this pattern. Third, I will give four examples — two drawn from past research, and two original cases taken from the study of midwestern secondary schools — that illustrate that high-quality instruction can occur in low-ability classes. Finally, I will consider the limitations and implications of these illustrations. (Gamoran 4–5)

Forecasts can also show up in "agentless" forms — that is, without either the text itself or "I" promising a particular course of discussion.

PASSAGE 25

Before proceeding to a more precise description of the research methods used and a detailed discussion of sample matched reader-writer protocols, the relevance of this study to current theoretical disputes over appropriate rhetorical techniques and planning processes for appellate advocates should be put into sharper focus. Two basic issues will be addressed:

1) What rhetorical techniques in briefs do current brief writing theories recommend appellates use, and what conflicts exist between these theories?

2) What problems has empirical research investigating these theories encountered? (Stratman 7)

This passage achieves its "agentlessness" by using the *passive voice*:

"the research methods used"
— who used the methods?

"the relevance . . . should be put into sharper focus"
— who should do this?

"two basic issues will be addressed"
— who will address the issues?

The passive voice has been condemned by many, and defended by a few. Despite its bad reputation amongst people who compose rules-for-writing, however, it is very common in scholarly expression.

We have already identified forecasts as a distinguishing feature of the scholarly genres. Aside from tables of contents in larger works, and other such guides, we do not run across them very often in everyday life.

*What have you been up to?*

**In addressing your question, I will first express my philosophy of life. Next, I will show that philosophy operating in my recent activities. Finally, I will describe my plans for the future.**

Yet forecasts are extremely common in the scholarly genres. It seems that forecasts play an important role in helping readers manage the contents of their mental desktops. Forecasts instruct the desktop's information-management device. They guide readers in determining when one section is finished and another beginning — determining, that is, when to file lower-level information, compacting its gist into higher-level statements that can be kept handy as the discussion goes on to other areas. We have already observed the distinctive **coherence** patterns of the scholarly genres — patterns which summon every part to demonstrate its relevance to high-level, abstract and complex propositions. Demanding for both readers and writers, these conditions are served by forecasts.

They are also served by statements of emphasis. Here are some examples.

PASSAGE 26

The crucial point for this essay is that between 1939 and 1944 the organization attracted *popular support*. (92, underlining added, italic emphasis in original)

★ ★ ★

Our main interest here is the style of the printed language — how did it reconcile with the everyday language of the predominantly oral world? (93, underlining added)

Thiathu J. Nemutanzhela 1993 Cultural forms and literacy as resources for political mobilisation: A. M. Malivha and the Zoutpansberg Balemi Association. *African Studies* 52, 1, 89-102.

PASSAGE 27    What I want to <u>highlight</u> in Wittig's explanation of what
              bars lesbians from the category 'woman' is that it claims
              both too much and too little for lesbians as well as reads
              lesbianism from a peculiarly heterosexual viewpoint.
              (Calhoun 563, underlining added)

PASSAGE 28    The <u>general point here</u> is that there are instances — this
              [campaigns for non-sexist language] is one — where we
              can locate the specific and concrete steps leading to an
              observable change in some people's linguistic behaviour
              and in the system itself. (91, underlining added)

Deborah Cameron 1990 "Demythologizing sociolinguistics: Why
language does not reflect society." In *Ideologies of Language*, ed. John
E. Joseph and Talbot J. Taylor. London: Routledge.

Research articles can do without both forecasts and statements of emphasis. Movements along the hierarchy of generalization, from high-level abstraction to specifics and back again,
will arouse experienced readers' expectations, and alert them to
important points. Lots of scholarly essays provide neither forecasts nor emphasis pointers, relying instead on these movements
themselves to convey implicit messages about the argument.
But many do use expressions of emphasis, and most seem to
offer some kind of forecast. Both emphasis and forecasting enable the reader to grasp the relation between lower level information and the high-level abstractions which give the topic
persuasive force.

Similarly, most instances of "I" could be removed, and the
expression in which they occur adjusted to get across equivalent
information. But "I" occurs nevertheless, with some frequency.
Perhaps both techniques not only benefit readers' desktop-
management devices but also provide writers with greater **control** over the use that readers make of their texts. Perhaps forecast and emphasis pointers would have, on some occasions, controlled some of those unruly readers/instructors who missed
your point. While we could speculate that both forecasts and
emphasis (and the associated references to the text itself and its
writer) are signs that scholarly genres are domineering or over-
powering in their measures for controlling readers' interpretive

work, we can perhaps also sympathize with writers' desires to overrule the hazards of misunderstanding.

The scholarly genres can seem aloof productions, remote from the personal contact and proximities of more mundane genres, or of everyday conversation. Yet the features we have looked at in this section on "messages about the argument" each summon writer and reader to the same spot, putting the writer in close touch with the reader.

## exercise

Imagine a reader from outside the academic community encountering the passages below (both of which are first paragraphs of introductions). How could you prepare that reader for contact with these examples of scholarly expression? How would you explain the features of these passages so the imagined reader would understand them as functional expressions of the academic community's routines and procedures? (It might help to imagine a particular reader — a friend, family member, neighbour, co-worker, or maybe yourself at an earlier stage of your education.)

PASSAGE A

Recent research in the history of nineteenth century psychiatry has explored the expanding powers of the medical profession and the proliferation of the asylum, that "magic machine"[1] for curing insanity. This medicalization of madness has usually been portrayed as a "top-down" process: "social control imposed from above with greater or lesser success on a population now the unwitting object of medical encadrement."[2] But as historians have begun to study individual asylums and the complexities of committal, more emphasis is being placed on the role played by families in the process. Asylum doctors, it has been suggested, merely confirmed a diagnosis of insanity already made by families, by neighbors, or by non-medical authorities.[3] Consequently, as the American historian Nancy Tomes has argued, "the composition of a nineteenth century asylum population tells more about the family's response to insanity than the incidence or definition of the condition itself."[4] Such arguments imply a more "dynamic and dialectical"[5] interpretation of the process of medicalization, one that requires a careful assessment of family demands for medical services and the degree to which these demands were met, willingly or unwillingly, by the emerging psychiatric profession.[6] In the present stage of research on mental illness and its treatment, it is vital to expand the range of institutional studies.

Patricia E. Prestwich 1994 Family strategies and medical power: "Voluntary" committal in a Parisian asylum, 1876-1914. *Journal of Social History* 27, 4, 799-818, 719.

PASSAGE B   It is now well known that optimizing governments face a credibility problem when agents form rational or model-consistent expectations because of the time inconsistency of the resulting policy (Kydland and Prescott, 1977). A time-inconsistent policy is one which is optimal at the beginning of the planning period but becomes sub-optimal at subsequent times thereby creating an incentive to renege. Assuming that the private sector has complete information of the nature of the policy-maker's calculations, the incentive to renege can be anticipated. Thus time-inconsistent policies may not be believed in the absence of some institutional arrangements which force policy-makers to precommit.

Paul L. Levine and Joseph G. Pearlman 1994 Credibility, ambiguity and asymmetric information with wage stickiness. *The Manchester School* 62, 1, 21-39, 21.

# 7

# The state of knowledge: positions, conditions, limits

## 7.1 Knowledge

In this chapter we take a closer look at two identifiable segments of the conventional arrangement of research writing: introductions and conclusions. All utterances have beginnings and endings, so we could say that the scholarly genres share with other genres the requirements of introductions and conclusions. And from previous chapters we have an idea of what scholarly beginnings and endings are like: they tend to be more general and abstract than other parts of the discussion. But in this chapter we will try to pin down the exact quality of that generality.

There are no doubt various ways to go about such an investigation. Here I have chosen to use the theme of **knowledge** to explore the styles of scholarly introductions and conclusions. In the research genres, beginnings and endings are, among other things, explicit or implicit claims about the **state of knowledge** of a topic. And, in between introductions and conclusions, certain forms of expression maintain and refine these claims through the body of the discussion. The "knowledge" theme will help us understand features that congregate in introductions, conclusions, and the space between.

## 7.2    Introductions: generalization and citation

Most people would probably agree that introductions typically begin at and sustain a relatively high level of generality. For the schoolroom essay, the height of a generality is often enough to get the essay under way.

Throughout history, humans have sought their identity.

Or

Imagination is a powerful force in our daily lives.

But if we transferred this habit of generality directly to the academic essay, we might find that academic readers' expectations are not entirely satisfied by generalities like these.

Here the "issues management structures" article that provided some examples in the last chapter begins with general statements:

PASSAGE I    In the last 20 years, business organizations have been increasingly held accountable for their corporate social performance in a variety of areas (Wood, 1991). Firms have been confronted by an organized, activist, and concerned set of stakeholders (Ansoff, 1975; Freeman, 1984) clamoring for improved corporate performance on a wide range of social and political issues, from clean air and nutritional labelling to equal employment opportunities.

Daniel W. Greening and Barbara Gray 1994 Testing a model of organizational response to social and political issues. *Academy of Management Journal* 37, 3, 467-498, 467.

It seems to me that most people know this: most people are aware that public consciousness of business and industry has changed, and corporate spokespersons appear often on TV, and are often quoted in the print media to answer complaints about their products and practices. But, even though these circumstances seem to be part of common knowledge, this passage attributes their mention to particular writers. Did the authors of the present article *not know* about this development in business domains until they read the three articles cited? This seems unlikely. Why are statements that could easily be justified as belonging to the present writer attributed to other writers?

John Swales, in his study of the introductions to research papers (1990 *Genre Analysis: English in academic and research settings*), observes that one of the moves writers typically make is to confirm that they are carrying on a **tradition** of inquiry. This topic has been ratified — as the parenthetical citations show. It is not just anybody who mentioned that firms must deal with social issues — not Ms. Blink, or Mr. Blonde, neighbour of one of the authors. It is published researchers who have said this. In the academic community to which this article is addressed, people recognize this topic.

But then we might ask, if this ratification is not just a constraining formality, does it have any *use*? Recalling Halliday and Martin's idea of research producing *uncommon sense*, we can see that, by attributing the generalization to other (published) speakers, the present writers place a control on common sense: maybe everybody "knows" this, but a lot of things that are commonly "known" can turn out to be in some way mistaken. The citation shows that this perception is verifiable by measures valued in the academic community.

As well as putting a check on common sense — on widely held views — attributing generalizations to others can also put a check on personal perceptions. We may notice, in our daily life, that the servers at fastfood outlets are young people. So we construct a generalization: "The fastfood franchise industries hire young people." (The socioeconomics of this circumstance would be interesting to explore.) But what if it is only the one or two outlets that serve the fried chicken we like that actually do hire young people? What if, in the next district or province, most servers are elders? Our limited experience — our particular position in the world — has distorted our knowledge of the situation. And what if our experience is limited in another way, by attitudes and interests? Maybe we have a grudge against young people, and feel the world is overrun with them. We see them everywhere. Our unchecked personal perception would produce an unwarranted generalization, one which reflected our position in the world, our point of view.

So, in academic writing, we find generalizations of this kind, which typify sections of the population, verified with citation.

PASSAGE 2

This article analyzes labour supply decision-making for a particular group of women workers in a particular segment of the London clothing industry. It takes as its starting point the concentration of Bangladeshi women in the homeworking sector of the East London rag trade (Mitter, 1986a).

Naila Kabeer 1994 The structure of 'revealed' preference: Race, community and female labour supply in the London clothing industry. *Development and Change* 25, 307-331, 307.

This example suggests, too, that citation can be a check on stereotypes as well as personal perceptions.

---
## exercise
---

Here are two examples of generalization occurring in opening sections of research articles. What would be the "commonsense" versions of these generalizations? Why is the commonsense version not adequate to the scholarly situation? That is, why are these generalizations secured by citation?

PASSAGE A

Just as people are unable to ignore discredited information in making personality judgments (Wyer and Budesheim, 1987; Wyer and Unverzagt, 1985) or revising social theories (Anderson, Lepper, and Ross, 1980), so mock jurors are unable to ignore evidence that had been ruled inadmissible (Carretta and Moreland, 1983; Sue, Smith, and Caldwell, 1973; Thompson, Fong, and Rosenhan, 1981; Wolf and Montgomery, 1977). As new information is presented, it is immediately processed into people's ongoing belief revisions, or schemata, which are then resistant to change and colour the evaluation of subsequent evidence and instructions. (Wrightsman, 1991, Ch. 13)

Brian H. Bornstein 1994 David, Goliath, and Reverend Hayes: Prior beliefs about defendants' status in personal injury cases. *Applied Cognitive Psychology* 8, 233-258, 235.

PASSAGE B     Gender is one of the most important categories — if not the most important category — in human social life. The dichotomy between female and male is of crucial relevance to virtually every domain of human experience (Bem, 1981; Huston, 1983; Ruble & Ruble, 1982). All known cultures specify that female-male is a fundamental distinction. They provide terms to distinguish boys from girls and men from women. More importantly, they associate men and women with different sets of characteristic features and with different sets of behavioral expectations (see Williams & Best, 1990).

Thomas Eckes 1994 Features of men, features of women: Assessing stereotypic beliefs about gender subtypes. *British Journal of Social Psychology* 33, 107-123, 107.

For the student writer, this scholarly habit of assigning to someone else statements writers could easily make on their own may seem like a strange and prohibitive condition.

> We should take our holiday
> in July. July is in summer
> (Hopkins 1991). Summer
> is warmer than winter
> (Sooter 1972).

And, on its own, such a practice does seem prohibitive, tending to deprive speakers in the scholarly genres of rights to independent speech, and leaving them speechless if they can't find someone to cite. Scholars themselves may even feel these prohibitions, as they wait for or look for precedent-setting statements regarding a topic they want to research. (Sometimes, in some fields, these precedent-setting generalizations come from the most famous scholars: distinguished thinkers whose long careers or brilliant contributions give them rights to speech others do not enjoy. Then the generalizations produced by these thinkers are used over and over again, by more humble scholars, to secure the generalities which frame their research.) And this system of dependence may have overall constraining effects on research products in our culture. We will consider this possibility in Chapter Eight.

But the custom of secured generalization does not operate on its own. It is part of a larger system of customary practices in the scholarly genres which represent the **quality** or **state of knowledge**. When a general statement is represented as *reported* from another source, it is offered as knowledge validated by research procedures recognized in the discipline. (These procedures include as a final step review by the editorial committees of the journals and presses that publish scholarly writing.) The citation signifies that this knowledge has been produced by certain identifiable people. It is not *common* sense, but knowledge issuing from a recognizable source. All reported statements in the scholarly genres implicitly remind us that knowledge has a source: it is made by somebody.

Other features of the scholarly genres also mark statements for the quality of knowledge they present: in particular, a set of expressions which signal the greater or lesser probability of a statement or the source and distribution of knowledge. (We will look at these expressions in section 7.5.2.) But it is probably the practice of reporting the speech of others that is the scholarly genres' most conspicuous way of constantly, relentlessly representing knowledge as something made by members of research communities.

## 7.3    Introductions: reported speech

As we noted in Chapter Three, reported speech in scholarly writing is so crucial a feature that the research genres have developed their distinctive ways of incorporating the speech of writers other than the primary writer — ways elaborate beyond anything observable in any other genre. (This elaborateness in itself should be a sign to us that quotation and documentation are far more than niceties. They play a big role in signifying the social meaning of research itself.) Systems of documentation — footnotes, endnotes, lists of works cited, parenthetical clusters of names and dates — are intricate and rule-governed, although the rules vary from discipline to discipline.

Equally intricate are the systems that direct writers to quote a lot, or not much, or quote directly, or to paraphrase, to put other writers' names in the reporting sentence, or to put them in parentheses, or even to leave the other speakers unidentified. In the samples which follow, we may find some guides to this unrecorded system, but we will not find the kind of rules that govern, for example, the preparation of a Works Cited page or the punctuation of a parenthetical citation in a certain discipline. Instead, we will find tendencies and signs of preferences, traces of the habits of academic communities.

So we observe, for example, that, while reported speech can occur at any point in a scholarly essay, it is most likely to occur in the introduction, somewhat less likely to occur in the conclusion, and least likely to occur in the space between. Not all of the samples we will look at show up at the very beginnings of the articles, but most are part of the writers' introductory moves. In the sections which follow we will see why reported speech plays such a big role in getting writers started in their address to their reader.

## 7.3.1   *Reported speech: direct and indirect*

When we say what someone else has said, we have choices as to how to go about it. We can use the words the other person used:

This is called direct speech. In writing, direct speech is supposed to be verbatim; in talking, as some research has shown, people are not always accurate in their repetition of others' words.

Instead of direct speech, we can use our own words — which can be more or less close to the original:

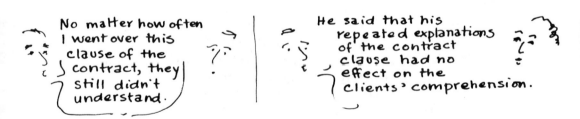

This is called indirect speech. When you are summarizing, you can often find yourself using indirect speech: the exact words of the original have to be transformed to fit into smaller space.

You may notice that my second example of indirect speech moves towards the nominalized style of scholarly writing. "I/he explained" becomes "explanations"; "they . . . understand" becomes "clients' comprehension"; and these two noun phrases are linked by a *cause* relation — "no effect." Not all indirect speech will take this nominal route, but in the scholarly genres, especially where longer chains are compacted, as in summary, we may find Indirect Speech heading this way.

Reported speech, mostly in indirect form, can take another step towards nominal style, by transforming the reporting verb itself into a noun.

So

|    |          |         |
|----|----------|---------|
| he | suggests | that ... |
|    | assumes  |         |
|    | argues   |         |

can become

|         |            |         |
|---------|------------|---------|
| his/the | suggestion | that ... |
|         | assumption |         |
|         | argument.  |         |

The choice between direct and indirect speech is reflected in questions students sometimes ask about their writing.

How much should I quote?
Do I quote too much? Do I
need _more_ quotations? How
much should I quote?

These are good questions, for it appears not only that there are certain tendencies in the proportion of direct to indirect speech, according to the function of the summary (to confirm what has been said, to dispute it, to go further), but also that, in different disciplines, direct speech is used differently. Greg Myers (1989 The pragmatics of politeness in scientific articles *Applied Linguistics* 10, 1–35) finds, for example, that direct speech is used ironically in the samples of articles in the biological sciences he analyzed: that is, writers quote directly when they don't agree with the original source. You will see that this finding does not hold for our samples.

## 7.3.2    Reported speech: identifying the speaker

The simplest, base-line case of reported speech is *x* said *y*.

Ms. Blink said, "The shopping is great. I got so many bargains."

Ms. Blink said that the shopping was great and she got a lot of bargains.

**Or x said [gist of y]:**

Ms. Blink expressed enthusiasm about shopping opportunities and reported getting "bargains."

Scholarly writing can often depart from these base-line cases. Commonly, the reported speaker can leave the sentence itself and relocate in parentheses.

> The shopping is good, and bargains are available (Blink 1994).

This form can eliminate the speech verb (*say* and its many substitutes, such as *report*, *suggest*, etc.) as above, or retain it:

> It has been reported that the shopping is good, and bargains are available (Blink 1994).

Sometimes the speaker or speakers can disappear entirely, the act of speech represented as **agentless**:

It has been reported that the shopping is good, and bargains are available.

This form of expression seems to defy the research community's practice of exactly attributing statements. Yet our samples will show that Indirect Speech can occur without an identifiable speaker. On non-scholarly occasions, agentless reports of statements may tend to make the statement seem more valid — coming from not just one person (who may or may not be reliable) but from more widely distributed sources.

The Prime Minister is said to be considering tax increases.

So the agentless report of speech can suggest some consensus. Inspecting the samples of reported speech below, you will have a chance to see if this is the case in scholarly publications.

In a variation on the agentless report of speech, statements can sometimes be attributed to a **typified group** — "researchers, "linguists," "neo-classical economists," for example, in the scholarly genres; "experts," or "officials" or "business leaders," for example, in other genres. So our sample, in a "group-speaker" form, could be rewritten as

Consumers report that the shopping is good, and bargains are available.

When statements are presented as reported speech, their quality as knowledge is indicated: the statement has been produced — somewhere. At first it may appear that, in the scholarly genres, to present a statement as coming from a position other than that of the present speaker may implicitly ratify the statement as true: "this is not just *my* idea." But, in fact, things are more complicated than this. Statements are reported not simply to ensure that only true things get down on paper. Writers also report statements to sketch a community of speakers producing knowledge in a particular area. Reported statements produce a map of that knowledge domain. And writers' main concern, as we will see, is to locate themselves on that map — maybe close to some speakers, or far away from others, maybe starting in densely populated locales where a lot has been said, but heading out into sparsely settled regions from which few statements have been transmitted so far.

## 7.3.3    *Reported speech: naming the speech action*

We have called the simplest or "base-line" case of reported speech **x says y**. In the variation on the shopping example, we picked up the verb *report* (which could turn into a noun, producing "the report that shopping is good"). But *report* is by no means the only other verb for reporting speech. *State, propose, suggest, maintain, claim* are some others (see Chapter Three for another inventory of reporting verbs). And associated with verbs of speech are a set of verbs we could call "knowledge-making" (following the current way of talking about scholarly writing as belonging to the "knowledge-making" genres). Among the knowledge-making verbs we find words like *analyze, investigate, examine, discover, find, identify, observe.*

> <u>Analyzing</u> shopping opportunities, Blink (1994) <u>found</u>
> that bargains were available.

Like the verbs of speech, many of these verbs can turn into nouns. So we might come across sentences like this:

> The <u>analysis</u> of shopping opportunities has led to the <u>identification</u> of bargains (Blink 1994).

Where a range of wordings presents choices, the different choices can tend to be associated with different functions. So, in everyday speech, to use "claim" as a reporting verb may in some situations have the effect of discrediting the statement, or at least suggesting that it needs review.

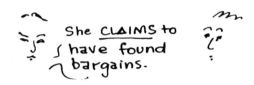

It is not clear whether claim — as just one example — has the same function of negative evaluation in scholarly writing. Nor is there extensive evidence as to which kinds of reporting verbs position the writer *near* the reported speaker (in agreement) or *far away* (in some form of disagreement). But some research (e.g., Sarah Thomas and Thomas P. Hawkes 1994 Reporting verbs in medical journal articles, *English for Special Purposes* 13, 2, 129-148) has found some correlation between the choice of reporting verb and the position of the writer vis-à-vis the sources reported.

---

## exercise

---

Below you will find six samples of scholarly writing which report the statements of others. The samples illustrate the range of expression and function described above: the summoning of the voices of others to gesture to a Big Issue, or established line of research; the variation between direct and indirect speech; the naming, obscuring, or typifying of other speakers; the characterization of the production of statements with various words for speaking and/or making knowledge.

Examine each sample to identify these features. From these limited data, can you generalize your results? What do you notice about the reporting of statements in scholarly prose? Can you see any correlation between the features you identify and the disciplines in which the writers are working?

PASSAGE A

One topic of recurring interest in the analysis of written discourse has been the identification of various text *types*. This identification has frequently involved linking a rhetorical 'mode' or 'aim' of discourse with the particular linguistic categories which realize that mode or aim in a text (Jakobsen, 1960; Hausenblas, 1966; Barthes, 1970; Benveniste, 1971; Colezel, 1973; Werlich, 1975; Faigley and Meyer, 1983). In that this method links discourse functions to linguistic features, it continues the Prague School tradition of functional linguistics begun by Mathesius (1975; see Vacheck, 1964) and Mukarovsky (see Garvin, 1964; Burbank and Steiner, 1977) and associated today with the work of Danes (1964, 1974), Firbas (1964), Sgall and Hajivoca (1977, 1978). There are also strong analogues to the Prague School method in the functional analyses of texts performed by British linguists in the neo-Firthian school (especially following Halliday, 1976a, 1967b) and by American linguists working with Longacre's (1976) version of tagmemics. While there have been functional analyses of specifically scientific texts by neo-Firthian linguists — most notably Widdowson (1974), Widdowson and Allen (1978), and MacKay (1978) — there has thus far been no comparable analysis of scientific texts using Longacre's tagmemic taxonomy.

Edward L. Smith, Jr. 1985 *Text.* 5, 3, 229-247, 229-30.

In the second paradigm, gender is construed as a global personality construct. The concepts of *masculinity, femininity* and *androgyny* exemplify this approach (see, e.g., Archer, 1989; Cook, 1985, Morawski, 1987). In reviewing the literature concerning the sex-differences and the gender-as-a-personality-construct approaches, Deaux & Kite (1987) come to the following conclusion: 'The scientific record on questions of sex differences, based on either biological or psychological distinctions, is shaky at best. . . . Yet despite evidence of considerable overlap and situational specificity of gender-related behaviors, beliefs in sex differences are held tenaciously' (p. 97).

Researchers adopting the third and most recent approach conceive of *gender as a social category*, that is, as a category on which perceivers base judgements, inferences and social actions. The central research issue here is not 'how men and women actually differ, but how people *think* that they differ' (Deaux, 1984, p. 110).

Thomas Eckes 1994 Features of men, features of women: Assessing stereo-typic beliefs about gender subtypes. *British Journal of Social Psychology* 33, 107-123, 107-08.

PASSAGE C

Although lesbian feminist theorizing has significantly contributed to feminist thought, it has also generally treated lesbianism as a kind of applied issue. Feminist theories developed outside of the context of lesbianism are brought to bear on lesbianism in order to illuminate the nature of lesbian oppression, and women's relation to women within lesbianism. So, for example, early radical lesbians played off the feminist claim that all male-female relationships are dominance relationships. They argued either that the lesbian is *the* paradigm case of patriarchal resister because she refuses to be heterosexual or that she fits in a continuum of types of patriarchal resisters.[2] In taking this line, lesbian theorists made a space for lesbianism by focusing on what they took to be the inherently feminist and antipatriarchal nature of lesbian existence. Contemporary lesbian theorists are less inclined to read lesbianism as feminist resistance to male dominance.[3] Instead, following the trend that feminist theory has itself taken, the focus has largely shifted to women's relation to women: the presence of ageism, racism, and anti-Semitism among lesbians, the problem of avoiding a totalizing discourse that speaks for all lesbians without being sensitive to differences, the difficulty of creating community in the face of political difference (e.g., on the issue of sadomasochism [s/m]), and the need to construct new conceptions of female agency and female friendship.4

2. On the former, see, e.g., Charlotte Bunch, "Lesbians in Revolt," in her *Passionate Politics, Essays 1968-1986* (New York: St. Martin's, 1987); and Monique Wittig, *The Straight Mind and Other Essays* (Boston: Beacon, 1992). Regarding the latter, see Adrienne Rich, "Compulsory Heterosexuality and the Lesbian Continuum," in *The Signs Reader: Women, Gender, and Scholarship*, ed. Elizabeth Abel and Emily K. Abel (Chicago: University of Chicago Press, 1983).

3. For instance, Jeffner Allen states in her introduction to the anthology *Lesbian Philosophies and Cultures*, ed. Jeffner Allen (Albany, N.Y.: SUNY Press, 1990), "The primary emphasis of this book is *lesbian* philosophies

and cultures, rather than lesbianism considered in relation to or in contrast to, patriarchy, or heterosexuality" (p. 1).

4. See e.g., the recent anthology, Allen. ed., *Lesbian Philosophies and Cultures;* as well as Sarah Lucia Hoagland's *Lesbian Ethics: Toward New Value* (Palo Alto, Calif.: Institute of Lesbian Studies, 1990; and Janice G. Raymond's *A Passion for Friends* (Boston: Beacon, 1986).

Cheshire Calhoun 1994 Separating lesbian theory from feminist theory. *Ethics* 104, 558-581, 558-559.

PASSAGE D    Many commentators on post-war Britain have suggested that the workforce and its unions must accept a large part of the responsibility for the country's continuing economic ills. British workers may or may not have been unusually strike prone, but they have certainly long colluded, it is believed, in a range of restrictive practices on the shopfloor, thus increasing costs, curtailing output and drastically limiting the scope for necessary industrial modernisation. As the distinguished Anglo-German academic Ralf Dahrendorf has recently put it, working people in Britain have tended to 'stretch their work so that it begins to look like leisure'.[1] In this situation, the inevitable consequence has been economic stagnation.

Over the following pages we aim to challenge this view and demonstrate that restrictive practices of this type have been nowhere near as common or serious as some have argued.

1. R. Dahrendorf, *On Britain* (1982) p. 46.

Nick Tiratsoo and Jim Tomlinson 1994 Restrictive practices on the shopfloor in Britain, 1945-60: Myth and reality. *Business History* 36, 2, 65-84, 65.

PASSAGE E    The diverse ways in which people of areas considered peripheral to advanced capitalism confront the problems of survival force us to rethink theories of the crisis that take into account subsistence systems and the question of survival in a holistic context. Economists of the neoclassical school have always left subsistence production out of their equations, and they have done little to update their supply-demand functions to explain the present crisis except to invent a term, *stagflation,* for why their market theory does not work. Marxists start with the proposition that the cyclical crises of capitalism result from the decline int he rate of profit as the organic components of capital (technology and administrative expenses) rise in relation to the variable component (labor costs); but they end with a critique limited to national policies. Neo-Marxists have extended the analysis to show how countries with mature economies, trying to overcome their own cycles of recession, tie peripheral economies into an unequal exchange that subverts their development (Amin 1970; Frank 1967, 1980; Wallerstein 1983). Some have demonstrated how, since the decade of the 1960s, the expansion of investments in low-wage areas throughout the world has intensified competition among workers, thereby depressing wages and reducing the basis for organization in the worksite (Frobel et al. 1980; MacEwan and Tabb 1989; Nash and Fernandez-Kelly 1983; Safa 1981).

June Nash 1994 Global integration and subsistence insecurity. *American Anthropologist* 96, 1, 7-30, 8.

PASSAGE F     The problem of teenage parenthood, acknowledged to be a significant social problem in the United States since the late 1960s, has been the subject of much study (Alan Guttmacher Institute, 1985; Chilman, 1980; Furstenberg, Lincoln, & Menken, 1981; Lancaster & Hamburg, 1986; Hayes, 1987). Efforts to understand its causes have generally focused on the issue of individual choice regarding the decision to engage in sexual behavior (Chilman, 1978; Pete & DeSantis, 1990) and to use contraceptive devices (Finkel & Finkel, 1975; Goldsmith, Gabrielson, 1972). The association of teenage motherhood with dropping out of school prematurely (Gray & Ramsey, 1986; Roosa, 1986), not being employed (Trussell, 1976), and becoming dependent on government subsidies (Klerman, 1986; Moore, 1978) is well-documented. In general, consideration of how schools and educational policies contribute to the high rate of teenage motherhood has been limited to how dropping out affects the likelihood of a girl becoming pregnant, how pregnancy affects the probability of dropping out, and the relationship between education aspirations and pregnancy rates (Moore, Simms, & Betsey, 1986).

Helen Rauch-Elnekave 1994 Teenage motherhood: its relationship to undetected learning problems. *Adolescence* 19, 113, 91-103, 91-92.

# exercise

To appreciate the effect of reporting expressions in creating the sound of the scholarly voice, choose two of the samples above to rewrite *without* reporting expressions. This won't be easy, for the act of reporting is deeply embedded in scholarly style, and not easy to root out. But a rewrite of the last passage might go something like this:

Teenage parenthood is a significant social problem in the United States. Teenage mothers drop out of school prematurely, don't have jobs, and depend on government subsidies. Individual choice is involved in deciding to engage in sexual behaviour, and to use contraceptive devices. Schools and educational policy also contribute to the high rate of teenage of motherhood. Dropping out affects the likelihood of a girl becoming pregnant, and, in turn, pregnancy affects the probability of dropping out. There is also a relationship between education aspirations and pregnancy rates.

# exercise

Examine essays you have written recently or are currently drafting. How do you go about stating the generalities which introduce your work? How do these generalities resemble or differ from those in the sample passages?

# exercise

While reported speech is a conspicuous feature of the scholarly genres, it is also evident in an everyday genre we are all familiar with: the newspaper report. An example of such a report appears below. Analyze this example for reported speech: underline all reported statements, direct and indirect. If all the reported statements were eliminated, what would be left? Going on what you know about the function of reported speech in the research genres, how would you describe the difference between the function and meaning of reported speech in the research genres and its meaning and function in newspaper genres?

## Don Hauka "Bouchard visit has fur flying" Vancouver Province 1994 May 3

A visit to Vancouver by Bloc Quebecois leader Lucien Bouchard sparked allegations of treason and separatism in the B.C. legislature yesterday.

Former Liberal leader Gordon Wilson called for an emergency debate to condemn Bouchard for advocating Quebec sovereignty while visiting B.C.

But the current Liberal caucus said that's a case of the pot calling the kettle black.

Liberal house leader Gary Farrell-Collins went so far as to accuse his former leader of "treason," noting Wilson himself had last week suggested B.C. should be prepared to separate if Canada starts to break up.

Wilson charged that the Liberals are falling flat by not questioning why the NDP government isn't doing more to show its opposition to Bouchard.

Wilson, now head of the fledgling Progressive Democratic Alliance, defended his suggestion that B.C. have a contingency plan in place should Quebec decide to leave confederation. Going it alone, he said, would be better than getting sucked into the U.S. through the concept of a regional Cascadia.

Farrell-Collins countered that Wilson is dredging up the constitution issue because it brought him brief popularity as Liberal leader.

He also defended his use of the word "treason."

"I think it's been used by a large number of people on behalf of Mr. Bouchard in his attempt to try to take his province out of Canada, so I think it can be used just as readily on behalf of Mr. Wilson for trying to take B.C. out of Canada."

Bouchard told a meeting of the Canadian Bar Association in Vancouver that he's sure the separatist Parti Quebecois will win the coming election in Quebec, but is still not sure if Quebecers will vote to actually separate in a later referendum.

He was greeted by various protesters, including members of the National party and two members of a Christian prayer group who waylaid the leader after the speech to tell him they're "praying for Canada to stay intact."

Acerbic Vancouver radio host Rafe Mair told Bouchard that Quebec should have the guts to stop taking federal money — some of it from B.C. — and start proving it can stand on its own fiscal feet. "You have no trouble taking my tax dollars to pay your salary, your expenses and, indeed, your pension."

Bouchard flies to Alberta today.

---

## exercise

The samples which we have been examining are typical: that is, they conform to general tendencies in introductions in research genres, and they compactly display distinguishing features. (That's why I chose them.) In real life, you will find many variations on these features and their arrangement. In one discipline in particular you are likely to find significant and fairly frequent variation from the patterns we have been observing. Below are two sample of introductions from articles in history journals. Examine these introductions and describe the ways they depart from what we have come to regard as typical of scholarly introductions and their way of establishing the generalities that frame the writer's contributions to research.

PASSAGE A Toward the end of the eighteenth century, a young Philadelphia merchant confided to his uncle that a recent series of business reversals had "wholly unmanned" him. Another, writing in 1798 to a friend who was in debtors' prison pending a bankruptcy hearing, dubbed his friend's creditors "relentless harpies" and congratulated him for "driving" them "off."[1] Philadelphia's eighteenth-century merchants punctuated the voluminous correspondence upon which much of their trade depended with narratives of business failures that used gender imagery in striking ways. The cumulative effect was a sustained meditation on the precariousness of manly identity and reputation, a precariousness linked not only to the competitiveness and volatility of markets but also to the difficulties of defining a reputable self within the world of patronage and connection that still structured market relations. This essay undertakes a close reading of those narratives of failure as a way of illuminating the history of male subjectivity and the formation of gender conventions in a specific market milieu.

The essay focuses on the correspondence of Philadelphia's largest wholesale merchants — men who traded actively in the Caribbean and overseas to London and southern Europe. They were, for the most part, among the wealthiest of the Philadelphia merchants. Most amassed sufficient wealth to appear among the richest 15 percent of all wholesalers active in the last half of the eighteenth century, a group defined by a net worth of at least fifteen thousand pounds in 1770. Such wealth allowed these men, albeit with difficulty, to "emulate, if not quite duplicate the lives of the lesser gentry of England."[2] The history of these merchants' subjectivity is thus bound up not only with the creation of — or obstacles to the creation of — an occupational ethos but also with the formation of an elite identity.[3] Moreover, the merchants were implicated in the articulation of a conservative and deeply masculinist discourse of civil inclusion and exclusion that circulated among elites, some of whom dominated the national leadership after the Revolution, at least for a time.

1   Robert Lamar Bisset to Henry Hill, July 2, 1794, correspondence file, 1790s, Lamar, Hill, Bisset, & Company Box 1, Sarah A. G. Smith Family Papers, 1732-1826, collection no. 1864 (Historical Society of Pennsylvania, Philadelphia); Charles Young to Henry Banks, Sept. 12, 1798, correspondence file, 1798, box 4, Ball Collection, collection no. 28, *ibid.*

2   Thomas M. Doerflinger, *A Vigorous Spirit of Enterprise: Merchants and Economic Development in Revolutionary Philadelphia* (Chapel Hill, 1986), 20-22, es. 21, 25-26, 31-32. See also Gary B. Nash, *The Urban Crucible: Social Change, Political Consciousness, and the Origins of the American Revolution* (Cambridge, Mass., 1986), 256-59; Frederick B. Tolles, *Meeting House and Counting House: The Quaker Merchants of Colonial Philadelphia, 1682-1763* (New York, 1948), 109-14, 131-34; Gordon S. Wood, *The Radicalism of the American Revolution* (New York, 1992), 110-20.

3   These merchants also mediated between Philadelphia's elite and traders of the middling sort. Although mercantile wealth became more concentrated in the late eighteenth century, wholesale trade remained open to new recruits from among shopkeepers and artisans. Doerflinger, *Vigor-*

*ous Spirit of Enterprise*, 20-40, 51, 126-34; Nash, *Urban Crucible*, 120-21. Elite merchants, interacting with fellow traders, suppliers, and purchasers who were at ease in the social and cultural milieu of mechanics and shopkeepers, experienced diverse, class-related cultural styles. As a result, individual merchants were prone to hesitate between, alternate between, or amalgamate styles in ways that contributed to the interesting *bricolage* qualities of their writing.

Toby L. Ditz 1994 Shipwrecked; or, masculinity imperiled: Mercantile representations of failure and the gendered self in eighteenth-century Philadelphia. *The Journal of American History* 81, 1, 51-80, 51-53.

In October 1888 the Colonial Office expressed deep disquiet at news that an officer of the Gold Coast Constabulary, Inspector Akers, while involved on an expedition to subdue Krepi, had inflicted harsh sentences of flogging upon men under his command who were accused of attempting to strike an NCO, drunkenness and cowardice. The nine accused Hausa constables were flogged publicly before the whole force, the worst offender receiving 72 lashes. Both the method of flogging and the number of lashes given were extremely severe and contrary to the standing orders of the Constabulary. In an enquiry that consumed a considerable amount of Colonial Office time and paper the matter was thoroughly investigated and Akers, an officer with 'many good qualities' but 'having a violent and hasty temper,' was invalided home.[1]

European use of physical violence, even excessive violence, against African subordinates was not particularly unusual in the late nineteenth and early twentieth centuries. However, the Akers case, coming less than ten years after flogging had been abolished in the British Army, marks an approximate point at which the Colonial Office began to exercise concern, and seek to regulate, the extent and severity of officially sanctioned corporal punishment inflicted on African soldiers and also labour. A discussion of official and colonial attitudes to the use of coporal punishment in British Africa is a large subject and beyond the compass of a brief article. What is attempted here is much more manageable: a discussion of the attempts by the Colonial Office, over a period of more than sixty years, first to regulate more closely and then to bring to an end corporal punishment in the African Colonial Forces. Colonial Office officials were agreed on the need to regulate corporal punishment; those advocating abolition steadily increased with the progress of the century. Both regulators and reformers in London had to contend with military officers and colonial administrators who argued that corporal punishment was necessary for the control and discipline of African troops, especially when on active service, and the steady pressure from various humanitarian lobbies in Britain denouncing severe practices in the colonies.

1  Public Record Office, Kew [PRO], CO96/197/3064, 31 Dec. 1888; and CO96/197/3080, Griffith to Knutsford, conf., 31 Nov. 1888.

David Killingray 1994 The 'rod of empire': The debate over corporal punishment in the British African colonial forces, 1888-1946. *Journal of African History* 35, 201-216, 201.

## 7.4    Documentation

Sections 7.3.1 to 7.3.3 have brought you into contact with many instances of reporting expressions, from a variety of disciplines. Reporting expressions summon a community of voices, and position the present writer amongst them. But everybody knows that these expressions are only part of the system that situates research amidst other research. Like the leafy, aboveground part of a plant, they are secured by an underground part, a root system of documentation — footnotes, endnotes, lists of "references" and "works cited."

It is also well known that styles of documentation differ from discipline to discipline. So the distinctive appearance of the passages cited in the exercise above is characteristic of publications in history. And, in fact, most disciplines do not use the heavy footnotes characteristic of history publications. Most use some variation on a system of parenthetical expressions in the body of the text which are keyed to an alphabetical list at the end. So, these entries in a section called "References" —

Linn, R. L. (1987). Accountability: The comparison of education systems and the quality of test results. *Educational Policy 1* (2), 181-198.

Madaus, G., West, M.M., Harmon, M.C., Lomax, R.G., & Viator, K.A. (1992). *The influence of testing on teaching math and science in grades 4-12*. Chestnut Hill, MA: Boston College Center for the Study of Testing, Evaluation, and Educational Policy.

Madaus, G.F. (1985). Can we help dropouts? Thinking about the undoable. In G. Natriello (Ed.), *School dropouts: Patterns and policies* (pp. 3-19). New York: Teachers College Press.

— are signalled by reporting expressions in the body of the text:

The idea of using assessment as a lever for school change is not a new one: many accountability tools in the 1970s and 1980s tried to link policy decisions to test scores (Linn, 1987; Madaus, 1985; Wise, 1979).

Linda Darling-Hammond 1994 Performance-based assessment and educational equity. *Harvard Educational Review* 64, 1, 5-30.

The parenthetical "(Linn, 1987)" sends the reader (if he or she is interested) to the first entry above, while "(Madaus, 1985)" sends the reader to the third rather than the second entry under "Madaus." (If Madaus had two entries, both by himself and both from 1985, the writer could have distinguished them as "1985a" and "1985b.") While documenting systems vary in detail, they all operate to achieve one principal effect: the reader's easy movement from the body of the text to the full citation in the "References" or "References Cited" or "Works Cited" pages. So, although this entry in an anthropology journal

Rouse, Roger
   1991 Mexican Migration and the Social Space of Postmodernism. Diaspora 1:8-23.

looks a little different from the ones in an education journal, it nevertheless operates the same way, as an easy-to-arrive at destination for the reader setting out from this passage in the body of the article:

Although many examples exist, a recent example was presented by Rouse (1991), who carried out ethnographic research among immigrants from the Mexican community of Aguililla living in Redwood City, California. In developing the notion of "transnational communities," Rouse presents a novel challenge to spatial images, highlighting the social nature of postmodern space.

Leo R. Chavez 1994 The power of imagined community: The settlement of undocumented Mexicans and Central Americans in the United States. *American Anthropologist* 96, 1, 52-73.

---

# exercise

Below are four samples of entries from reference pages at the end of articles in scholarly journals. Inspect these samples to determine the points at which they vary (e.g., punctuation, use of capitals, order of information, and so on).

## From a "Works Cited" list in PMLA (a literary-critical journal, Publications of the Modern Language Association of America):

Baudrillard, Jean. *For a Critique of the Political Economy of the Sign.* Trans. Charles Levin. Saint Louis: Telos, 1981.

Eisenstein, Sergei. "Dickens, Griffith, and the Film Today." *Film Form.* New York: Harcourt, 1949. 195-255.

Geertz, Clifford. *The Interpretation of Cultures.* New York: Basic, 1973.

Gilbert, Elliot. "The Ceremony of Innocence: Charles Dickens's *A Christmas Carol.*" *PMLA* 90 (1975): 22-31.

## From a "References" list in Environment and Planning:

Frobel F, Heinrichs J, Kreye O, 1980, *The New International Division of Labor: Structural Unemployment in Industrialized Countries and Industrialization in Developing Countries* (Cambridge University Press, Cambridge)

Johnson H T, 1991, "Managing by remote control: recent management accounting practices in historical perspective", in *Inside the Business Enterprise: Historical Perspectives on the Use of Information* Ed. P Temin (University of Chicago Press, Chicago, IL) pp. 41-70

Monden Y, 1981, "What makes the Toyota production system really tick?" *Industrial Engineering* (January) 36-46

## From a "References" list in Language and Communication:

AUDEN, W.H. 1962 Dingley Dell and the fleet. In *The Dyer's Hand and Other Essays,* pp. 407-428. Random House, New York.

JAYNES, J. 1976 *The Origin of Consciousness in the Breakdown of the Bicameral Mind.* Houghton Mifflin, Boston.

JAYNES, J. 1986 Consciousness and the voices of the mind. *Canadian Psychology* 27, 128-137.

LAWSON, L. 1989 Walker Percy's prodigal son. In Crowley, J. D. (Ed.), *Critical Essays on Walker Percy,* pp. 243-258. G. K. Hall, Boston.

## From a "References" list in Genetic, Social, and General Psychology Monographs:

Eisenstadt,S. (1989). *Israeli society* (2nd ed.). New York: Stockten.

El-Sarrag, A. (1968). Psychiatry in northern Sudan: A study in comparative psychiatry. *British Journal of Psychiatry, 114* , 946-948.

Spiro, M.E. (1983). Introduction: Thirty years of kibbutz research. In E. Krausz (Ed.), *The sociology of the kibbutz: Studies in Israeli society II.* New Brunswick, NJ: Transaction Books.

---

# exercise

Referring to the samples above or to a sample of articles you have collected from the discipline you are majoring in, answer these questions:

How do scholars document a source that is (a) an article in a journal? (b) a book? (c) a chapter in a book? (d) an article in a book?

## 7.5  The knowledge deficit

Investigating the role of reported speech in getting the scholarly discussion under way, we observed that, when statements are presented as issuing not from the present writer but from other writers, they include an implicit comment on their status as knowledge. They were produced by someone; they came from a site in the research community.

If we take this perspective on scholarly statements, we can see reported speech as mapping a set of positions in the territory of knowledge producers. On this map, no spot can be occupied simultaneously by more than one publication: that is, the publication must be "original." Some disciplinary locations on the map are very heavily populated. In these locations, you will find the majority of scholars working. Competition for space is keen, and researchers vie for position.

One way they can get title to a location on the map is by claiming to add to existing knowledge: a space that has been recognized as unoccupied or only tentatively claimed gets filled up with new data and further reasoning. Sometimes the space has not yet been recognized: it has gone unnoticed by others. Another way scholars get title to a position on the map is to evict the current occupant. They show that previously established knowledge cannot hold that ground because it is faulty or undeserving in some way.

Making these moves, the writer identifies a **knowledge deficit**. There is something we don't know, some space on the map where there is a gap, a spot where no one has so far settled to take careful account of the place. The only way such a deficit — a gap, a space unsurveyed or inadequately surveyed — can be identified is through a review of what *is* known, or taken to be known. So reported speech — in fact, the whole practice of summary — *constructs the deficit*. While on the one hand reported speech warrants the speech of the current writer *positively*, by connecting it with ratified statements and established concerns, it also, on the other hand, warrants the speech of the current writer *negatively*, as a response to a deficit. The samples in the exercise which follows show various ways writers identify knowledge deficits.

---

## exercise

Inspect the following passages and identify the ways each one establishes the writer's (or writers') right to speak positively (i.e., by connecting the present work with established concerns) and negatively (i.e., by identifying a knowledge deficit).

PASSAGE A

In this article, we examine the cultural categories and the conceptual logic that underlie the orthography debates about kreyòl that have taken place over the last 50 years. In Haiti, as in many countries concerned with nation building, the development of an orthography for vernacular literacy has been neither a neutral activity nor simply about how to mechanically reduce a spoken language to written form. The processes of transforming a spoken language to written form have often been viewed as scientific, arbitrary, or unproblematic. However, the creation of supposedly arbitrary sound-sign (signified/signifier) relationships that constitute an orthography always involves choices based on someone's idea of what is important. This process of representing the sounds of language in written form is thus an activity deeply grounded in frameworks of value.

Bambi B. Shieffelin and Rachelle Charlier Doucet 1994 The "real Haitian creole: Ideology, metalinguistics, and orthographic choice. *American Ethnologist* 21, 1, 176-200, 176.

PASSAGE B

[This] study directly compares, for the first time, the thought processes of professional appellate attorneys as they researched, composed, and revised a brief for litigation with the subsequent thought processes of two independent appellate court readers, charged with pronouncing a decision.

★ ★ ★

. . . the large professional and academic literature on writing effective appeal briefs has appropriately emphasized that briefs lie at the "headwaters" of judges' and their staff attorney's [sic] decision-making process.

Despite this emphasis, the thought processes of opposing brief writers while they compose has never been systematically studied in real time (Stratman, 1990a). Similarly, the thought processes of appellate judges and their supporting staff as they actually read and evaluate these briefs have never been directly studied (Becker, 1964; Benoit, 1981, 1989; Benoit & France, 1980; Hazard, 1982; Jones, 1976; Llewellyn, 1960; Schubert, 1964; Wassertron, 1961). Most of the extant theories abut the difficulties real brief writers face in understanding court readers' response to their text are drown from secondary data, primarily commentaries by judges. These commentaries have rarely, if ever, presented a real-time account of what thinking occurs in the readers' minds during brief review. The neglect of the brief-reading process in empirical research not only hinders the development of theory describing appellate judges' decision-making processes, but also hinders the development of a theory of the skills and strategic decision processes required to successfully compose appellate briefs (Ashley & Rissland, 1985; Lundeberg, 1987; Rissland, 1984, 1985; Skinner, 1988; Stratman, 1990b).

James F. Stratman 1994 Investigating persuasive processes in legal discourse in real time: Cognitive Biases and rhetorical strategy in appeal court briefs. *Discourse Processes* 17, 1-57, 1-2.

PASSAGE C    Despite the vociferous debate surrounding the ordination of women to the priesthood of the Church of England, the issue of gender and the rural church has been remarkably little studied. Whilst it may be argued that this neglect is due to a lack of scholarly interest in the rural church rather than in gender relations in the Anglican Church as a whole, even the recently published *Faith in the Countryside* pays noticeably scant regard to the issue of gender (ACORA 1990). Furthermore, the rural Church Project from which the material for this paper has been drawn, was set up primarily to address the dearth of information on rural churches, and gender did not form a specific focus (Davies *et al* 1990a, 1990b, 1990d; Davies *et al* 1991). Indeed this lack of research support Little's assertion that, despite recent work, the study of gender issues generally in rural areas remains relatively neglected (Little 1991).

This paper is an attempt to begin to redress the balance by concentrating on the gender division apparent in the material collected by the rural Church Project, and aims also to highlight the need for further specific study of gender and the rural church.

Susanne Seymour 1994 Gender, Church and people in rural areas. *Area* 25, 1, 45-56, 45. [This is a geography journal.]

PASSAGE D   There are several studies which have analyzed the discourse functions of quotation. Some researchers have analyzed languages other than English (e.g., Larson 1978; Besnier 1986; Glock 1986). Others have analyzed English, but most did not examine discourse samples to determine if their analyses are actually supported by data (e.g., Wiersbicka 1974; Halliday 1985; Li 1986; Haiman 1989). Additionally, these studies have not addressed the question of whether direct quotations are really quotations. In other words, how authentic are direct quotes? Do they represent actual previous utterances, or are they inventions of the speaker? This paper focuses on these questions as well as on the functions of quotation in informal spoken English. Unlike these other studies, my analysis is based on discourse samples.

Patricia Mayes 1990 Quotation in spoken English. *Studies in Language* 14, 2, 325-363, 326.

*Student versions of the statement of the knowledge deficit.* As a student writer, you may be reluctant to say that *nobody* has ever studied this before, or that *everybody* has got it wrong so far. But, with some adjustments, you can still replicate the move which identifies a knowledge deficit. So, for example, the last passage above could be recast to show that there is something interesting to be found out:

PASSAGE 3   Although speakers often resort to sayings which they attribute to other speakers and listeners accept these sayings as appropriate elements of conversation and other speech genres, we might still ask what role such quotations play in these speech acts. What conditions motivate speakers to repeat others' claims? Is the repetition exact or approximate? authentic or fictionalized? In short, how and why do we represent our own speech as originating with someone else?

Or it could be recast to mark the writer's position in relation to one other speaker (instead of seven):

PASSAGE 4    Halliday (1985) provides a useful account of the functional grammar of reported speech, but his analyses do not explain the role of quotation in conversation and other speech acts. What conditions motivate speakers to repeat others' claims?

And where a professional version of the statement of the knowledge deficit would summarize many (if not all) published claims about a research entity, the student version can summarize one or two — or even none. In that case, the introduction can propose plausible ideas about the object of inquiry and then show that these ideas, reasonable as they seem, are **problematic**: they leave some questions unanswered.

PASSAGE 5    *As For Me and My House* can be read as a system of concealment: Mrs. Bentley skips days at a time, shifts her focus suddenly to the weather, offers little information about her own background while she relentlessly exposes her husband's personal history. Yet the idea of concealment suggests an audience — and *As For Me and My House* is represented as a diary, a genre which assumes no audience but the writer herself. If the narrative is indeed a pattern of withholdings, how can we reconcile this condition with the book's generic presuppositions about audience? From whom is the missing information being concealed? Perhaps by revising the idea of concealment, and recasting it as a *system of attention* to painful matters, we can understand Mrs. Bentley's diary on its own terms, as a diligent, deliberate — and sometimes desperate — personal inquiry into the circumstances of her life.

## 7.6    Making and maintaining knowledge

Consider for a minute what it means to *make* knowledge. Say you felt a need to know, on a particular summer day, if that day was warmer or cooler than the day before. You might consult your own sensations, and find that, yes, this day was hotter. Reporting your sensations, you get some corroboration.

whew. It's hot. This is the hottest day.

Yes. A real scorcher. This is the hottest day.

We could say that you and your corroborator have made some knowledge of the relative temperatures of the season in question. (You might go on to compare this season to others, and generalize about climatic conditions.)

But say both you and your corroborator had, the day before, gone for a long swim in a mountain lake. The swim cooled your bodies, and you found the air temperate, not scorching. You could say that your *position* — your point of view, your experience of the world — had affected your findings about relative temperature. Aware of variables like swimming in glacial waters, the next time you construct knowledge of relative temperatures you look for some sign outside yourself and your closely positioned corroborator.

> This is the hottest day. The butter is melting. It didn't melt yesterday. This is the hottest day.

Now you could be said to have made knowledge by consulting a sign, reading it, and citing this evidence. (Conceivably, there might be, in some possible world, a community where melting butter was a weather-forecast sign: "The current heat-wave will intensify today. Expect butter to melt.")

But somebody might question your evidence.

> Our butter melted a bit yesterday, too. Where do you keep your butter?

You have made *some* knowledge of relative temperature, but it is vulnerable. Or, to put it another way, this knowledge is not conclusive: it provokes further knowledge-making.

Finally, if you wanted to make knowledge that was independent of your position — your swimming experience, your habits in storing and observing your butter — you might consult a widely recognized and respected instrument of measurement: a thermometer.

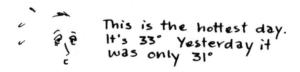

> This is the hottest day. It's 33° Yesterday it was only 31°

.  This may seem to put an end to knowledge-making on this topic, but someone could go further (claiming a knowledge deficit), questioning your instrument or its use.

> Are you sure? Did you move the thermometer? I keep mine in the shade. Have you had your thermometer checked?

Or someone could question the use of the instrument itself.

> Yesterday was hotter for me. I was tarring a roof. I've never been so hot in my life. It's very well to say this is the hottest day, but you aren't taking into account the experience of roofers.

In this sequence of knowledge-making actions, we have, very roughly, travelled through the range of *methods* of the research disciplines, from "soft" (so-called "subjective" interpretations of data corroborated by members of a community occupying similar positions) to "hard" (so-called "objective" interpretation sustained by research instruments which produce quantitative readings of the world) and back to what we might call "critical" (sort of "reflexive-soft" interpretations which question whether any knowledge can ever be produced independent of the interpreter's position).

Even without the critical techniques of current theory, we can see that knowledge-making procedures differ from discipline to discipline. These differences are reflected in stylistic differences: different ways of representing the production of knowledge. The most conspicuous of these differences is that which distinguishes publications with lots of numbers from those with no numbers. This difference has been characterized

as the difference between **quantitative** and **qualitative** study
— a distinction we will encounter again in Chapter Eight.
Along these lines that distinguish quantitative from non-quanti-
tative study, research genres are also distributed according to
whether they make provision for a "Methods" section — an explicit account of how the researchers produced the knowledge
they are now reporting — or they leave method implicit. We
will look at some examples of "Methods" sections below, and
look again at the description of methods in Chapter 8, when we
investigate the genre of ethnography. Despite these differences,
however, the scholarly genres share a concern for the sources of
knowledge, and an interest in tracing the production of knowledge. The prominence of reported speech is an obvious sign of
these interests and concerns. But it is not the only sign of them.
Appearing with some regularity throughout reports of research
are typical expressions which signify that knowledge is under
construction, and in the process of being made, and that it
comes from a position in the research community. In Section
7.6.2 below we will inspect some of these expressions, and try to
arrive at generalizations about their use. First, though, we will
glance at the scholarly genres' most explicit demonstration that
knowledge is made.

## 7.6.1    *Methods*

Method sections expose the procedures by which knowledge
has been produced.

> Method: A thermometer was placed on
> an east-facing wall of an average-
> size dwelling. Readings were taken
> on two successive days at midday.
> The readings were compared.

The rhetoric of method sections has been much studied, for
these sections show some interesting stylistic features. For one

thing, they tend towards **agentless** expressions. So you will find in one of the samples in the exercise below these wordings: "[t]he conversations to be examined here . . ."; "[t]he groups were formed after consultation with the children's teachers." In these cases, the people who examine, form groups, and consult with teachers are missing from the statement. This feature of style has excited a lot of commentary, and sometimes it is interpreted as a way of persuading readers that the researchers' methods were very "scientific" and "objective," and not open to personal bias.

Another interesting feature of method sections is their unusual pattern of coherence: although sentences are all, roughly, about "method," sometimes the relation between sentences is obscure, if measured by ordinary standards of connectedness. So, in the first sample in the exercise below, you will find

The participants in this study were educationally and socially advantaged, middle-class, urban children who were predominantly white. The children attended the day-care centre for full days, year round, and had known each other for 1 - 3 years.

If this were not a method section, a reader could very well ask, "what is the connection between, on the one hand, race and socioeconomic status and, on the other hand, full-time attendance in daycare? Is it a causal connection? And what does any of this have to do with the topic of the article?" But it is a method section, so readers don't ask these questions.

---

## exercise

Four samples from appear below. (None of the first three is complete: the first two are each only half of the full method section in the articles in which they appear; the third is in an account of a series of experiments, and relies on the reader having gone through a much longer description of the method of another experiment.) Analyze these samples for agentlessness and coherence. Then consider the overall function of these passages: if you were to generalize from these limited data, what would you identify as the main concerns of researchers composing an account of their methods?

PASSAGE A The conversations to be examined here are from an extensive research project with 3- to 5-year-old children at a day-care center in a large midwestern city. The children were grouped into 12 same-sex triads on the basis of friendship and age. The groups were formed after consultation with the children's teachers. The participants in this study were educationally and socially advantaged, middle-class, urban children who were predominantly white. The children attended the day-care centre for full days, year round, and had known each other for 1 - 3 years.

The triads were videotaped during the regular day-care day in one of the children's usual play areas, which was separate from the larger group. The only children in the room were those being filmed. They were not supervised by an adult, although an assistant and I sat somewhat out of sight in a play loft above and behind the children's play area. The children knew we were there. They were videotaped on three separate occasions, each time playing at one of three types of activities. Each group was videotaped for a total of approximately 75 minutes (25 minutes per session).

Amy Sheldon 1990 Pickle fights: Gendered talk in preschool disputes. *Discourse Processes* 13, 5-31, 12-13.

PASSAGE B We analyzed a corpus of 15 "high-brow level" articles (see Huddleston 1971) distributed as follows: 10 CR [case reports] (making up a total of 13,958 running words) and 5 RP [research papers] (making up a total of 11,871 running words). The articles, all published between 1980 and 1990, were drawn from leading medical journals such as *The British Medical Journal, Annals of Internal Medicine, The Lancet, Archives of Internal Medicine* and *The New England Journal of Medicine*. These journals were chosen because they are considered to contain the best medical journalism.

The number of hedging devices was recorded in each rhetorical section in each article separately, and the percentage of hedges (with respect to the total number of running words making up each rhetorical section in each article) was computed. The results were analyzed by means of $\chi 2$ tests. The alpha value was set up at .05.

For the reasons stated in the Introduction and in order to identify hedges as accurately as possible, we carried out a rigorous contextual analysis (both from a linguistic and medical standpoint) of the linguistic expressions commonly considered as hedges. This is why the taxonomy we adopted in this research (see below) considers both formal *and* functional criteria. Obviously, such a procedure does not guarantee a 100% reliability rate in the ascription of a given linguistic form to a hedge, but we believe that it is much more reliable than a "blind" (i.e., non-functional, purely formal) identification which would undoubtedly lead to the distortion of the data both in their quantity and their distribution.

Françoise Salager-Meyer 1994 Hedges and textual communicative function in medical English written discourse. *English for Specific Purposes* 13, 2, 149-170, 153-54.

PASSAGE C    Observers. Caucasian volunteers were recruited from the University of Texas at Dallas undergraduate psychology program and again received a research credit for a core course as compensation. Each observer participated in only one of the rating subexperiments. Twenty-five observers rated faces for typicality, 20 observers rated familiarity and repetition, and 20 observers rated memorability and attractiveness.

Stimuli. The stimuli were the recognition test sections of the videotapes described above. Each tape contained all 240 faces, blocked by race. The order of rating Japanese versus Caucasian faces was counterbalanced across the observers in each of the subexperiments.

Procedure. Observers were tested in groups of 1 to 5 and were given response sheets to make the appropriate ratings. Again, because of the length of the list, the observers were given breaks periodically.

Alice O'Toole, Kenneth A. Deffenbacher, Dominque Valentin, and Hervé Abdi 1994 Structural aspects of face recognition and the other-race effect. *Memory and Cognition* 22, 2, 208-224, 211.

PASSAGE D    *Subjects*

The subjects were 64 girls, ranging in age from 12 to 17, who voluntarily enroled in a comprehensive program for teenage mothers and their infants that was provided by the local public health department in a large city in North Carolina. Of the 64 girls, four were white and 60 were African-American. They had been sexually active from a young age, the average age at first intercourse having been 13.3 years (range 10 to 16, median 14). Average age at the time of first birth was 15.5 years (range 12.5 to 17; median 15). One girl who gave birth at the age of 12 1/2 years had been raped by her mother's boyfriend. Leszs than half of the girls' mothers had been teenage mothers themselves. Although 43% of the fathers frequently participated in the care of their infants, 19% maintained only minimal contact, and 38% had none. Half contributed to the support of their child. Although school attendance by parenting teenagers was encouraged in the school district, 12 of them (18%) were not attending school at the time of initial intake into the program.

Procedure

Girls were required to attend the clinic at regular intervals, depending upon the age of their infant (i.e., mothers of younger infants attended more frequently), although many appointments were not kept. Efforts were made to administer a structured interview and a measure of self-esteem (Piers-Harris Children's Self-Concept Scale). In addition, the records of some of the girls' performances on the California Achievement Tests (CAT) were obtained from local public schools (N = 39). The scores reported were those most recently completed by each girl. They include the results of testing done in the sixth (N = 9), seventh (N = 8), eighth (N = 20), and ninth (N = 2) grades between 1984 and 1988.

The Mental Scale of the Bayley Scales of Infant Development was administered to infants at their 9th and 18th month clinic visits, where possible. Because of logistical difficulties (e.g., missed appointments, attrition) all data are not available for every girl.

Helen Rauch-Elnekave 1994 Teenage motherhood: its relationship to undetected learning problems. *Adolescence* 29, 113, 91-103, 93.

# exercise

Practise writing in "method-section" style: describe how you found out what your bank balance was; how you came to a decision about how to vote in a recent election; or how you determined the cost of an airline ticket to a holiday destination.

As we noted above, not all disciplines use method sections. Research in disciplines in which scholars do not share recognized instruments and procedures do not explicitly expose the means by which knowledge has been made. So, in literary criticism, you will not find

> The novel was read and notes were taken. Annotation took place at each point where the annotator could detect mentions which might signify something.

But even in disciplines where methods are tacit — generally but silently understood, and not much talked about — there can still appear implicit traces of method. Theories and concepts take the place of instruments and procedures, producing knowledge by operating on a particular set of data.

## 7.6.2     *Modality and other limiting expressions*

In Chapter Six we met the "discursive I" — the being who arranged and forecast discussion, who pointed to parts of the text, summing up and emphasizing. Discursive "I" can also become the knowledge-making "I", although this being is perhaps more shy than the discursive "I". For example, in summarizing the views of another writer, this writer appears in the surface of text as a reasoning being, evaluating the statements of others:

PASSAGE 6

> Because lesbians and heterosexual resisters must have, on [Wittig's] account, the same relation to the category 'woman,' there can be no interesting differences between the two. This, I think, is a mistake, and I will argue in a moment that lesbians are in a quite special sense not-women. (Calhoun 564, emphasis added)

Since the scholarly genres impose many restrictions on the presentation of the writing *self*, we might well scrutinize this appearance of the writing self to find out what conditions permit it.

What we will find is that the "I think" in the passage above is by no means an isolated case. Rather, it is a variation on a set of expressions that are in fact abundant in the research genres, and that tend to occur in just such situations as the passage above exemplifies: situations where the writer is taking a step beyond established knowledge, moving to offer new statements to the academic community. To develop some perspective on this set of expressions and their range of occurrence, we will first see how the grammar of "I think" is related to the grammar of some other expressions which are related to it in function.

*Estimates from positions of limited knowledge.* Say you are inside on a dark night. You hear a sound on the roof. You report

It's raining.

Since you are inside, where it is dry, you are *inferring* that it is raining. Another way of reporting your finding would mark your statement as such an inference — an estimate from a position of limited knowledge.

*I think it's raining.*

Equally, you could mark your statement as such an estimate by other means. You could say

*It seems to be raining*

Or "It must be raining," *must* signalling that your claim is an estimate. Or, if you and your companion are new to the area, and less certain about local night sounds, you could express your estimate with less certainty:

*What's that noise?*

It could be rain.
It might be rain.
Maybe it's raining.

Embedded in the statement, all these expressions — along with others like *evidently, apparently, perhaps, possibly, appears* — condition the statement as the product of inference from a position of limited knowledge. They **modalize** statements. Roughly speaking, they are equivalents of "I think." Although they erase "I" from the surface of the expression, they nevertheless maintain the sense of the statement being knowledge under construction from a certain location: the writer's position in the world.

From a distance, we might think that the research genres would be the ones *without* these markers of limitation — possibility rather than certainty, "maybe" rather than "yes" or "no" — and even of "subjectivity" in that these expressions indicate the writer's reasoning, inference, speculation. If we think of research and the sciences — from hard to soft — as sources of authority and ultimate fact, we would not expect these traces of indeterminacy in the research genres. But in fact they are abundant. As the examples we examine below will show, they occur especially, but not exclusively, in introductions and conclusions. And perhaps we would not be surprised at this abundance if we thought of the scholarly genres' distinctive dependence on reported speech. In a way, the expressions which make a statement indeterminate by showing that it is the speaker's inference from incomplete evidence are something like the statements which are reported as coming from someone other than the writer. So, to return to our rain example, the speaker could also make a claim about the weather by reporting the speech of someone else.

If the speaker's companion knows that Tanya has just come in from outside, then he is likely to credit the statement as valid. It seems to come from a reliable position. (On the other hand, if Tanya has not been out, and is only speculating, and tends to interpret all noises as rain, the addressee might not be convinced.)

Both modal expressions and reported statements monitor the state of knowledge by attaching statements to the positions from which they issue. Their presence in scholarly writing is a sign of the research genres' relentless preoccupation with the making of knowledge.

*Modality in introductions.* One place we might expect to find modal expressions signifying that the statement is only an estimate is in writers' formal statements of their *hypothesis*: the statement which, for accountable reasons, is deemed plausible but which is so far untested and will be shown to be tested in the course of the article. And, in fact, modalized expressions do show up in such locations.

PASSAGE 7
Two main hypotheses are addressed in this study: (1) that unidentified and untreated learning difficulties <u>may</u> be related to teenage girls becoming pregnant, deciding to raise their children, and dropping out of school, and (2) that teenage pregnancies <u>may</u> *not* be characteristically "unintended." (Rauch-Elnekave 92, italic emphasis in original, underlining added)

But many research publications do not specify the "hypothesis" in this way, and still make use of modal expressions. So, rather than attach modality simply to the "hypothesis," it may be better to locate it in the larger process of constructing a **knowledge deficit**. Then we spot it showing up as a writer poses his research question about "low-ability" classes where "high-quality instruction fosters significant learning among students":

PASSAGE 8
What characterizes such classes? To address this question, I draw on evidence from earlier studies by other authors, and I provide two new illustrations taken from a larger study of eighth- and ninth-grade English classes in 25 midwestern schools. Although these examples are far from conclusive, common elements emerge that, taken together, <u>may</u> help to characterize effective instruction low-ability classes in secondary schools. (Gamoran 2, emphasis added)

The question identifies a location on the knowledge map so far unoccupied. We don't know what goes on in these classes. Plotting his approach to this space, the writer moves speculatively. Conceding the limits of the evidence available to him, he says his work "*may* help" to make this unknown area known. Compare the unmodalized, unqualified version of the same statement:

Common elements emerge that characterize effective instruction in low-ability classes in secondary schools.

While the unmodalized version may actually be more in keeping with the traditions of the schoolroom essay, where students are often advised to take a stand and be decisive, the modalized version is more typical of scholarly writing, where knowledge is laboriously constructed, and statements trail behind them traces of their sources and status. In scholarly writing, statements leave footprints.

To confirm that we do not in fact know enough about what goes on in classes where less successful students, grouped together, do enjoy success, this writer must first, as he says "[reinterpret]" standing ideas that "low-ability" grouping does not benefit students significantly, or, at least, has no regular effect on overall achievement. To identify the knowledge-deficit, he must show that the current state of knowledge is inadequate.

According to this view, observed differences among studies in the effects of grouping are due to chance; taken together, the studies indicate that no real effects on achievement exist.

Another interpretation seems equally plausible. The inconsistent findings may have resulted from uncontrolled differences in the way ability grouping was implemented in the various school systems under investigation. (Gamoran 3-4 emphasis added).

In moving to show that a published view from a respected source comes up short, and leaves the state of knowledge in this area unfinished, the writer does not simply deny the view: "This interpretation is wrong." He doesn't even say that "another interpretation is equally plausible," or "more plausible" — it only "seems equally plausible." And the reinterpretation is itself modalized: "inconsistent findings may have resulted from uncontrolled differences . . ." rather than "inconsistent findings resulted from uncontrolled differences. . . ."

These traces of reasoning from positions of limited knowledge are typical of scholarly expression. They signify the research community's persistent interest in the production of knowledge. On the one hand, they permit the individual re-searcher to move into unconfirmed territory — a lone explorer, estimating and reckoning — and, on the other hand, they signal respect for the community's cooperative work of corroborating and recognizing established positions.

So strong is this tradition of respect for properly established positions that even when the current researchers are evidently impatient with the dominance of accepted views, and when their own research defies those views, they still identify knowl-edge deficits through modalized statements. So, when two re-searchers report extensive evidence to overturn the standing idea that trade-union activities have a lot to do with Britain's post-war economic decline ("Many commentators on post-war Britain have suggested that the workforce and its unions must accept a large part of the responsibility for the country's con-tinuing economic ills" (65)), they nevertheless approach the standing view with signs of respect, expressed through modality. Here they treat the work of a distinguished and "widely cited" scholar:

PASSAGE 11    Olson's work demands to be taken seriously, yet it, too, seems to be flawed. Olson has attracted considerable sup-port from economists and economic historians because his methodology conforms to the tenets of individual ra-tional action theory inherent in neo-classical economics. However, this choice of approach can be criticised be-cause it encourages a misleadingly simplified view of real-ity. (67)

★ ★ ★

It may be right to conclude about Olson, therefore, that what he has produced is not an explanation, but merely an historical set of abstractions. His theory seems to pro-vide little more satisfaction than the offerings of far less sophisticated analysts.

At this point, it appears wise to turn from the current literature and re-examine the contemporary evidence. Many recent authorities have argued, as we have shown, that restrictionism was strongly evident on Britain's shopfloor after 1945, but not much of what has been written, it <u>seems</u> fair to conclude, is very persuasive. (Tiratsoo and Tomlinson 69, emphasis added)

The modalizing expressions of introductions situate the present writer in relation to others working nearby. Each of the modalizing expressions emphasized above says, in effect, *"from our position of limited knowledge, we think that. . . ."* As Greg Myers (1989) suggests in his study of "politeness" in scientific articles, these situating moves are intensely **social** — they represent relations among members of the research community, and between individual members and the larger collective.

**Knowledge** is both product of the community and index to the standing of individual members of the community. As is true of most social situations deeply cultivated with politeness expressions, power and the competition it inspires operate at these moments when one researcher identifies current knowledge as inadequate, or mistaken, and offers his or her own knowledge products as a replacement for current knowledge. In scholarly writing, politeness takes a particular form — signs of inferences from a limited position. These signs attach themselves to statements as reporting expressions (the statement issues from the position of other writers) or as modality (the statement issues from the position of the present writer). Only when a generalizing statement is widely accepted in a particular research community does it appear without reporting or modalizing expressions. Then it is "fact." (Even then, "facts" can be subject to revision or rejection by later generations of the research community.) Before generalizing statements are treated as "fact," their expression triggers complex politeness behaviours (and we can speculate that student writers unaware of this intricate etiquette could seem "rude" to academic readers). This form of politeness could be called **epistemic** — to do, that is, with **knowledge**.

Epistemic modality clusters around the researcher's step away from the reported statements which summarize the current state of knowledge in the field towards the knowledge deficit. It also clusters around the researcher's concluding statements, where the newly-constructed knowledge product is presented in its final form. So, after the hypotheses on teenage motherhood are screened through the available evidence, the writer estimates their status as knowledge.

PASSAGE 12  The findings of this study, although preliminary in nature, <u>suggest</u> that learning issues <u>may</u> represent a significant contributing factor to the high rate of births to teenage girls in the United States. That is, unidentified and untreated learning difficulties <u>may</u> be a factor that is common both to becoming pregnant and deciding to raise one's child, and to dropping out of school. Further, the findings <u>suggest</u> that substantial numbers of teenage pregnancies <u>may</u> not be "unplanned," but represent choices that conform to current peer values and pressures. If these observations are correct, school failure <u>may</u> not *result* from girls' pregnancies and early parenthood but <u>may</u> — like the pregnancy itself — bear a close relation to unidentified and untreated learning problems. (Rauch-Elnekave 101-02, italic emphasis in original, underlining added)

But conclusions, as we will see in Section 7.7 below, confirm rather than announce claims: they consolidate statements that have been arrived at earlier in the paper. So, in the long approach to the conclusion, modalized statements can show up as researchers arrive at interpretations of their data. These statements can also be associated with established knowledge — in a positive or negative way. Here, a writer offers an interpretation of evidence she has presented as to the conditions of labour after the abolition of slavery in Brazil, these conditions comprising an element of a three-part comparison including Louisiana and Cuba.

PASSAGE 13  It was this process that Peter Isenberg called "modernization without change" and that has generally been interpreted as implying a crushing continuity of dependence and poverty for former slaves. While this is in one sense quite accurate — indeed, rural northeasterners <u>may</u> have been even more malnourished after emancipation that before — an overemphasis on continuity <u>may</u> ob-

scure the importance of the access to land that many former slaves did achieve. . . .

Even though the physical work performed by labor
tenants <u>might</u> differ little from that performed by slaves,
the orbits of their lives now had a somewhat different
shape. While slaves had lived in a centralized set of quarters under direct supervision, *moradores* usually built their
huts "at scattered points on the estates." An even more
general dispersion of the population was <u>probably</u> prevented by the development of central mills, but the small-
scale dispersion within estates <u>could</u> be of crucial importance to the development of a life oriented toward family
and neighbors rather that employer. And, to the extent
that freedom of movement could be maintained, it provided some constraint on the exactions that could be imposed on rural dwellers.

Rebecca J. Scott 1994 Defining the boundaries of freedom in the
word of cane: Cuba, Brazil, and Louisiana after emancipation.
*American Historical Review* February 70-102, 96,

In the next example, the writer has just presented the results
of her interviews with Bangladeshi women on their decision to
work at home, using a combination of the women's own words
(direct speech) and summary of what they said (indirect speech).
Now she combines a mention of the text ("To summarize this
section") with direct-speech reports of "other studies" in the
context of modalized interpretation of the interview data ("it
appeared," "It seems clear"):

PASSAGE 14

To summarize this section, therefore, it <u>appeared</u> that for
the majority of the women interviewed, the chief advantage of homework was its compatibility with the different cultural dimensions of being a housewife within the
Bengali community — primarily looking after children
and keeping the house in order, but also servicing the
needs of male breadwinners, usually husbands, and
fulfilling the family's hospitality obligations. This finding
echoes those of other studies of homeworkers, which

have included women from a variety of majority and minority ethnic groups:

> Any explanation of why it is mainly women who do
> homework ... cannot ignore the family roles of these
> women.... All the women in our sample considered
> housework and child-care to be their responsibility
> and regarded help from their husbands as a generous
> concession. (Hope, Kennedy and de Winter, 1976:
> 98-9)
> The explanatory emphasis put on the care of young
> children obscures what is a life-long experience of
> women, namely that of servicing others on an un-
> waged basis. (Allen and Wolkowitz, 1987:79)

Naila Kabeer 1994 The structure of 'revealed' preference: Race
community and female labour supply in the London clothing
industry. *Development and Change* 25, 307-331, 315-316.

*Other markers of the status of knowledge.* Modal expressions are
perhaps the most obvious way of marking a statement as issuing
from a position of limited knowledge. But they are not the only
way. Just as modality is linked to the practice of reporting statements of others, it is also linked to a set of expressions which
some research (Chafe 1986) has shown to characterize the
speech of academics. So, while the opening generalization of
the passage below appears at first to defy the modalizing and reporting tendencies we have been observing ("During the
course of the twentieth century relationships between minorities and dominant societies have fundamentally altered in wartime. . . ."), on closer inspection we will see that it in fact conforms to traditions of marking statements for their status as
knowledge.

PASSAGE 15      During the course of the twentieth century relationships
between minorities and dominant societies have fundamentally altered in wartime, an assertion which applies to
all states. The position of minorities usually deteriorates,
particularly if they represent a group which has acted as
the traditional scapegoat for the dominant society, or if

they are identified with the state facing their land of settlement in war. In such a situation the minorities almost
invariably face persecution, varying from controls on
movement and expression to internment and even geno-
cide. The response of the dominant group varies according to the political traditions upon which it is grounded.
A liberal democracy will usually retain traces of tolera-
tions, while an autocratic state will exercise more arbitrary anti-minority policies (Panayi 1990b). Few exceptions exist to this state of affairs, although in some cases
opportunities may arise that allow a minority to make
some socio-economic progress. The experience of Afro-
Americans and American Indians in the first world war
provides an example (Dippie 1982, p. 194; Grossman
1989).

Mark Ellis and Panikos Panayi 1994 German minorities in World
War I: A comparative study of Britain and the U.S.A. *Ethnic and
Racial Studies* 17, 2, 238-259.

The writers seem to be aware of the risk they take in offering
a generalization that is neither **reported** nor **modalized**, for
they quickly move to characterize it and insist on its generality:
"During the course of twentieth century relationships between
minorities and dominant societies have fundamentally altered in
wartime, *an assertion* which applies to *all* states." Then, as they
develop this generality, they gradually and slightly reduce the
application of its parts: *all* gives way to *usually, almost invariably,
usually, [f]ew exceptions exist, some cases.* Each of these expressions
conditions the statement in which it occurs as in some way
**limited**. The writers do not commit themselves to saying that
this is universally true. That would be too much.

In effect, expressions like these **control** the extent of statements' application, reducing and monitoring their power to apply to all cases, leaving spaces around them to signify the limits
of knowledge. Given the scholarly genres' preoccupation with
the status and production of knowledge, we could expect expressions like these —

| usually   | in part   |
|-----------|-----------|
| most      | at least  |
| some      | partly    |
| many      | often     |
| generally | sometimes |
| roughly   | typically |

— to cooperate with reporting and modality to sketch the limits of knowledge. And notice the effect the insertion of appropriate limiting expressions can have in conditioning a broad statement for use in a research setting. Compare

> Family-wage campaigns supported both patriarchal and corporate interests.

to

> Typically
> Often
> Generally      family-wage campaigns supported both patriarchal and
> Most      corporate interests.
> Usually

And inspection of the passage on former slaves' access to land (p. 307) reveals just such a cooperation of reporting, a modality, and limiting expressions:

> "in one sense quite accurate"
> "many former slaves"
> "differ little"
> "somewhat different shape"
> "usually built"
> "some constraint"

All these expressions limit the scope of the statement. In that respect, they are pointers to the statements' status as knowledge, and to the writers' limited position: they are not in a position to say such-and-such is true for all cases.

## exercise

In the passage below, the writers begin to reinterpret evidence. Identify the modal and limiting expressions they use as they begin to evaluate available knowledge.

Taken together, these various accounts appear to constitute a formidable indictment, yet closer inspection once again exposes flaws. Some industrial correspondents did, of course, have good contacts in business and may have accurately reported what they were told. Nevertheless, it is not certain what employers' complaints really added up to: grumbles from the boardroom were, of course, nothing new. Moreover, some of the press accounts have a formulatory ring and may well have been shaped more by the pressure to grab the reader's attention than the desire to present accurate facts. (Tiratsoo and Tomlinson 69-70)

## exercise

Inspect essays you have recently written or are currently drafting. Do you find the modalizing and limiting expressions we have been examining in examples of published scholarship? If you find them missing, can you explain their absence? (That is, does your writing situation differ from that of professional scholars in ways that lead you away from such expressions of position and limitation? Or have you been unaware of the role these expressions play in making statements in the research genres?) If you find modalizing and limiting expressions missing from your academic writing, try introducing them at appropriate points, and observe the effect.

Linguists have described these limiting expressions as belonging to a larger family of wordings all of which index statements for their status as knowledge. If we see these expressions as part of a larger family of sayings, we can regard them as establishing writers' attitudes towards or opinion of the statement they are offering. And we find scholarly writers favouring not only attitudes about the limits of statements but also about their obviousness. So we have seen writers using words like *suggest*, or *indicate*. We see them saying

Certainly, *x*
It is evident that *x*
Surely *x*
Apparently *x*
Undoubtedly *x*

as well as possibly, may, might and so on. They can even combine apparent confidence with seeming reservation. Summarizing the research of "social investigator Ferdinand Zweig," these writers say

> He concentrated five main sectors (building and civil engineering, cotton, engineering, iron and steel, and printing) and found that restrictive practices of various kinds were <u>certainly</u> <u>sometimes</u> <u>evident</u>. (Tiratsoo and Tomlinson 70, emphasis added)

rather than

> . . . found restrictive practices of various kinds.

This complex trace of reasoning — the phenomenon is "evident" (to an observer/interpreter), but only "sometimes," but then "certainly" — indicates the status of this statement as knowledge.

To say that something is *evident* — or *apparent,* or *observable,* or *recognizable* — is to say that is so to **someone**. Remembering that scholarly writing makes big efforts to attach statements to their sources, we might confront wordings like these and ask, well, *who* finds something evident or apparent, or *who* observes it or recognizes it? At first, these wordings might seem vague, and at odds with other features we have been looking at.

But we can account for these typical wordings by noticing how they resemble some other forms we have seen. *Observable, evident, identifiable* are **agentless**: they take away the person who observes, identifies, or finds something evident. So they are like other agentless forms we have seen — for example

it is known that *x*

*x* is acknowledged as. . .

These expressions seem to **distribute** knowledge: it is not just the present speaker or one other person who sees this or knows it. Similarly, in the case of expressions like "evident" or "observable," the commentary on the status of knowledge includes not so much an estimate of its probability (as "possibly" or "may," for example, would provide), or not only a trace of its source (something someone reported) but a measure of the position from which x is known. As

it is known that *x*
*x* is acknowledged as . . .

suggest that more than one person knows this, so

evident
apparent
observable
identifiable

suggest that, from any reasonable position, people would see this.

These markers of obviousness can take the form of "evident," or "apparent," "recognized/recognizable," or "observed/observable," or the more pronounced forms of "surely," "certainly," "clearly," which insist that the statement should be accepted by reasonable readers. Most compelling, perhaps, of these forms is "of course." "Of course" signals that the statement is so evident that readers are only being reminded of what they already know.

It is now well-established, of course, that the majority of British employers looked to the apprenticeship system rather than formal education in the classroom as the appropriate training for the bulk of their employees.

Keith Burgess 1994 British employers and education policy, 1935–45: A decade of missed opportunities? Business History , 36, 3, 29–61, 32.

"Of course" signals that the writer takes his readers as already knowing that it is known that British employers favoured apprenticeship training. "Of course" describes that status of this knowledge as widely distributed in the community which forms the audience for this article.

In a way, "of course" is a politeness — it constructs readers as knowledgeable, as not needing to be told something they already know. But what if you <u>didn't</u> know that apprenticeship was the preferred form of training? Or, after reading most of the article, which describes the efforts of school administrators to design programmes to satisfy the training needs of British employers, you had not come to the same conclusion as the author, reported here with "of course"?

> In the post-1945 period, a survey of business histories shows that the selection and training of managers was still based largely on non-credentialist criteria, and that the public education system was seen to play a marginal or at best an indirect role in this process. This explains the [Federation of British Industries'] 1944 booklet on the qualities of character, loyalty and team spirit, regarded as so important in industry, and which were seen as the chief advantage enjoyed by those educated in the independent schools. What was absent, <u>of course</u>, was a recognition of the significance of accredited cognitive capabilities, grounded in a knowledge of the principles of production processes, which could not be acquired solely in a firm-specific organisational career based around internal labour markets. (Burgess 55, emphasis added)

In my reading of this article, I expected a class interpretation of employers' attitudes and training preferences: employers wanted lower-level employees trained only in the specific skills appropriate to specific firms and industries, and they wanted upper-level employees — managers and supervisors — conditioned to middle-class attitudes. So I was surprised by *of course*, and took it as a signal that this assumption or topic — the necessity of advanced technical training (engineering would be an example) to industrial prosperity — was **common ground** for the intended audience. I did not belong to that audience.

So, while markers of obviousness can create the impression of consensus, and signs of a community of agreement, they can also suddenly alienate a reader. On the one hand, you should be aware of the power of certain expressions to appear to distribute knowledge: you can use them in your own writing to signal to your readers that you know you are not delivering brand-new ideas, but, rather, ideas that are broadly entertained in the community. On the other hand, these expressions incur some risk that your reader may not find something as clear, evident, or matter-of-course as you suggest.

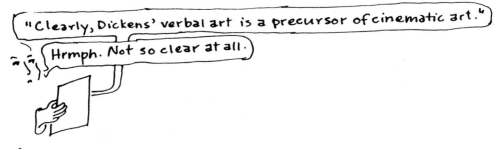

## 7.6.3   *Presupposing* vs. *asserting*

"Of course" draws boundaries around knowledge communities: people who belong to these communities know the things marked with "of course," and other signs of obviousness. In Chapter Two we looked at the social implications of telling people what they already know; now we can add the markers of obviousness to our strategies for dealing with these implications. In Chapter Two we also reflected on some of the difficulties students face in estimating the distribution of knowledge in different disciplines. Sometimes things should **not** be taken for granted, and should be attributed, defined, or explained, to show that the writer respects certain ideas as having been painstakingly constructed by the research community. But other times writers appear to satisfy their readers by representing things as understood, and by not explaining.

"Of course" and the other signs of a statement's obviousness are not the only ways of signalling that knowledge is shared. In the example which follows, the first sentences of an article, the writer makes several assumptions about readers' knowledge of the topic, through **definite expressions** — "the" or "this" phrases.

PASSAGE 18    Recent research in the history of nineteenth century psychiatry has explored the expanding powers of the medical profession and the proliferation of the asylum, that "magic machine" for curing insanity. This medicalization of madness has been portrayed as a "top-down" process...

Patricia E. Prestwich 1994 Family strategies and medical power: 'Voluntary' committal in a Parisian asylum, 1876-1914. *Journal of Social History* 27, 4, 799-818, 799 (emphasis added).

An alternative version of these sentences shows just how much the original takes for granted, and assumes as already known by the reader.

PASSAGE 19    Psychiatry was practised in the nineteenth century. In the nineteenth century, the powers of the medical profession expanded, and asylums proliferated. Madness was medicalized.

Whereas the original version **presupposes** this knowledge, the alternative version **asserts** it. Perhaps you can hear how the first version constructs the reader as *knowing*, and the second constructs the reader as *unknowing*, and needing to be told.

In any social situation, the choice between presupposing and asserting can be tricky, for, as we see, it conveys messages about the speaker's ideas of the addressee. It can also convey messages about the speaker: by always asserting, the speaker can seem naïve, or appear to have just learned something that is in fact well known. In the research genres, the choice between presupposing and asserting can be particularly tricky in that knowingness is so crucial to status and power. And it seems that students can sometimes make the mistake of starting too far back, explaining too much, and thereby offending their expert readers. John Swales (1990: 204-08) reports a case study of just this situation, where a PhD student's dissertation in the biological sciences explained too much, presupposed too little, and excited sarcastic and impatient comments from her readers. At the same time, however, readers can react negatively to a writer's offhand mention of a complicated concept, and can appreciate an explanatory account of it. (In the sample above, for example, what does it *mean*, exactly, for something to be *medicalized*? These days, lots of people are finding instances of "medicalization" here or there, but we may have been neglecting the concept itself, taking too much for granted.)

Presupposing expressions can take many forms (proper nouns are among these forms — to say simply "Chomsky" rather than "Noam Chomsky is a transformational linguist" presupposes that readers know who "Chomsky" is, and can identify him for themselves). We will not go into all these forms here. Nor can we come to any conclusions about what kinds of knowledge students should presuppose and what kinds they should assert, for, at this point, we don't know a lot about this aspect of the style of the research genres — or any other genres. What we do know, however, is that readers are sensitive to patterns of presupposition, and that these patterns signal information about the state of knowledge and its distribution.

## exercise

The first four of the following statements are opening sentences from articles in a variety of disciplines; the fifth occurs at the end of the first paragraph of an article. Some (but not all) presupposing expressions are underlined in each. To develop your awareness of the effect of these expressions, rewrite each passage to assert what the original presupposes. You may find yourself resorting to "there" expressions (e.g., "the three aspects of readability" becomes "there are three aspects of readability"); "there" expressions in English are specially designed for asserting. You may also notice that many of the underlined expressions are nominalizations— a stylistic feature we have become familiar with in our study of the research genres.

PASSAGE A

In recent years, <u>the school reform movement</u> has engendered widespread efforts to transform <u>the ways in which students' work and learning are assessed in schools</u> (emphasis added).

Linda Darlington-Hammond 1994 Performance-based assessment and educational equity. *Harvard Educational Review* 64, 1, 5-30.

PASSAGE B     Scholars have long noted, often with disapproval, <u>the tardiness of the introduction of printing to the Muslim world</u>, but <u>the consequences of that introduction on the production, reproduction, and transmission of knowledge in Muslim societies</u> are now only beginning to be understood.

Adeeb Khalid 1994 Printing, publishing, and reform in Tsarist Central Asia. *International Journal of Middle East Studies* 26, 187-200 (emphasis added).

PASSAGE C     <u>When Margaret Fuller's *Woman in the Nineteenth Century* first appeared in the winter of 1845</u>, few readers were prepared to accept her <u>uncompromising proposition that "inward and outward freedom for woman as for man shall be as a right, not yielded as a concessions"</u>.

Annette Kolodny 1994 Inventing a feminist discourse: Rhetoric and resistance in Margaret Fuller's *Woman in the Nineteenth Century*. *New Literary History* 25, 2, 355-382 (emphasis added).

PASSAGE D     During the 1980s and 1990s a number of factors emerged in various countries of western Europe to raise anew questions about <u>the meanings of national identity</u>. <u>The finally acknowledged presence of settled immigrant populations</u> (as opposed to transient-worker populations), <u>the arrival in western Europe of large numbers of asylum-seekers from southern and eastern Europe and from the Third World</u> and, most recently, debates in the countries of the European community about some of <u>the provisions of the Maastricht Treaty</u> have been among the most significant factors that have fuelled controversies about national identity.

Christopher T. Husbands 1994 Crises of national identity as the 'new moral panics': Political agenda-setting about definitions of nationhood. *New Community* 20, 2, 191-206 (emphasis added).

PASSAGE E     To put it bluntly, <u>the new cultural politics of difference</u> consists of creative responses to the precise circumstances of our present moment — especially those of marginalized First World agents who shun degraded self-representations, articulating instead <u>their</u> <u>sense of the flow of history</u> in light of <u>the contemporary terrors,</u> <u>anxieties and fears of highly commercialized North Atlantic capi-</u><u>talist cultures</u> (with <u>their escalating xenophobias against people of</u> <u>color, Jews, women, gays, lesbians and the elderly</u>). <u>The thawing,</u> <u>yet still rigid, Second World ex-communist cultures</u> (with increasing nationalist revolts against <u>the legacy of hegemonic party hench-</u><u>men</u>), and <u>the diverse cultures of the majority of inhabitants on the</u> <u>globe smothered by international communication cartels and re-</u><u>pressive postcolonial elites</u> (sometimes in the name of commu-nism, as in Ethiopia) or starved by austere World Bank and IMF policies that subordinate them to the North (as in free-market capi-talism in Chile) also locate vital areas of analysis in this new cul-tural terrain.

Cornel West 1990 The new cultural politics of difference. In *Out There: Mar-ginalization and Contemporary Cultures*, ed. Russell Ferguson, Martha Gever, Trinh T. Minh-ha, Cornel West. Cambridge, Mass.: MIT Press 19 (em-phasis added).

## 7.7   Conclusions

Looking at conclusions from a cognitive perspective — that is, examining the role they play in readers' understanding what you have written — it is best to think of them as **confirming** what has gone before. The conclusion is your last chance to make sure that connections between parts of the argument are secure in your reader's mind; it is your last chance to invoke the complex, high-level proposition that was your topic. The sam-ples provided below will show scholarly writers using their conclusions to confirm their arguments.

A cognitive perspective also predicts that conclusions which merely restate the introduction can be troubling for readers. Such conclusions can sound strange, for the reader who is ad-dressed at the end of an essay is not exactly the same reader who is addressed at the beginning. At the end, the reader is familiar with the details and course of the argument: he or she has been through it. To simply repeat the introduction suggests that the reader hasn't heard a word you said.

But, all along, we have tried to keep in mind that reading is not only a process of reasoning and understanding, not only a cognitive process. It is also a **social process**. Like any use of language, scholarly reading and writing maintain the values and practices of the communities that use the genres we have been studying. So, in conclusions, scholarly writers not only see to their readers' cognitive needs, but also advance their claims in ways that are in keeping with the representations of knowledge typical of the research genres.

In that the conclusion advances the writer's claim in its final form, we might expect that it will be seeded with modality and other signs of **limits**. So here, in the last paragraph of their article on plain language, researchers are still speculating and inferring:

PASSAGE 20   As in the case of consultation between health-care professionals and consumers, it is <u>possible</u> that legal concepts are difficult to understand because, even when explained in plain language, they are complex or because they are in conflict with folk theories of the law. The subjects in this study (and lay people in general), <u>may</u> have been relying on inaccurate prior knowledge of the law or on their own intuition about justice, which <u>frequently</u> does not reflect the legal reality. These results <u>suggest</u> that plain language drafting alone will take us only part way to the goal of making the law more broadly understood. It must be supported by other measures such as public legal education and individual counselling of persons faced with legal obligations.

Michael E. J. Masson and Mary Anne Waldron 1994
Comprehension of legal contracts by non-experts: Effectiveness of
plain language redrafting. *Applied Cognitive Psychology* 8, 67-85, 79.
(emphasis added)

We could say that, in the research genres, conclusions are not
conclusive. While scholarly articles begin with the identification
of a knowledge deficit, they can also **end** by gesturing towards
what is not known for sure. (It is yet to be established that "folk
theories" are in fact interfering with people's understanding of
the language of legal contracts.) So, in the next example, where
few modals appear, the work modals might have done is performed by an explicit remark on **what we don't know** —
even after reading this article on the rhetorical techniques of A.
M. Malivha, leader of a South African political organization, the
Zoutspanberg Balemi Association (ZBA):

PASSAGE 21      Through his association of writing with speech, Malivha
immersed *Inkululeko* in the pre-existing forms of communication, and thus ensured the paper's accessibility to its
audience. As *Inkululeko* was read some fifty years ago, we
are at a disadvantage in getting a clearer picture of how
readers interacted with the newspaper. Questions about
how the paper was distributed, read and discussed among
the people would undoubtedly enrich our understanding
of the role played by *Inkululeko* in mobilising for the
ZBA, but what is left of these today will certainly be general impressions and memories.

In spite of these limitations, it is hoped that this essay
has highlighted issues otherwise largely overlooked by existing social-historical studies seeking to understand questions of popular responses to political mobilisation in the
countryside. The processes of forced removal, disposses-
sion, and community destruction undoubtedly generated
political consciousness which varied with region and
time. But a focus on these processes alone, this essay argued, ignores a host of other factors which can also help
explain questions of popular responses to political mobilisation in the countryside. Using the ZBA as a case study,
the essay focused on *how* ideas about these process were

communicated to the Zoutpansberg people by looking at the language and style of mobilisation, and the methods as well as the media of communication the organisation used. We believe that a more detailed and thorough research in this direction will enrich our understanding of how some organisations are able to attract popular following in the countryside.

Thiathu J. Nemutanzhela 1993 Cultural forms and literacy as resources for political mobilisation: A. M. Malivha and the Zoutspansberg Balemi Association, 1939-1944 *African Studies* 52, 1, 89-102, 100-01.

As well as confirming the main point of the essay, and the knowledge deficit it addressed, this conclusion directly refers to its own "limitations" by mentioning them, and indirectly refers to limitations by saying what still has to be done.

After getting under way by identifying a knowledge deficit, and then labouring to correct that deficit, many scholarly articles end by sketching a **new** knowledge deficit, gesturing to the future, and the on-going process of constructing knowledge. So we find

> The findings of this study, although preliminary in nature, suggest. . . . (Rauch-Elnekave 101, emphasis added)

And, accompanying such a gesture towards the future, we can find **promise** for greater knowledge still, as above in the conclusion to the article about the ZBA, or here:

PASSAGE 22

. . . it might be of some interest to explicate the relation between the cognition of gender subtypes and the cognition of situations in which they are assumed to function. Two-mode clustering seems to be particularly well suited to the study of such topics. Alternatively, one might be interested in introducing a third mode, for instance the sample of subjects providing type-by-feature co-occurrence data, and investigating the construal of interactions between classes of types and classes of situations specific to classes of individuals. Research into these diverse and fascinating issues <u>promises</u> to yield important new insights into the intricate nature of social stereotypes.

Thomas Eckes 1994 Features of men, features of women: Assessing stereotypic beliefs about gender subtypes. *British Journal of Social Psychology* 33, 107-123, 121 (emphasis added).

## exercise

Inspect essays you have recently written or are currently drafting. Do your conclusions sketch the limits of your findings (through modality or limiting expressions)? Do they gesture towards other opportunities for study? If not, try rewriting them to adopt these attitudes of limited knowledge and unfolding possibility for knowledge-making. (For example: "This essay has examined only one episode in the current controversy over the judicial treatment of young offenders. While it suggests that expressed attitudes towards young offenders may be linked to broader political trends, investigation of other episodes may reveal further complexities. Moreover, further study may reveal connections between public attitudes towards young offenders and public attitudes towards other policy issues, such as welfare reform.")

As the last example, from the article on gender subtypes, shows, conclusions also tend to return the reader to the highest level of abstraction: there, "the intricate nature of social stereotypes." Cognitively, this move makes sense because it puts the finishing touches on the product on the reader's mental desktop. But it makes sense socially too, for these abstractions are often the high-status terms that gave the introduction rhetorical force — the Big Issues which warrant claims on readers' attention and identify the writer as someone in touch with established concerns.

Accordingly, it is mainly in conclusions that we see the rather rare appearance of what we could call "moral" statements. The research genres are relatively free of statements of moral obligation like these:

the government <u>ought</u> to put a stop to this

people <u>should</u> learn to respect the environment

we <u>must</u> preserve our neighbourhoods

But there are occasions when obligation is expressed. Sometimes these obligations are about research itself. Something <u>needs</u> to be examined more closely; something <u>should</u> be explained in relation to something else. We can see an example of such an expression of obligation here, in the last sentence of the article on the experience of German minorities in Britain and the U.S. in World War I (notice as well the major abstractions — "xenophobia," "control," "intolerance" — that are invoked by this ending):

PASSAGE 23    In each case, the experience of the German minority
<u>needs</u> to be placed within traditions of xenophobia in the
two countries, but, more especially, the war atmosphere
which led to increasing control of all citizens towards and
a growth of more general intolerance towards all perceived outgroups. (Ellis and Panayi 255-56, emphasis
added)

Sometimes the expression of obligation extends to the application of the research, as in an example we looked at above. Plain language redrafting is not enough to make legal documents understandable:

PASSAGE 24    It <u>must</u> be supported by other measures such as public legal education and individual counselling of persons faced
with legal obligations (Masson and Waldron 79, emphasis
added)

And, sometimes, researchers can conclude with statements that resemble the calls to specific action or attitude we find in other genres, such as newspaper editorials or partisan political briefs. This is from a conclusion the writer has labelled "Policy implications":

PASSAGE 25    Human capital differences may be addressed by establishing programs to help women complete their educa-

tion. We should offer scholarships and financial aid for women at both the high school and college levels. We must also establish programs to allow women who were forced to drop out of school to return and complete their education. These educational programs must be supplemented by others that provide job training and retraining. Many women worked prior to leaving the waged labor force to bear and/or rear children. Their occupational skills often became outdated during their absence and must be brought up to date. Other women may never have developed relevant occupational skills because they grew up in an era or community where it was not expected that women would work for wages and will need to develop initial job skills. Programs of job training and retraining will be expensive without any possible source of funds other than the federal government.

My own analysis has revealed that young children in the home are a major barrier to married women's participation in the waged labor force. It is possible that this reflects a negative evaluation of mothers with young children working outside the home, but it could also reflect the absence of safe, affordable day care. We cannot or perhaps should not do anything about the former possibility, but we can certainly address the latter. We must establish federally funded and federally supervised day care centers. It would be especially desirable if these day care centers could combine custodial with educational functions to provide a "head start" where needed.

James A. Geschwender 1992 Ethgender, women's waged labor, and economic mobility. *Social Problems.* 39, 1, 1-16, 12, (emphasis added).

This conclusion seems to me unusually strongly stated. It goes further towards real-world action/application than most research genres would permit. But the preceding examples show that "moral" statements are not entirely missing from the scholarly genres, although they may occur in different degrees and with different focus in different disciplines. Moreover, we should keep in mind that high-status abstractions — ethnicity, class, gender, community, for example — which exert rhetorical force can also carry with them their own moral force as they expose circumstances of inequality or disturbing applications of power, or risks to valued ways of life.

---

## exercise

The passage below comes from the conclusion of the article on the educational effects of low-ability grouping. Identify the writer's techniques for sketching the limits of his findings. ("Mrs. Turner" and "Mrs. Grant" were two of the successful teachers of low-ability classes observed by the writer.)

Yet another limitation of this study, also a form of narrowness, is that it relied on higher-than-expected achievement as a sign of effectiveness without considering other sorts of outcomes. Critics of ability grouping, however, maintain that low-track assignment is stigmatizing, producing harmful social outcomes apart from effects on achievement (see, e.g., Schwartz 1981; Oakes 1985). Cases studied by Valli (1986) and by Camarena (1990) seemed to open the possibility of counteracting this problem. However, in this study, Mrs. Turner commented in the year-end interview that assigning students to a remedial class stigmatizes them and depresses their motivation, and she views this as reason to avoid assigning them to a separate class. In fact, both Mrs. Turner and Mrs. Grant told us that, although they see the ability-grouping question as complex and multisided, on balance they both prefer mixing low-track students with other students. Thus, our examples of teachers who succeeded with low tracks — at least with respect to instruction and achievement — would actually prefer to end that arrangement. Perhaps, then, these are simply examples of good teachers, who would be effective regardless of how students were assigned. In any case, given the likelihood that ability grouping will continue to be used, we need to know much more about how to use it well. (Gamoran 18-19)

# 8

# The politics of knowledge and the case of ethnography

Part of this chapter examines **ethnography** — a type of scholarly writing that develops from firsthand observation of a social group and its ways. Ethnography is an important member of the family of research genres. It also offers an opportunity for students to take an authentic research position. So this chapter assigns an ethnographic project, along with practice in two genres that often accompany research activities: the **proposal** and the **oral presentation**.

This chapter also reviews criticisms of scholarly expression, bringing together issues which have come up throughout our discussion of the research genres. It is not accidental that ethnography and criticism of research discourse appear together in this chapter. Ethnography has been a focus of scholarly innovations that seek to correct some of the conditions under which research makes knowledge. Yet, historically, it has also been one of the most powerful genres in producing just the kind of distortions in our knowledge of the world that leave scholarly practices open to serious political criticism.

We will begin by reviewing some of the more general concerns about scholarly expression, sketching a political context for our approach to ethnography.

## 8.1  Difficulty and "objectivity"

We have already considered some broad complaints about scholarly writing: it is too difficult, unnecessarily complicated and obscure, inaccessible to outsiders. (Or, to put it another way, its difficulty makes outsiders of too many people.) Often these complaints come from people who are not members of a research community.

We replied to these complaints with genre theory. The style of scholarly writing is suited to research situations. It maintains and represents those situations, and, as long as they remain unchanged, scholarly style will probably not change much. When scholarly style drifts out of research situations, however, it may indeed be inappropriate — obscuring and exclusionary.

Harder to answer are complaints that come from inside research communities themselves. These complaints currently emerge from reasoning we can roughly label "post-modern" — although that term is itself open to lots of criticism as covering too much and saying too little. So we will customize the word for our present purposes, and take post-modern reasoning as those attitudes which regard knowledge as "socially constructed." Such reasoning challenges views of knowledge as **fact** existing independent of the people who make it, know it, say, use it, and exchange it. Post-modern analyses of knowledge suggest that the "objectivity" of the products of research is, at worst, a hoax, at best a useful illusion. Any statement, the argument goes, issues from some **position** in the social order, and is contingent on that position. (From a different position, some other statement entirely might be transmitted.)

Let us look at this claim at the micro level. Again and again, our investigations of scholarly style turned up **agentless** expressions. We found good explanations for this agentlessness (nominalizations of verbs and qualities tend to eliminate the agent of the action or the possessor of the quality; nominalization in turn contributes to the distinctive coherence patterns of scholarly writing). But, on the whole, agentlessness can tend to erase from the surface of the expression the people who act, and the people acted upon — all the experience of the event described. So the expression

voluntary employee turnover

directs our attention away from some active elements of the thing referred to: people quitting their jobs, people who get fed up, or disappointed, or look for more meaning in life, or hate bosses who impose on them or harass them. At the same time, the expression itself seems to observe this thing from a manager's point of view — or **position**: it is hard to picture a person walking away from her desk and heading out the door, and thinking of the event as "turnover."

So, even as the expression seems to promise an abstract "objectivity," creating an entity that can be measured and reasoned about, it is "subjective" — that is, it is an observation **from a position in the social order**. From this, two lines of reasoning develop. The first credits knowledge on the basis of that very subjectivity. The second tends to discredit knowledge. We will look first at the ideas which embrace subjectivity.

## 8.2    Embracing the subject

Although many might disagree with what I am about to propose, I will risk it anyway: it is feminist reasoning, at the end of the twentieth century, which has most sincerely invited the subject — the thinking, feeling being, experienced in the complexities of daily life — back into scholarly writing. (Or at least drafted such an invitation. It is not entirely clear whether the invitation has actually been received and accepted.) Feminist reasoning has criticized research practices for being carried out from a masculinist **position** or point of view, and then representing that position as universal. So feminist research would be inclined to dismantle the form of knowledge constructed by traditional research practices, and expose that knowledge as not only not "objective" but also as serving the interests of those who work at it. But some tracks of feminist research would also do more than expose the subjectivity of established regimes of knowledge. They would acknowledge the impossibility of the independent "fact" (and possibly even deny its desirability), and require that the researcher **identify** himself or herself. Fleshed out beyond the "discursive I" we met in Chapter Six, the "subjective" researcher would expose the relevant social and political — **personal** — elements of his or her experience of the world. These elements would constitute the full **subject position** from which the researcher speaks. The "knowledge" which the researcher then offers would be contingent on that position — not absolute or universal, but relative to that position.

It is hard to say how far this project for remodelling scholarly writing has advanced. Publications in disciplines which deal with gender-related topics are still perhaps the most likely to invite the fleshed-out subject to the page (and even then, in the presence of gender issues, as we have seen from the many excerpts from articles on gender-related topics in previous chapters, the traditional scholarly voice can still prevail). But, even amongst the articles which we have consulted for samples of standard scholarly expression, and which are not about gender issues, we can also find the writer stepping out from traditional styles and saying who she is, and what happened to her, personally, to make her think the way she does now.

PASSAGE I    In the forty years that I have been doing fieldwork in Latin America and the United States, my own awareness of how the events I recorded are related to the world around them has expanded along with (and sometimes belatedly to) that of my informants. This follows trends in the field as the unit of investigation has progressed from one of bounded cultures where the task was to recapture a traditional past to a multilayered, historically situated inquiry where the authoritative stance of a privileged observer was no longer condoned. In tracing my own enthnographic journey, I shall try to capture some of those experiences in which I was forced to encounter the world dimensions of everyday struggles for survival. (13)

★★★

I found interpretation of these events [homocides in a village in the Mayan area of Chiapas, Mexico] difficult,
given the dominant paradigm of structural functionalism
in the field of anthropology. (14)

★★★

When I completed the monograph on the Maya, I felt
the need to escape the involuted conflicts of Mayan
semisubsistence farmers and work in a society where the
hostility was turned outward against class enemies. I visited the mining communities of Bolivia in the summer
of 1967, just three weeks after the massacre of San Juan in
Siglo-XXCatavi. (17)

★★★

I borrowed some books from my informants and acquired a library of publications by current Latin American theorists to cope with the confusion of ideological
currents and social movements that I found in the mining community.

★★★

Clearly, all of this turmoil [coup, debt crisis] exceeded
the anthropological models available for analysis of field
data. I tried to keep the life of the community at the center of my thinking about what was coming in, allowing it
to be filtered through the people's sense of what was hap-
pening. The life narratives that I undertook with a few of
my informants provided the ballast that kept me from
sliding into metatheories concerning the consciousness
of workers. (19)

June Nash 1994 Global integration and subsistence insecurity.
*American Anthropologist* 96, 1, 7-30.

This article is not about gender issues, yet perhaps its style has
been influenced by the feminist reasoning which suggests that
researchers identify themselves.

# exercise

Two excerpts from the beginning of introductory sections of scholarly articles follow. Examine them to determine how each writer steps beyond the traditional role of the "discursive I." (The second excerpt comes from a co-authored article innovatively structured as a dialogue.)

PASSAGE A    About 2 years ago, I conversed with an American businessman in Mexico about how difficult replacement parts were to come by in that country. Over the next several months, he formed an alliance with Mexican and American partners and investors and formed a company, one with a more specific business goal, namely, to provide rebuilt engine parts from the U.S. to commercial transportation fleets in Mexico.

During meetings over the following year, the American and Mexican partners saw me in action, doing what linguistic anthropologists naturally do — mediating worlds — sometimes in English, sometimes in rusty Spanish, sometimes in both. We mutually decided that I would spend the summer in Mexico City to help start up the company. I dealt with Mexican and American partners, government offices, lawyers, and customers. I worked in the cracks between two different "cultures," cracks described in recent books on Mexican-American relations, books whose titles foreshadow the examples to come: *Distant Neighbors* (Riding, 1985) and *Limits to Friendship* (Pastor & Castaneda, 1988).

Kismet turned me into something I had never been before — an "intercultural communicator." The rest of this article is dedicated to figuring out what, in light of that experience, the phrase might mean.

## INTERCULTURAL COMMUNICATION

After my baptism by fire, I returned to the university in the autumn and approached the library with a naive question in mind: "What is the field of intercultural communication all about?" The question was naive because the literature is huge, diverse, without agreement on any particular unifying focus (see Hinnenkamp, 1990, for a related concern with the fundamentals of the field).

Michael Agar 1994 The intercultural frame. *International Journal of Intercultural Relations* 18, 2, 221-237, 221-222.

## I. INTRODUCTION: MULTIPLE OPENINGS WITH(IN) A DIALOGUE

What, then, are the limitations of our practice? How is our practice complicit with certain established societal structures?
— Ming-Yeung Lu

MING-YUEN S. MA: This quote brings up many of the questions that keep coming up in my mind as I work on this project, and I think that they point out the uncertainties in my motives: who am I, a first generation Chinese gay man, who was born but did not grow up in the United States, whose higher education was enabled by my privileged, upper-middle-class background, to write about Asian lesbian and gay writers? What is my placement in the text? What does it mean for us to be writing about works by persons of Asian and Pacific Islander descent in a language that is not our own — though most of us communicate by it?

ALICE Y. HOM: As a second-generation Chinese American, raised in a working-class immigrant family but educated in an Ivy League college, I think there are some complexities to the language issue. Many second-, third-, and fourth-generation Asian Americans do not feel their native language is an Asian language. When talking about Asian Pacific Islander lesbian and gay writing, we have to address the definition of "Asian Pacific Islander." In this case we are speaking of Asian and Pacific Islander immigrants and those born in the United States. The diaspora is limited to the United States although some of the Asian Pacific Islander lesbian writings are coming from Canada. For the most part, we will concentrate in this United States-centred context because most of our research and experiences are from here.

Alice Y. Hom and Ming-Yuen S. Ma 1993 Premature gestures: a speculative dialogue on Asian Pacific lesbian and gay writing. *Journal of Homosexuality* 26, 2/3, 21-31, 22.

Perhaps in your career as a scholarly writer, you have wanted to say who you are. Perhaps the roles available to you as a scholarly writer — and the topics that accompany those roles — have not been quite the right ones. Maybe you quit your job one day, in frustration or in hopefulness, and you have something to say about "voluntary employee turnover." Maybe you know something about what makes a woman decide to do piecework at home, and you have something to say about "labour supply decision-making." But the arrangements of the scholarly genres don't seem to give you space to speak, or permission to identify yourself. Perhaps the changes suggested or inspired by feminist reasoning would allow you to speak up, from a position closer to home.

From the ground laid out by feminist reasoning, we might also see the coherence structures of the scholarly genres as hospitable to some kinds of knowledge and inhospitable to others. In earlier chapters we noted that other writing and reading situations don't call for the same laborious descents from high-level generalities to specifics, or the persistent restatements of topical abstractions to hold the parts of the text together. (Those genres which are least hierarchically ordered, flattest and most list-like, may be the ones to which readers bring their own "topic" — from their own immediate experience of life.) There may be some important kinds of knowledge that can't be captured in the controlling claims of introductions and conclusions where high-level abstractions concentrate details. Those controlling abstractions may distort some details, or eliminate others that won't fit, or that tend to wander off and suggest other notions.

Moreover, the coherence structures of the scholarly genres exert strict authority over readers' work, controlling their response to every passage of text, managing readers' mental desktops with a firm hand. Some writers may not want this authority. It may seem to misrepresent not only their own character and view but also the character of the knowledge they want to present. Sometimes questions remain open, even after careful inquiry; sometimes answers defy one another.

If the research genres were to speak in their own defence, they might say that these criticisms are in some way satisfied by features we have identified as typical of scholarly expression. They would point to the system of reported statements with their repertoire of reporting verbs that get scholarly discussion under way by summoning a community of (often competing) voices. They would point to the system of modality which renders claims as issuing from the writer's limited knowledge. Supporters of the conventions of the research genres might argue that the "discursive I" is more tangible and active than people think. And they would say that all these features — reporting, modality, "discursive I" — constitute **position**, and subjectivity.

To adjudicate between arguments which say that scholarly writing conceals subjectivity and those which say it adequately represents the subject, we may have to look to the second line of reasoning which questions the political result of research practice and its expression in writing.

## 8.3   Knowledge and power

It may be commonplace to say that knowledge gives us power. The more we know about the world around us, the better we are able to manage it, or control it, or at least ward off some of its more harmful effects on us.

Suspecting that there is more to knowledge than this simple benefit, many thinkers in the last part of the twentieth century have inspected the relations between knowledge and power. Findings in this area may not be welcome news to everyone, and they are quite complex. To establish their relations to academic writing, we will start with a familiar instance.

Say you feel sick and visit your doctor. You tell her how you feel; she takes your blood pressure, looks down your throat, listens to your heart, maybe sends you for x-ray, or other imaging, depending on the nature of your complaint. Consulting her expert knowledge of the human body and its frailties, she tells you what is wrong with you, and what to do about it. You must subject yourself to a regime of medication; you must alter your diet, temporarily or permanently; you must stay in bed, or get up and move around, depending on complaint. You must come back next week to be checked. You both hope you will get better soon.

You have been subjected to the modern knowledge of human health — products of the investigative practices of many researchers, those products reported in many publications. If you get better, we could say that knowledge has given you power (at least for a while) over the hazards to which human flesh is prone. But reflect for a minute on that visit to the doctor's office. If you look at it from a social point of view, as an instance of typical interaction (and a number of researchers have in fact inquired into patients' visits to their doctors as a **genre**), you may sense that power resided with the doctor. With her expert knowledge, she read the signess of illness — deviations from the norms of health — interpreting them as you could not, and, from the interpretation, directed your behaviour, achieving (depending on your compliance) even some physical control over your body. From a social point of view, knowledge conferred **power** on the doctor — not the patient. The doctor enjoyed some advantage over the patient, and patients' often submissive behaviour in doctors' office may signify recognition of this power differential.

Now let's take an example closer to the site where knowledge is actually produced. The previous chapter excerpted passages from a psychologist's article on teenage motherhood. We could say that the researcher **constructed knowledge** of young women who become pregnant and drop out of school. She made this knowledge by interviewing a group of young women who fit this description, by reviewing their scores on the California Achievement Tests, by measuring their babies' development by administering the Mental Scale of the Bayley Scales of Infant Development, and by measuring their self-esteem with the Piers-Harris Children's Self-Concept Scale. (You could say that these tests are like the x-ray machine or other imaging device that produces knowledge of conditions otherwise detectable only by intuition, or perhaps entirely undetectable.) The psychologist found that a significantly high number of these young women had "untreated learning disabilities." (If the young women, in the meantime, found out anything about the psychologist, these findings have gone unreported, or, at least, unpublished.) From this new knowledge about teenage mothers, we might expect some activity to follow. If this knowledge gets institutionalized, we might find teenage mothers routinely checked for learning disabilities — and subjected to a regime of treatment. Without the tests and the new knowledge about teenage mothers, people like the subjects of this study might be left alone, to continue their lives without this intervention.

Moreover, while the researcher identifies teenage motherhood as a recognized "social problem," the interviews revealed that the young women did not see it this way. Nor did their families, on the whole. Yet once the research community identifies the life condition of this population as a "problem" and develops more detailed, expert knowledge of the problem (it is associated with learning disability, also a "problem"), we can imagine that programmes and policies will develop to capture this group and its potential members in more detailed, expert systems of testing, surveillance and treatment — implementing more exhaustive systems of control.

Knowledge has been produced from the subject position — or point of view — of the researcher. The young women are the **object** of knowledge, and as such become susceptible to the exercise of **power**. Perhaps they will resist, and go their own way. What they won't be able to do is construct publishable counter-knowledge of the research community which studies them.

## 8.4   Qualitative research

Moved by intellectual currents like those which have carried feminist thought and the analysis of power and knowledge, other critics of scholarly practice have suggested that research with a strictly **quantitative** emphasis produces distorted versions of people's experience of the world. Once phenomena — events and attitudes, and the people who are involved in those events or harbour those attitudes — are translated into **numbers**, and those numbers are subjected to routines of statistical interpretation, they get separated from the meaningful complexities of real-life contexts. So a study of, for example, "learning outcomes" in a hundred classrooms might identify three relevant conditions — the socioeconomic identity of the learners (as measured by a standard scale), their learning styles (as measured by a standard taxonomy), and their performance in a subject area (as measured by a standardized, norm-referenced test). The results could lead to changes in curriculum or teaching strategies.

Critics of this kind of research argue that such quantifications erase the classroom moment, the experience of students and teachers, the complex interactions amongst them. Research quantifications produce a limited or distorted version of the world, and their applications can be unrealistic. In place of quantitative research they propose **qualitative** research.

Qualitative research can take various forms. One overall way to look at it is to say that it distinguishes itself from quantitative research by replacing the **many** instances (open to statistical interpretation) with **one** instance or a few instances. The one instance is examined in detail. The long-distance panoramas of quantitative research are replaced by close-up views. So, in the qualitative version of the "learning-outcomes" study, researchers would locate themselves in one classroom, and watch — for days, months, even years. They would record what they saw, taking notes, using video or audio tapes; they would collect documents and artefacts (the teacher's lesson plans, tests, students' work, and so on); they would talk to the teacher and the students. Unlike quantitative researchers who arrange measurable situations (controlled instruction, perhaps; tests administered solely for the purpose of the study), qualitative researchers try to leave things as they are. The only change is the presence of the researchers themselves.

Back at their desks, the researchers interpret the material they have gathered. Surveying their data, they look for patterns and regularities, and, consulting the theoretical tools available to them, they develop explanations for what they have observed.

Both quantitative and qualitative techniques seek generalizations, but they establish the authority of their generalizations by different means. While quantitative studies respresent their validity by **numerousness** and recognized means of manipulating numerous instances to coax out statistically significant results, qualitative studies have only the **one instance** (as in a "case study") or the **one group** (such as a group of young women who read teen romance fiction). So, while much has been made of the "objective" style of quantitative research, and the rhetorical force of that style, qualitative research may actually be even more dependent on **style** of reporting to persuade readers to accept generalizations developed from limited instances. More-over, as qualitative study generates an abundance of detail, the means of controlling these data, and transforming them into **text** readers can understand, are perhaps more demanding for writers than the conventions used for producing text to report quantitative research.

Qualitative techniques show up in various disciplines, and, while many scholarly journals are exclusively quantitative in the submissions they publish, and some tend towards qualitative research, many others publish both quantitative and qualitative work. You will also find individual pieces that are themselves a mix of quantitative and qualitative techniques. Given this variety in form and occurrence, it would be rash to list rules for reporting qualitative research. But we can observe some regularities, especially if we focus on the genre of **ethnography**. This focus also leads us to a research genre particularly hospitable to student writers — a genre which offers them a research **position** from which they can conduct and report original inquiry.

## 8.5 Ethnography

In the last ten or fifteen years, ethnographic research has illuminated many otherwise obscured situations. For example, Shirley Brice Heath's *Ways with Words: Language, life, and work in communities and classrooms* (1983) was a landmark contribution that changed views of learning and language among researchers in several fields — education, sociolinguistics, rhetoric and composition. Heath brought about such a change through her method of making knowledge about the lives of the people in two communitites in the Piedmont Carolinas. She spent ten years associating with families in the two communities, participating in their activities, and observing and recording their ways of using oral and written language,. The products of her techniques — those of a **participant-observer** — revised attitudes about the success of Afroamerican children and Euroamerican children in public schools, showing that Afroamerican children's relatively less successful performance could be attributed not to deficits in their home environments but to differences in ways of valuing and using language. (Her study tends to credit the linguistic habitat of the Afroamerican community as richer and more complex than that of the Euroamerican community.) Heath's **qualitative** findings corrected knowledge constructed by **quantitative** research: large-scale testing and statistical measurement of the school performance and socioeconomic profile of large populations. Whereas quantitative research instruments maintained the researchers' **distance** from the object of inquiry, qualitative, ethnographic instruments brought the researcher into close contact with the people and situations she was studying.

# 8.5.1   *Post-colonial views of ethnography*

While major ethnographies like Heath's, or Bruno Latour and Steve Woolgar's *Laboratory Life: The Construction of Scientific Fact* (1979), which reports two years of observation of the behaviours, routines and beliefs of workers in a neuroendocrinological lab, appear to initiate a new era in research, ethnography is in fact not new but very old. And, while ethnography appears to correct many distortions in research practice, in its history are many episodes which, nowadays, look politically suspect.

We can trace ethnography to, first, the eras of "discovery," when Europeans set out to explore areas of the world unknown to them, and, second, to the periods of imperial expansion and colonization which followed. When navigators and explorers encountered people in distant places, they wrote down what they saw. So, Jacques Cartier, exploring what was to become known as the Gulf of St. Lawrence, came across an indigenous community, and wrote down what he saw.

PASSAGE 2

While making our way along the shore, we caught sight of the Indians on the side of a lagoon and low beach, who were making many fires that smoked. We rowed over to the spot, and finding there was an entrance from the sea into the lagoon, we placed our long-boats on one side of the entrance. The savages came over in one of their canoes and brought us some strips of cooked seal, which they placed on bits of wood and then withdrew, making signs to us that they were making us a present of them. We sent two men on shore with hatchets, knives, beads and other wares, at which the Indians showed great pleasure. And at once they came over in a crowd in their canoes to the side where we were, bringing furs and whatever else they possessed, in order to obtain some of our wares. They numbered, both men, women and children, more than 300 persons. Some of their women, who did not come over, danced and sang, standing in the water up to their knees. The other women, who had come over to the side where we were, advanced freely towards us and rubbed our arms with their hands. Then they joined their hands together and raised them to heaven, exhibiting many signs of joy. And so much at ease did the savages feel in our presence, that at length we bartered with them, hand to hand, for everything they possessed, so that nothing was left to them but their naked bodies; for they offered us everything they owned, which was, all told, of little value. We perceived that they are people who would be easy to convert, who go from place to place maintaining themselves and catching fish in the fishing-season for food. . . . I am more than ever of the opinion that these people would be easy to convert to our holy faith.

from *The Voyages of Jacques Cartier, 1534* , trans. H. P. Biggar 1924. In *Literature in Canada, Vol. 1,* ed. Douglas Daymond and Leslie Monkman. Toronto, Gage, 3.

He took this report home, and it played a role in **constructing knowledge** of the faraway people — the "Other," the exotic, foreign, strange, non-European inhabitants of a distant place. (Perhaps you can see from just this short excerpt how Cartier's point of view, or subject position, determines the kind of knowledge he constructs about the people of the Gulf of St. Lawrence.)

As colonizers followed, and settled and dominated regions explorers had pointed out, they too wrote about the people who originally inhabited those regions. Indeed, some colonizers and colonial travellers made a specialty of describing local people, dispatching their reports of the "Other" to a home audience, and developing the writing traditions that became a basis for the anthropological genres. Like Cartier, they wrote from a European point of view — a position, increasingly, of dominance and economic interest. (So, for example, as colonizers in the Pacific Northwest needed land for settlement, natives of the area were described as having no sense of land title. This "fact" became part of the knowledge made about these people.)

While many people who produced reports about non-European communities were amateur observers, others adopted an increasingly professional or "scientific" stance. They published their reports in journals devoted to the study of faraway peoples, founded associations, and organized meetings. In other words, they developed a **research community**, and ways of writing — genres — which served and embodied the research routines which characterized their work. As we encounter ethnography now, we encounter the descendants of these genres which are traceable to the interests of imperial domination. So it is reasonable to ask, as many people have, whose interests are served by the ethnographic genres? How is the writer's position embodied in the style of ethnography, and what is this position? Is it still a position of dominance — to the advantage of the writer and the interests he or she represents, and to the disadvantage of the social group described?

Addressing such questions, we also need to take into account changes to ethnographers' typical itineraries, for the objects of investigation have tended, in recent times, to move closer to home. While the traditional anthropologist/ethnographer made a long trip to a remote place (the longer the trip and the more remote the location, the more valuable the knowledge), ethnographers in current practice often don't go very far. Sometimes they just go across town, or to a classroom around the corner. Do these foreshortened journeys change the political implications of ethnography?

In this chapter and previous ones we have pursued the idea that a genre's **style** — language itself — represents the routines and values of the situation the genre serves. So one way we can approach this question about the political implications of current ethnographic writing is to examine its style. How does the wording transform people and groups into research objects? Is the transformation to the advantage of the researcher? What does research practice — which values "uncommon sense" — **do** to the people it operates on? If knowledge is power, in the simple sense or the complicated sense, where does power accrue as a result of knowledge being constructed about a particular social group? Are generalities illuminating typifications or demeaning stereotypes? Here, for example, in an ethnographic account of a social group typified as RVers (Americans and Canadians who spend most if not all of their year living in their recreational vehicles), the "commonsense" term *potluck dinner* is transformed into the "uncommonsense" abstraction *ritual food-sharing* .

PASSAGE 5    Among RVers the most common food-sharing ritual is the potluck dinner. Weekly potluck dinners are a regular event at resort parks, at many Arizona state parks during the winter season and at RV parks of all sorts at Thanksgiving and Christmas. RVers who are away from their families during the holiday season may pool their funds to buy a turkey and share a holdiay meal. Some RVers travel every year to the same park where they meet friends to share Christmas or Thanksgiving dinner. Finally, any important celebration — such as a wedding — includes a potluck dinner. Newcomers join the community by participating in ritual food-sharing.

Dorothy Ayers Counts and David R. Counts 1992 "They're my family now": The creation of community among RVers. *Anthropologica* 34, 2, 153-182, 167-68.

The word the RVers themselves use — "potluck dinner" — is replaced by a term at a higher level of abstraction — "ritual food-sharing" — which is a word the RVers themselves would probably never use.

The transformation moves the description away from the social milieu of the RVers themselves — moves it to another social circle, where the wordings "community" and "ritual" are valued ways of speaking. Out of earshot of RVers, ethnographic style turns them into a distant tribe, remote as African nomads (to whom they are eventually compared). We could speculate that RVers will not read "'They're my family now': The creation of community among RVers," just as African nomads, or other foreign peoples who were the object of colonial accounts, did not read what Europeans wrote about them.

Here (and everywhere) genre instates the social order — an order which separates RVers from professional researchers, making RVers into the "Other," and objects of knowledge. In colonial times, this separation was mapped across power differentials: ethnographers were allied with the political and economic interests of European peoples. In post-colonial times, questions about knowledge and power persist, and challenge scholarly writers to account for the political dimensions of the research routines represented and maintained by the research genres.

## exercise

Following are three excerpts from recent ethnographic descriptions of social groups, products of qualitative research practices. Inspect each sample for its ways of transforming the people described into objects of knowledge: look for abstractions which belong to the research community rather than the group described (that is, "words these people would never use to describe themselves"), and for typifications which you would estimate that the described people would not apply to themselves. Consider how the interests of the researchers are represented in their ways of speaking. How are these people made into the "Other"?

PASSAGE A

(From an account of the experience of one of the author's students in an "undergraduate feminist theory class.")

In her opening entry E. L. reveals the first stage of Lacan's stages or "patterns" of psychoanalytic transference by identifying with the "teacher," suggesting, at this early stage, as Ragland-Sullivan notes, that "the emphasis is on likeness and the analyst [in this case the teacher] is perceived as a counterpart" (37). She assumes that her "ideas and interests," her desires, correspond to those of her teachers and that this correspondence gives her a kind of control or mastery over the process of writing.

E. L.'s reaction five days later to her own first exploratory efforts at producing feminist theory reveals the fragility of her own hard-won sense of identity, of control and mastery.

I think [the assignment to write an exploratory essay on the topic chosen for the term project] distracted me from my original idea. That is fine, I guess — but I don't like being confused. I like knowing what I am trying to say when I write. I don't think I knew what I was trying to say in that essay.

This was to become a persistent theme in E. L.'s diary. The harder she pressed me to reveal "what kind of paper I wanted," the more unwilling or unable I was to tell her what she wanted to hear. I say this without complacency because it was both frustrating and embarrassing to realize that perhaps I did not know myself what I wanted. In the psychoanalytic situation, as the ideal "subject supposed to know" is revealed as an illusion, an "imaginary projection," there is a parallel "disintegration of the analysand's supposition of knowing." Ragland-Sullivan describes this process in the analysand as a disintegration of the self. Because the unified *moi* (the ideal ego) gives the subject a sense of "self cohesion," "any unraveling of the strands that went into weaving that identity as a conviction of 'being' causes a debeing of being: a sense of fragmenting" (37).

Laurie Finke 1993 Knowledge as bait: feminism, voice, and the pedagogical unconscious. *College English* 55, 1, 7-27, 21.

PASSAGE B Jankowski's study is unique in that he studied gangs as organizations, addressing a void in the literature. His work is limited, however, because of his adoption of the rational choice model: Both the gangs he studied and their individual members made rational decisions based on self-interest. Organizational theorists have found rationality of decision making in even formal organizations to be "rare in nature" (Weick 1976; also cf. Zey 1992; March and Olsen 1976). There is a deep literature describing organizations as "myths" (Meyer and Rowan 1981), as being "loosely coupled"

(Weick 1976), or even comparing them to "garbage cans" of solutions waiting for the proper problem to solve (Cohen et al. 1972). Any of these theories might fruitfully be applied to a study of gangs, but Jankowski chose not to examine perspectives other than rational choice. One serious deficiency is his neglect of those theories that look at the relationship of the environment to organizational type.

For example, Jankowski's (1991) claim that gangs with loose organization fade away and only those with "tight structures" endure is inconsistent with contingency theory, one of the main strands of organizational thought. Lawrence and Lorsch (1969) point out that vertically structured organizations are better suited to stable environments, whereas more decentralized or loosely organized structures are more appropriate for dynamic environments. The main thesis of their classic work, *Organizations and Environments*, is that organizations do not perform well if their organizational structures do not fit the environment they face.

Overall, the environment where drug dealing takes place is as "dynamic" as anything in the organizational literature. The fear of police raids, customers who are erratically acting addicts, potentially violent competition from other dealers or gangs, surveillance by hostile neighbours, and uncertainty in maintaining supplies are everyday occurrences. The task of drug dealing is also far from routine. The fear of violence or arrest makes every sale risky and demands varying methods of getting supplies, bagging or cooking the cocaine, and safely delivering the goods to the house or corner salesman. Even the location where the product is sold might suddenly have to change.

John M. Hagedorn 1994 Neighborhoods, markets, and gang drug organizations. *Journal of Research in Crime and Delinquency* 31, 3, 264-294, 267.

PASSAGE C       . . . Masciarotte (1991:90) analyses *Oprah Winfrey* in terms of the feminist debate over women's voices and empowerment, claiming that 'talk shows afford women the political gesture of overcoming their alienation through talking about their particular experience as women in society.' These commentators see the genre as offering more opportunities than dangers for the audience, countering the undermining of the authentic self which critical theorists see as the effect of the mass media. The genre draws on the ways in which feminism has 'redefined the relationship between the public and the private,' transforming the political towards a reliance on the 'circulation of discursive practices [rather] than on formal political agendas' (Carpignano et al., 1990: 51-2). Masciarotte concurs: 'Oprah Winfrey is not a simulated self, and so a fetish for the endless lack of consumer desire, but a tool or a device of identity that organizes new antagonisms in the contemporary formations of democratic struggle' (Masciarotte, 1991:84).

Access and public participation genres are growing in number, spreading into prime-time as well as more marginal slots in the schedule. The operation of different interest groups who gain representation through these genres and the rules of engagement which regulate their interaction in a mass media public sphere have consequences for the public expression of women's experiences, for assumptions about rationality and for the gendering of social spaces (Benhabib, 1992) and social representation (Moscovici, 1984). Audience discussion programmes may be seen to act communicatively as a forum for the expression of multiple voices or subject positions, particularly because they confront members of powerful elites with the lived experience of ordinary people.

Sonia Livingstone 1994 Watching talk: gender and engagement in the viewing of audience discussion programmes *Media, Culture & Society* 16, 429-447, 432-33

## 8.5.2  *Constructing ethnographic topics*

The preceding sections have focussed on the social and political implications of ethnographers' project: where do they stand in relation to the people they study? How does the style of ethnography itself represent their position? This section and following ones also focus on the ethnographer's position, but in more practical, working terms: how does the ethnographer turn a classroom or an RV park or a gang's hangout into a research site? How do teen readers of romance fiction or prison inmates studying French or people watching *Oprah* become objects of scholarly interest?

One step in this transformation of everyday sites into research sites is a process we are already familiar with: a **prestige abstraction** enters the picture. So, the researchers who investigated the customs of RVers, invoke "community" and "social change."

PASSAGE 4

There is a concern that social change has resulted in the destruction of community in contemporary North America (Bender 1978:4). For instance, Bellah et al., argue that although North Americans value mobility and privacy, these values "rob us" of "opportunities to get to know each other at a reasonably intimate level in casual, unforced circumstances" (1985:135). North Americans' high regard for these values have, in other words, robbed them of a sense of belonging — of a sense of community. If this is true, we would expect RVers, who choose their lifestyle at least partially *for* its mobility, to be isolated, lonely people who have difficulty in establishing a network or a community to help them cope with crisis. Such is not the case. (Counts and Counts 154-55, emphasis in original)

An ethnographic study of the behaviours and routines of workers and clients in a credit union invokes "literacy," and people's functioning in "modern society":

PASSAGE 5

During the last decade there has been a good deal of public outcry over the problem of literacy skills. In particular, this discussion has come to focus on the literacy skills individuals must possess in order to function in modern society. This competence, known as *functional literacy* (cf. Pattison 1982), entails skilled interaction with such materials as apartment leases, job application, and product instructions. Many have argued that the unintelligibility of these written materials has contributed significantly to the absence of literacy.

Deborah Keller-Cohen 1987 Literate practices in a modern credit union. *Language in Society* 15, 7-24, 7.

The ethnographic study of readers of teen romance fiction summons "ideological struggles," "social control," "social identities," "gender, class, racial, ethnic, age, and sexual identities":

PASSAGE 6

> An important theme in this volume is the cultural role played by written texts in ongoing and ideological struggles for students' hearts and minds. School texts have often been a mode of social control through the "selective tradition" contained within their pages, which elevates the stories of powerful groups to the level of canon. However, students are not some tabula rasa upon which the text inscribes their social identities. Rather, students approach texts from the position of their previously acquired gender, class, ethnic, age, and sexual identities.
>
> Linda K. Christian-Smith 1991 Readers, texts, and contexts: Adolescent romance fiction in schools. In *The Politics of the Textbook*, ed. Michael W. Apple and Linka K. Christian-Smith. Routledge, New York, 191-212, 191

Like those we have observed in other introductions, these abstractions come with a reputation: they are recognized topics in the research community. Accordingly, they have been addressed before, and the current writers cite instances from other research publications. The investigators of RVers' ways report the statements of other commentators on community; the writer who researched the practices of a credit union attributes statements about literacy to other researchers. And even here, where the invoked abstraction — "racism" — is so compelling as to warrant an opening generality unsecured by citation, the authors soon turn to reported statements.

PASSAGE 7

> To combat racism it is necessary to understand its complex features and underlying themes. In Britain it has recently been argued that such understanding is lacking in many anti-racism strategies (see Gilroy 1990; Rattansi 1992).

Maykel Verkuyten, Wiebe de Jong and Kees Masson 1994
Similarities in anti-racist and racist discourse: Dutch local residents
talking about ethnic minorities. *New Community* 20, 2, 253-267, 253.

This example also shows ethnographers — like researchers using other techniques of inquiry — establishing a **knowledge deficit**: there is something we need to understand, and this understanding is "lacking." The rest of this first introductory paragraph goes on to weave together the dominant abstractions "racism" and "anti-racism," the statements of others, and persistent gestures towards the gap in our knowledge.

PASSAGE 8    Anti-racist understanding of racist thinking is not very sophisticated. Cohen (1992), for instance, typifies anti-racism as the disavowal of complexity for the sake of pursuing moral certainties. Anti-racism appears to be lacking in effectiveness because of its doctrinaire form and its lack of powerful arguments which go beyond a moral appeal to tolerance. What seems to be required is a more complex understanding of the nature of racism and critical reflection on the ideas and approaches used in anti-racist work. (Verkuyten, de Jong, and Masson 253)

Like other researchers, ethnographers sketch a map of existing knowledge, showing routes currently under construction, and desirable destinations not yet reached. In the sample above, the mapping of knowledge begins to turn several evenings of conversation among people living in Rotterdam into a research site, and a matter of scholarly interest.

Sometimes the statement of a knowledge deficit can be as brief and decisive as the traditional anthropologist saying, "No one has written about this faraway island before" (in which case the "knowledge map" would be nearly literal). After explaining that her work "falls into the tradition of narrative inquiry," the writer who investigates the learning of prison inmates studying French points to the as-yet unvisited spot she will journey to:

PASSAGE 9    Although not labeled as such, narrative inquiry probably accounted for *Life in Classrooms* (Jackson 1968). This portrait of schools serves as a benchmark in educational research. Ethnographic studies have also examined life in jail (Spradley 1979, 1980). No studies, however, have examined the interactions of these two institutions — school and prisons — and that is the intent of this research.

Ann Masters Salomone 1994 French behind bars: A qualitative and quantitative examination of college French training in prison. *The Modern Language Journal* 78, 1, 76-84,77.

Student writers could feel wary about making such a claim about the state of knowledge — "*no* studies. . . ." But they can replicate the sound of such a claim by pointing to the limits of *some* other research. So, for example, in establishing a knowledge deficit that a study of undergraduates' in-class note-taking will fill, a student writer might offer a summary of Heath's *Ways with Words* (1983), invoking abstractions like "literacy," and then show a route not taken by Heath.

PASSAGE 10

While Heath's account of each community's use of written aids to memory provides some basis for speculating on differences between men and women in this literate practice, she neither collected nor analyzed her data with a view to illuminating gender distinctions. This study explores a comparable literate practice — in-class note-taking — with the specific intention of discovering whether some of the gender differences we glimpse in Heath's work show up in other settings.

Equally, once the prestige abstraction is established, the student writer may be able to secure it by reporting statements of as few as one or two other writers. While the authors of theses and honours essays will need a much denser network of published voices to invoke the community of knowledge-producers, the writer of an assignment such as the one to which these sections are leading can take a scholarly position by reporting the statements of one or two others.

# 8.5.3　Representing ethnographic method and background

Ethnographers can spend weeks or months or even years amongst the people they are observing. In the reports of their research, they represent these periods of their lives in terms which focus on the experience as a research activity. So, under the heading "Research Methods and Sources of Data," the investigator of "Neighbourhoods, markets, and gang drug organization" identifies himself as a researcher, outlines the research relationship between himself and his objects of study, and defines part of that research population in terms he takes to be relevant to the current topic.

PASSAGE II

The interpretations presented here draw on observations and extensive field work over a number of years, specifically on data from studies in 1987 and in 1992. During the early 1980s, the author directed the first gang diversion program in the city and became acquainted with many leaders and other founders of Milwaukee's gangs. He has maintained a privileged relationship with many of them during subsequent years. The confidential interviews in this most recent study were conducted in late 1992 and early 1993. As in the original study, the research follows a collaborative model (cf. Moore 1978), in which gang members cooperate with academic staff to focus the research design, construct interview schedules, conduct interviews with their homeboys, and interpret findings.

As part of our current study, we conducted 3-hour interviews with 101 founding members of 18 gangs: 90 were male and 11 female; 60% were African American, 37% Latino, and 3% White. Their median age was 26 years, with three quarters between 23 and 30 years old.

John M. Hagedorn 1994 Neighborhoods, markets, and drug organizations. *Journal of Research in Crime and Delinquency* 31, 3, 264-294, 269.

Reading between the lines, we might catch sight of enduring and complicated relationships — and the routes of personal and professional life that led this researcher into the midst of gangs and drug dealing. But, on the surface, these matters are reduced, deleted, or transformed into a subject position constituted from research practice. (Even the "discursive I" is transformed into "the author"/ "he.") **Agentless** expressions —

| | | |
|---|---|---|
| *I observed* | — | "observation" |
| *I interpreted* | — | "interpretation" |
| *I worked in the field* | — | "extensive field work" |
| *I conducted interviews* | — | "interviews . . . were conducted" |

— shift the one making knowledge to the margins, not concealed but tacitly assumed. While both researchers and research objects are typified ("academic staff," "gang members"), there is more classifying information about the latter than about the former: although we know the principal researcher is male, we don't know his age or his ethnic category.

At the same time, however, this researcher's subject position is refined by mention of a "collaborative model": a set-up which invites the objects of knowledge to take part in the making of knowledge. Such a model replies to the post-colonial criticisms of ethnography, which would be suspicious of a research project investigating non-"White" people who were poor.

---

## exercise

---

Here are three samples of method sections in ethnography. Compare the rhetorical and stylistic features of these passages: that is, how do these convince readers that the researchers' methods produce reliable knowledge?

PASSAGE A

**Research Method**

Our field research on RVers was conducted between October 1 and December 15, 1990. Our goals were to interview as many different kinds of retired RVers as possible and to focus on Canadians travelling in the United States. We attempted to live and be like the people we wished to study. Our age and appearance facilitated this (we did not alienate potential informants by our youth, a problem encountered by some researchers attempting to work in retirement communities; see Streib, Folts and LaGreca 1984). We rented a 12-year-old, 25-foot Prowler trailer and pulled it from British Columbia to the U.S. southwest with an aging van. We stayed in private and public RV parks in British Columbia, Nevada, Arizona and California. We boondocked on U.S. Bureau of Land Managment (BLM) land in the southwestern desert and (with hundreds of others) we trespassed on an abandoned World War II Army training base — popularly known as The Slabs or Slab City — near Niland, California. We slept overnight in private parks, in public campgrounds, in roadside rest areas and in the parking lots of truck stops. In short, for two-and-one-half months we became RVers.

We conducted 50 interviews with retired RVers, some who were singles and others who were couples. Of our interviews, 34 were with full-timers and 16 were with part-timers; 25 were with Americans, 24 with Canadians and 1 was with a British couple. Of the 24 Canadians, 16 were full-timers, while 18 of the 25 Americans were full-timers. We were able to ascertain the ages of 81 of our informants: 2 of these (both women married to older men) were in their 40s, 13 were in their 50s, 45 in their 60s, 19 in their 70s and 2 in their 80s. Our youngest informant was 46, the oldest 86.

We followed an interview guide and asked everyone the same questions, although not necessarily in the same order (also see Kaufman 1986: 22-23). We did not tape our conversations, which were infomral and intended to encourage people to talk in a relaxed context about what was important to them. Some of our informants were curious about our project and asked us as many questions as we asked them; others seemed delighted to find an audience interested in RVing and talked with enthusiasm about their RVing experiences. Some of the interviews were brief, lasting only an hour or so. Others lasted for hours over several days. People were interested in our research and most were extremely cooperative and helpful. Many spoke of a need for the general population to know more about RVing and some hoped that wider exposure would dispel a lingering stereotyupe of RVers as "trailer trash." Others labelled themselves as trailer trash or "trailerites," with irony and fierce pride, as if daring the world to despise them. A number of people said they had thought about writing a book on

RVing themselves. Some brought us magazine articles relevant to our research; others introduced us to people whose stories they thought we should hear; and some sought us out to discuss the advantages of RV retirement. One couple even led us to a park 45 miles from where we and they were camped to show us where we could find Canadian booddockers.

We initially intended to supplement interviews with a questionnaire asking about age, former occupation, estimated income before and after retirement, length of time retired, type of RV selected, etc. Many people were suspicious of the questionnaire and resisted it. Some flatly refused to fill it out. Others declined to answer particular questions — especially the ones about income: "I forget," we were told. . . .[One] couple commented that they did not mind answering questions in conversation because this made us all equals and they could ask *us* questions too. They would, however, respond to a questionnaire either by throwing it away or by lying. And one man, when asked to fill out a questionnaire, inquired "Are you going to ask me if I eat dog food?" In his experience, he said, this was the sort of question asked by people who pass out questionnaires. We abandoned the questionnaire after two weeks. (Counts and Counts 156-67)

PASSAGE B

## Analyzing the audience of audience discussion programmes

*Sources of data concerning audience reception*

The empirical research reported in this article is based on a multi-method project on audience discussion programmes which consisted of twelve focus group discussions following viewing of an audience discussion programme, a series of individual in-depth interviews with viewers and programme participants, and a survey questionnaire from some 500 respondents from a diary panel. Each was considered in conjunction with textual analysis of a wide range of audience discussion programmes (see Livingstone and Lunt 1994a for details). These diverse sources of audience reception data are analyzed specifically in relation to gender for the present paper. Methodologically, the intention is for these different kinds of data to support one another, trading off considerations of sampling and interpretive validity to arrive at a multi-faceted picture of audience reception for the genre.

Sonia Livingstone 1994 Watching talk: Gender and engagement in the viewing of audience discussion programmes. *Media, Culture & Society* 16, 3, 429-447, 433.

PASSAGE C  Triangulation of data to support the narrative was achieved by collecting information in several ways: my daily journal, college inmate-student evaluation instruments, the inmate-student newspaper, informal conversations with inmate students, and inmate-students' written work. (Salomone 77)

Sometimes the representation of "method" calls for an account of "background" — a description of the observed group's social and/or physical context, their habitat. "Background" is somewhat discretionary in ethnography. Sometimes researchers leave it out; sometimes they figure it is relevant. And the grounds for this estimate of relevance can stay submerged, or tacit. For example, here, where the ethnographer of credit-union practices combines background and method, it is hard to say what is significant about staff reductions: how are we to see this circumstance in light of the larger topic of "literacy" or "literate practice" and in light of later findings regarding the use of documents?

PASSAGE 12  At the time of this study, the membership of the credit union was approximately 15,000 and was drawn from three institutions: a large midwestern state university, a community college, and a nonprofit research concern. Slightly more than 50 percet of the credit union's membership were nonacademic employees (e.g., trade, technical, clerical). The proportion of nonacademic members was great among borrowers of CU funds, where they comprised two-thirds of that group. Initially, the target site had thirty-three full-time and eleven part-time employees. Due to rising costs, staff size was trimmed to twenty-four full-time and eleven part-time employees during the period in which the data were collected. Over the bulk of the project, there were five major departments in this credit union: Loans (including Collections), Office, Operations, Education/Marketing, and Accounting. (Keller-Cohen 9)

We saw in Chapter Seven that method sections can depart from the rule of dominating (or domineering) coherence in the research genres, and background sections of ethnography also seem exempt from the strictest patterns of coherence. The account of background doesn't have to openly demonstrate its relevance to other sections or to higher level abstractions that control the discussion. So the writer who tells about inmates learning French also tells about where they live —

PASSAGE 13

*The institution.* Originally built for half as many prisoners as it now holds, this medium security prison suffers from overcrowding to perhaps a dangerous extent. Housed in red brick buildings over fifty years old, inmates sometimes have their sleeping quarters in hallways. The men are "counted" six times a day at approximately three-hour intervals. They eat in a common dining hall, have movies once a week, and engage in organized sports. Educational programs are available to qualified inmnates: a General Education Development (GED) program serves those working toward a High School Equivalency Certificate; a college program leads to Bachelor of Arts, Bachelor of General Studies, and Bachelor of Science degrees. (Salomone 77)

— although it is not clear how these statements are to be interpreted in relation to the study's overall findings and concerns: the transferability of established foreign-language-teaching techniques to prisons. Moreover, if we looked for the kind of tight, local connectedness typical of most research writing, we would come up with uncertain results: what, exactly, does being "'counted'" have to do with once-a-week movies, or Bachelor's degrees? What is the gist of this paragraph?

Sometimes, background sections make a more explicit point, as here where the neighbourhoods of Milwaukee gangs are described under a heading which itself interprets statements about the habitat of the observed social group:

## Background: Gangs And Decreased Legitimate Opportunities

Before we look at variation between neighborhoods, we need to briefly sketch the background for the growth of Milwaukee gang drug sales in the mid- to late 1980s. Economic conditions deteriorated in Milwaukee during that time. Manufacturing jobs declined precipitously in the 1979-83 recession and did not ever completely recover. During the 1980s, Milwaukee lost 19% of its manufacturing job base (McMahon, Moots, and White 1992)/ Of the large firms that paid high wages and where many minorities had been hired (Trotter 1985), 37% were shut down. The Milwaukee area lost 42,000 manufacturing jobs while gaining 100,000 service jobs. The majority of all metropolitan jobs are now located in the suburbs, accelerating spatial mismatch of Milwaukee's "hyper-segregated" minority population with new jobs (Kasarda 1985).

These trends hit Milwaukee central city neighborhoods especially hard, with 1990 African American male unemployment rates exceeding 45% (Rose, Edari, Quinn, and Pawasarat 1992) compared to less than 3.7% of all area workers. As African American and other youths who founded Milwaukee's gangs in the early 1980s reached adulthood, they found few good-paying jobs (Hagedorn 1988). Most of the founders of Milwaukee gangs bobbed in and out of conventional employment and periodically sold cocaine as a means of survival (Hagedorn 1994). But there were major differences between neighborhoods in the organizational form of gang cocaine sales as well as the rise and fall of a notorious citywide drug gang. We will begin our examination of variation in gang drug organization by examining Milwaukee's infamous "Citywide Drug Gang." (Hagedorn 271)

In this example, "background" is organized to demonstrate its relevance to the study's concerns, and it would not be hard to construct the gist of these paragraphs. But, on the whole, statements in background and method sections are under much less pressure to maintain coherence than other sections of the research genres. Some have suggested that the list-like quality of method sections is a sign of readers' assumed familiarity with research practice: they can fill in the missing parts with their background knowledge of research routines. (And to explain too much would alienate readers, and spoil the feeling of academic solidarity.) Perhaps something similar could be said for background sections. Reading a list-like set of statements about a prison, or an urban community in economic decline, or a financial institution, we fill in the gaps for ourselves, from our knowledge of the world, and get an implicit or tacit feeling rather than explicit proposition about the research population's habitat.

Besides this tendency to list-like flatness, background sections, and other parts of ethnography, can have the effect of making the *familiar* strange, and unfamiliar, an effect something like that which comes of transforming "potluck dinner" into "food-sharing ritual." So Shirley Brice Heath's ethnography of "ways with words" in two communities includes this account of a living room, attending to the elements of this cultural space as carefully as if they were a remote people's ritual artefacts:

PASSAGE 15

The screen door on the front porch of this first house on the street opens into a living room filled with showroom-like matching furniture: a suite of sofa and chairs, two end tables, and a coffee table fill the small room as they once did the display window of the furniture store. There have been a few additions: starched stand-up doilies encircle the bases of end table lamps, ashtrays, and vases. Flat crocheted doiles cover the arms of the chairs and sofa and the headrest position of the chairs. A hand-crocheted afghan in the suite's colors is thrown over the back of the sofa. A huge doily of four layers, and a large vase of plastic flowers top the television set. The wooden floor is covered with a large twist rug, and several small matching scatter rugs mark the path to the hall which leads to the bedroom and kitchen.

Shirley Brice Heath 1983 *Ways with Words: Language, life, and work in communities and classrooms.* Cambridge University Press, Cambridge, 30–31.

Or the enthography of literate practices in a credit union can make familiar occasions (going to the bank) seem new and somewhat unfamiliar:

PASSAGE 16     At the time this research project began, the money machine service was a relatively new one at the credit union. . . . The money machine document was presented to new members at the time they enrolled for services at the credit union. The document has two parts: a single page application (3.5" x 8") to use the automated teller and a ten-page foldout section (of equal paper size) describing the rights and obligations of a money machine user. In order to use the money machine you need only fill out the application; it is not necessary to read the agreement. . . . Many members left the agreement on the Coordinator's desk when the application procedure was complete. Some gave it a perfunctory treatment — picking it up, turning it over, and placing it back down on the desk. (Keller-Cohen 18)

Perhaps this defamiliarization is the modern descendant of ways of writing which got their authority from describing the truly unfamiliar — ways and customs of people remote from the European societies which used the early ethnographic genres. Perhaps, in now applying this technique closer to home, modern ethnographers inherit some of that authority.

## exercise

Here is a chance to try the defamiliarizing techniques of modern ethnography. Suppose you are writing an ethnography of routines of speaking (or not speaking) in food markets in the area where you live. Write a "background" section to account for the context of these uses of language.

# exercise

If you were to conduct such a study, what techniques of inquiry could you use? Describe those techniques in ways comparable to the method sections we have examined. One more such section follows, combining method and background, and showing one way of representing research method.

## The Research Context

During an eight-month period in 1985-86, I studied teen romance-fiction readers in three schools in a large American midwestern city that I will call "Lakeview." Once dominated by the automobile, farm-equipment, and alcoholic-beverage industries, the economic crisis of the late 1970s left its imprint on the city and surrounding communities. Plant closings have transformed Lakeview from a smokestack city to one of empty factories and glittering strip malls. Most new businesses are in the service sector, such as fast-food and insurance companies, and employ the bulk of the working- and middle-class women and men in Lakeview.

Lakeview School District is a large district that draws students from the inner city and some of the outlying areas that were annexed to the city thirty years ago. My sites of research were Jefferson Middle School and Sherwood Park Middle School, two outlying 7-8 schools, and Kominsky Junior High School, an inner city 7-9 school. At the time of the study, Lakeview was in the process of converting the junior high schools into middle schools. Jefferson and Sherwood Park each had about three hundred students. Sherwood Park's student population was mostly White. Like Sherwood Park, Jefferson was predominantly White, but had three Chinese students as well. Kominsky's 700+ student body was about one-half White, one-quarter each Black and Hispanic, with a small Vietnamese and Asian Indian population. Both Jefferson and Sherwood Park split their students into three tracks (low, medium, and high) for reading instruction. Reading placements were based on the results of the following: district-wide and individual-school standardized reading test scores, teacher recommendation, and students' previous grades. Kominsky and Sherwood Park also had an additional reading support service through the federally funded

Chapter I program, which enrolled one-half and one-quarter, respectively of their students.

In order to study readers and their romance novels I used a variety of methods combining ethnography with survey research. An initial sample of seventy-five young women from the three schools was assembled through interviews with teachers and librarians regarding who were heavy romance-fiction readers and by personal examination of school and classroom library checkout cards and bookclub order forms. A reading survey was given to all seventy-five young women. From this survey, I was able to identify the heaviest romance-fiction readers, some twenty-nine young women, whom I interviewed individually and in small group settings. These twenty-nine young women had five teachers for reading in the three schools. I observed these classes and interviewed the teachers. This chapter stems from the written reading survey of the seventy-five young women, and from observation of and interviews with the twenty-nine young women and their five teachers. (Christian-Smith 194)

---

## exercise

---

Again, if you were to conduct a study of routines of speaking in food markets, what abstractions could you invoke to begin the transformation of everyday, "commonsense" experience into an object of scholarly interest?

The researchers whose writings we have examined report having spent quite long periods observing the group targeted for study. Student writers are not likely to be able to spend so much time collecting data. But their representations of method can nevertheless construct an equally scholarly position. By specifying the ways data were collected (interviews, questionnaires, observation, analysis of documents) and recorded (by hand in notebooks, for example, or by audio-tape), and specifying the number and duration of research episodes (two one-hour periods of observation, for example, or a half-hour interview with each of three informants), and by typifying the research population and setting (shoppers in a large retail food outlet catering to a suburban neighbourhood in a Canadian metropolitan area of 1.3 million), student writers can establish as valid the sources of the knowledge they have made about the social group they have studied. "Method" and "background" can transform your real-life, commonsense, everyday experience as a shopper into a research project — controlled, calculated, and designed to produce research knowledge.

## 8.5.4 *Interpreting ethnographic data*

Months and years (or even just hours) spent observing people's ways and talking to them about their ways can produce a lot of material, some of it recorded, and some of it stored in memory. And this material is not only plentiful; it is also waiting to be transformed from its everyday, "commonsense" forms, as it originally occurred, into the "uncommonsense" forms of scholarly prose. So the ethnographer of the credit union had to convert the documents, routines, and values of the credit-union community —

— into forms other than those in which she had originally experienced them.

Some aspects of the ethnographer's experience — her research activities and the research population's habitat — have already been converted in method and background sections. These sections begin to re-organize and segment experience, and further operations continue that re-organization and segmentation. Although some ethnography adopts a narrative form, telling the story of the researcher's encounters with the research population, most ethnography *partitions* experience, dividing it into segments and naming their gist with a high-level abstraction. So, the results of a year and a half of observing activities in a credit union produce these abstractions, which *interpret* the data in terms relevant to the topic: "literate practices" and the limits on or opportunities for communication that arise from them:

## LITERATE PRACTICES: INSTITUTIONAL

*Characteristics of document availability*
*The structure of interactions*
*Attitudes and beliefs*

    *Compliance versus membership size*
    *Efficiency*
    *Consultative aids*
    *Conflicting views*

## LITERATE PRACTICES: CREDIT UNION MEMBERS DISCUSSION

Evenings of discussion among eleven residents of Rotterdam are reorganized under a series of headings which pick out abstractions which the authors argue are entertained by *both* anti-racist *and* racist talk.

| Equality: | Equal treatment |
| | Equal opportunities |
| Merit | |
| Rights | |
| Freedom | |
| Rationality | |

Two and a half months of life on the road with RVers produce abstractions which, serving as headings for sections presenting results of the study, interpret details:

Equality, Community and the Good Life
Community and Reciprocity
   Exchange of Personal History
      Ritual Sharing of Food
      Community, Space and Place
      RVers and the Problem of Limited Space

All these sets of interpretive headings (introducing abstractions which in turn control the lower level material which follows) are the products of operations which up-root information from its narrative sequence —

The first place we went was in Oregon. When we were setting up, a woman named Vanessa came over and invited us to potluck. We told her what we were doing, and arranged to interview her. She told us that some people have very expensive RVs and stay in private camps. She showed us her photo album.

— and reorganize it into interpretive orders characteristic of scholarly writing. The reordering establishes the hierarchical structures of generality which we have identified as characteristic of the research genres.

So a moment with Vanessa, or a particular utterance on a Rotterdam evening, doesn't *disappear*, but, rather, withdraws to re-emerge in a characteristically interpretive and hierarchical structure. Accordingly, the passage below establishes abstract concerns — "rite of passage" and "community" — in generalizing about RVers' custom of divesting themselves of their belongings, and then descends to a specific case and a particular moment of the research project.

PASSAGE 17    Giving up home and possessions is a rite of passage, especially for full-time RVers. Those who have done it share a unique experience that sets them apart, even from other RVers, and creates among them a sense of community. As onlookers we witnessed, but could not participate in, the comradeship shared by full-timers as they swapped stories about how they decided to give up their homes, how they established priorities in determining which of their possessions to keep and the difficulties of actually carrying through with their decision. Most full-timers said they spent a long time deciding to do it and many took several years and more than one start before they completed the process. As Randy expressed it:

> People who want to go full-time have a set of problems. The first is letting go of their house. You can't have a nest. You must strip your belongings down to the bare essentials and get rid of the rest. You can't take a lot of things with you. Too many people try to hang onto their house and rent it out. Renters tear the place up and they lose their shirts. I tell them, "Give it up and sell." (Counts and Counts 176)

Note that we don't know *when* "Randy" said what he is reported to have said. Although this passage occurs near the conclusion, the researchers may have met Randy on their first day on the road. The conversion of two and a half months of travel to a research document re-orders *time*.

Similarly, the remarks of some young women talking about characters in a teen romance are excerpted from the researcher's eight-month experience amongst them, and re-introduced under the heading "Creating and Pondering Femininity." Then they become elements relevant to the topic of "reading practices" and gender and "social identities":

PASSAGE 18     Although readers' life experiences are important in constructing meaning when reading, the text still exerts a measure of control over those meanings. In this regard, Iser claims that the text's control happens through "blanks" or gaps in the text. Many times the threads of the plot are suddenly broken off, as happens between chapters. Or they continue in unexpected directions. These textual features prompt readers to "read between the lines." The blanks call for combining what has been previously read with readers' own life experiences and expectations. Although teen romance novels are not characterized by many unexpected twists and turns, they nevertheless require a certain amount of constitutive activity on the part of readers. When female readers encounter blanks in romance texts that involve matters of femininity, two things occur. Readers are offered models of femininity, but are also given opportunities to think about femininity. I will exemplify this dynamic by recounting the readings by three young women of Marshall's *Against the Odds*.

★ ★ ★

Annie filled the blanks in this manner:

> A: It was fun trying to figure out what Trina and the other girls would do to get back at those boys. I thought that they would sneak into the boys' locker room and do something to their sports equipment. Marsha had the guts to do something like that.
>
> LKCS: Was that something you might have done?
>
> A: Are you kidding? No way! I'd never have the guts. Well, you'd have to do something, that's for sure. Hmm, I'd probably start a rumor about the guys or every time me and my friends would see them we would make like we were talking about them. They can't stand that!

Marcy's responses to the same passage also set up a conflict between who she is and who she would like to be:

> M: I figured Trina and Laurie would come up with something fantastic. I never thought in a million years that they would stuff confetti drenched in cheap perfume into the boys' lockers.
>
> LKCS: Would you do that, get even in this way?
>
> M: Well, I'd like to do something like that, to get even with some of the boys in my math class who are real pains. But I'd get chicken and probably just fume.
>
> LKCS: Can you tell me more?

M: It's kinda difficult, I mean, well, I guess I don't want to be seen as a girl who's too pushy with boys. You have to be careful about that. But then you can't let boys push you around. I don't know. (Christian-Smith 202-03)

The paragraph which follows the sections of transcript goes on to convert them to research knowledge by deeply interpreting the young women's remarks in abstract terms valued by the scholarly community: "reader-text-context relations," "femininity," "gender tensions" (203).

Ethnographers' **conclusions** recombine the abstractions which have interpreted the data or re-ordered experience.

PASSAGE 19     **Conclusion**

In her discussion of the Gabra of Kenya, Prussin observes that the repetition of fixed spatial pattern reinforces the cognitive structure of interior space for nomads (1989). We would take this further and argue that when RV nomads set up at a new site, their repetition of spatial patterns reinvents and reinforces their cognitive structure of home, society and community. Although RVers carry with them the form of their social structure, the form is empty. Because they share no history with their RV neighbours, there is no one to fill the status of "neighbour," "friend" or "family," but the ideal content of these forms is shared knowledge. Therefore, when a newcomer pulls in, the strangers who are instant neighbours immediately begin to perform the roles of friend and family by sharing substance and labour. They help the newcomer set up, bring food, give advice and exchange information and personal history. This sharing and exchange allows RVers, who have no common past, to recreate the structure of history from one park to another and to embed themselves in a familiar social structure given substance. Like the Gabra, their reconstruction of history and society enables them to insulate themselves from a hostile environment — the "Crazies" out there — and to transform the stranger who might "rip you off" into the

friend who will look after you in your time of need.
(Counts and Counts 179)

And before going on to speculate on the implications of their findings for developing effective strategies against racism ("how prejudice and racism should be approached in an old inner-city centre"), the researchers who observed evening discussions in Rotterdam recombine and confirm the interpretations that were expressed in ordering abstractions:

PASSAGE 20 **Conclusions**

> We have tried to show that there are basic principles
> which are being shared and used in an anti-racist as well
> as in a more racist discourse. Notions such as equality,
> freedom, human rights and rationality are used by Dutch
> local residents in their daily thinking and arguing about
> ethnic minorities living in the same inner-city quarter. In
> the discussions these principles are acknowledged and
> used by all participants: those who present themselves as
> anti-racists as well as those who describe themselves as
> racists. (Verkuyten, de Jong, and Masson 265)

## 8.5.5    *Assignment: ethnography*

*Finding a research site.* Ethnography involves researchers in the lives of others — sometimes marginally, sometimes deeply. We have discussed political implications which follow from this involvement. In developing an ethnographic project, you will have to take account of the politics of the position you assume in relation to the people and situations you observe, monitoring the transformations which turn them into objects of knowledge.

At the same time as ethnography intervenes in the lives of others, it also calls on ethnographers themselves to consult their own lives and experience for possible research sites. Although ethnographic style can conceal the personal connections between the researcher and the research site, it is often the designs of life itself that destine a researcher to investigate one site rather than another. Was the "modern credit union" Deborah Keller-Cohen's own bank? Did she notice how a bank official explained a loan agreement to her, and decide there was something there worth investigating? Did she have a friend working at the bank? Did Dorothy Counts and David Counts know some people who sold their home, divested themselves of their possessions, and set out to roam the American interstates? Did their friends suggest the research itinerary? Or were the Counts planning a trip anyway? Both Ann Salomone and John Hagedorn had jobs that led them to the situations that became the sites of their research: Salomone taught French in a prison; Hagedorn directed an inner-city social programme

In choosing a site for your research, examine your daily life for the access it may provide to situations where people behave in interestingly characteristic ways — situations you have witnessed or situations you may yourself be involved in. Here are some examples of situations students have written about using ethnographic techniques:

- sports-card trading sessions among preadolescent boys

- interactions between servers and Asian-Canadian patrons and between servers and non-Asian-Canadian patrons in a dim-sum restaurant

- purchase of sea-bus tickets from an automated wicket

- question-and-answer routines during a guided tour of an aquarium

- instruction-giving by instructors to novice and experienced divers on a dive boat

(You may notice that four of these topics have a regional quality to them. Developed by students living on the west coast of Canada, they arose out of their life experience.)

Topics need to meet certain criteria. First, you must have an opportunity to gather data. You need to be able to situate yourself to watch, take notes, use a tape recorder, and gather any relevant documents. Second, the situation needs to be narrow enough to permit firsthand observation. So, interesting as the topic "planning a wedding in a post-feminist era" might be, you may not have time to gather data on all phases of this often elaborate and prolonged procedure. (You might narrow it to "selection and preparation of the bride's ceremonial costume.")

Third, you need to be able to get your research population (even if it is only one person) to agree to be observed and written about. You need to be able to explain to them the purpose of your investigation, and to assure them of confidentiality: that is, you will write about them in such a way that readers will not be able to identify them. (Often, ethnographers use fictitious names for their subjects, if proper nouns make the reporting go better. Some even use fictitious names for the geographical location [e.g., "Lakeview"] or identify the place in general, typifying terms [e.g., "a small western Canadian city with a resource-based economy"].)

And, finally, your research site must be a place where you can cultivate **abstraction** relevant to other published scholarship. The Counts' article, for example, isn't only a report of RVers' ways. It also addresses a research question about *community*, one which has been addressed by other researchers whom they cite. Verkuyten, de Jong, and Masson don't just listen in on what people say about their neighbourhood. They address research questions about *racist and anti-racist discourse*, which they frame by citing other writers on racism and on the social psychology of "commonplaces" ("principles which speak for themselves and are not questioned as such" (254)).

Criteria for selecting a research site in effect combine two facets of your experience: (1) the avenues of your daily life that reveal behaviours and situations around you, and give you access to these situations; (2) the course of your life as a scholar and reader, which has brought you into contact with the research concerns of the academic community.

So the sample topics listed above tended to centre around the abstractions *literacy* and *genre*, issues addressed in publications we studied in the courses in which students arrived at these topics. Citing and summarizing Deborah Keller-Cohen and Shirley Brice Heath, the student who wrote about sports-card trading sessions interpreted three eleven-year-olds' use of documents to support their evaluations of the cards and their bids and counter-offers. (One of the eleven-year-olds was her son.) The student who wrote about ordering in a dim-sum restaurant cited and summarized Heath and Carolyn Miller ("Genre as social action" 1984) to invoke the abstraction *tacit knowledge* : the role of unspoken but mutually understood assumptions in defining group boundaries.

These are delicate negotiations between scholarly experience and everyday experience. And they offer important insights into the nature of this kind of research inquiry. Let me give an example. The student who wrote about tourists and commuters getting sea-bus tickets from an automated wicket was interested in how people coped with written instructions for a procedure that has been traditionally governed by an oral genre (spoken interactions between traveller and ticket-seller). After observing people using the wicket, successfully or unsuccessfully, and watching them confer with other travellers or with station attendants, and interviewing some of the sea-bus patrons, she drafted her introduction. The major abstraction she invoked was *transportation technology*. She made it a Big Issue by remarking on the need for attention to transportation in the context of population growth and environmental concerns (*"Technology,"* as a prestige abstraction in itself, tended to compete with *"transportation,"* bringing along its own related issues of social change, employment patterns, and so on.) But this Big Issue stalled when the writer turned to cite relevant research and sketch a knowledge map with the gaps and spaces her work would occupy: Heath, Keller-Cohen, and Miller on literate practice and the role of genre in housing common knowledge of social routines. It was hard to get from "transportation" to the domain of knowledge represented by the other writers she would cite to ratify her topic and situate herself amongst the voices of the research community. Inspecting this stalled essay, we saw that the writer's Big Issue was not transportation technology but *genre* and *literacy* . On those topics she was an expert — able to cite relevant statements by others. "Transportation" was her **research site**, not her topic.

Similarly, the student who wrote about communication between dive-boat instructors and novice and experienced divers also first invoked a Big Issue that seemed compelling but finally would not sustain the conventions of the research genres. A dive-boat instructor herself, she referred to and developed the topic *safety* in her introduction. This seemed to be an automatic Big Issue: everybody wants to be safe. But, despite being a dive-boat instructor, she was not in fact an expert — in the research sense — on safety. She was an expert on routines of communication (able to cite statements about oral and literate interaction). The dive-boat, along with the safety issues involved in its operation, was her **research site**.

## Suggested topics

*(A) Genre and literacy*

Because this course of studies has repeatedly consulted theories of genre, and because you have been involved in analyzing the written expression of research communities and the role of this expression in maintaining the values and routines of research communities, you have become (perhaps inadvertently) expert in genre and *literate practice*. You can exploit this expertise in an ethnographic project by focussing on a typical real-life situation in which people interact in routine ways, consciously or unconsciously complying with recognizable norms of expression. So, for example, you might secure the cooperation of two or three of your fellow students and observe their note-taking techniques in class, and their transformation of this genre into the essay genre. Or you might observe two or three of your friends who use email — a new genre emerging from technological change. Observing these behaviours, collecting relevant documents, and possibly interviewing your subjects, you will collect data sufficient to enable you to generalize about learning, language, and authority, or about technological change and literacy.

If you decide on a project related to genre and literacy, I suggest the following sources:

Amy Devitt 1993 Generalizing about genre: New concepts of an old concept. *College Composition and Communication* 44, 357-86

Shirley Brice Heath 1983 Chapter Six: Literate traditions. In *Ways with Words: Language, life, and work in communities and classrooms*. Cambridge University Press.

Deborah Keller-Cohen 1987 Literate practices in a modern credit union. *Language in Society* 16, 7-24.

Carolyn Miller 1984 Genre as social action. *Quarterly Journal of Speech* 70, 151-167.

John Swales 1990 Chapter Two: The concept of discourse community and Chapter Three: The concept of genre. In *Genre Analysis: English in academic and research settings*. Cambridge University Press.

Appearing in well-known journals or in books from widely distributed publishers, these should be available in your university library. **Summary** of two or three of these sources will enable you to invoke the voices of the research community, and to take a position among these voices. (Remember that, to identify the **knowledge deficit** you will address, you need only describe the limits of these sources: they propose a general framework which can direct your inquiry in a research site they do not explore.)

(B) Gender and language — politeness and other speech behaviours

Many of this textbook's examples of scholarly expression have dealt with gender issues: gender issues attract attention in many disciplines. At the same time, much of our inquiry into scholarly expression could be characterized as having to do with "politeness" — especially if we define politeness as the encoding in language of mutual recognition of social status. (So Myers (1989) has accounted for salient features of research articles in science journals as "politeness" — a configuration of relative distribution of power and a concern for the community's solidarity.) **Reporting** and **modality** — features we looked at in Chapter Seven — are often associated with politeness: reporting and modalized expressions leave space open around the speaker's statement — space available for a listener to occupy. By making statements somewhat indeterminate, reporting and modalizing expressions help speakers appear not to impose on addressees. So, instead of uttering the command

Bring me a glass of water.

a polite speaker might say

I wonder if you might be able to bring me a glass of water.

Or a speaker who wanted to express an opinion about his or her addressee's appearance might avoid the directness of

Your trousers are too short

and select instead a form that modalizes and minimizes the opinion:

Your trousers might possibly be just a little too short.

Folk theories of gender and politeness seem to associate politeness with women: people think women are more polite than men. Some research tends to confirm the folk view; other research does not. The following is a very brief list from the extensive research into differences in women's and men's speech and can provide a basis for inquiry into gender difference in communicative situations. (Greg Myers (1989 The pragmatics of politeness in scientific articles *Applied Linguistics* 10, 1-35) may also be useful to you. And you will find in Sheldon, below, especially, some definitions of speech styles that go beyond just "politeness.")

Penelope Brown 1990 Gender, politeness, and confrontation in Tenejapa. *Discourse Processes* 13, 123-141.

Jennifer Coates 1986 Chapter 6 Sex differences in communicative competence. In *Women, Men and Language* Longman, Harlow, Essex, 96-118.

B. L. Dubois and I. Crouch 1975 The question of tag questions in women's speech: they don't really use more of them, do they? *Language and Society* , 4, 289-94.

Amy Sheldon 1990 Pickle fights: gendered talk in preschool disputes. *Discourse Processes* 13, 5-31.

Summary of two or three of these sources (or any others you discover) will enable you to define an issue — a topic ratified by research. To investigate the topic, you can turn to the academic world around you — classroom discussion, comments addressed to university lecturers, responses to commentary on marked essays, for example — or to life beyond the academic world: the workplace or marketplace, or the home.

## (C) Disciplines and their discourses

Traditionally, ethnography has involved researchers in some degree of face-to-face contact with the groups they have undertaken to study: on-site observations and interviews, or some other form of limited participation in the group's activities. But, for the purposes of this assignment, we could loosen traditional definitions of ethnography to include research that involves no face-to-face contact with the groups targeted for inquiry. So differences in different disciplines' styles of expression could be investigated by examining a selection of articles from scholarly journals. After all, genre theory tells us that communities leave traces of their values and practices in the documents they typically use. Accordingly, these articles will be a source of knowledge about the social groups which produce them.

This book's course of studies offers some guides for examining documents representing the habits and routines of different academic communities. Concentrating on introductions and conclusions, you might attempt to characterize

- the role and qualities of generalities

- the quality of "prestige abstractions"

- the use of reported statements and the practice of documentation

- the use of modality and limiting expressions

- the ways a knowledge deficit is identified

- the presence and quality of descriptions of method

- the presence of "discursive I" and messages about the argument (including headings and other types of partitioning).

To position yourself as a researcher, you could cite and summarize one (or more) of the studies listed above as frames for studying genre (Devitt, Swales or Miller would be most relevant), and cite and summarize the findings of

> Susan Peck MacDonald 1994 Chapter Two: Patterns in disciplinary variation. In *Professional Academic Writing in the Humanities and Social Sciences.* Southern Illinois University Press.
> Greg Myers 1989 The pragmatics of politeness in scientific articles Applied Linguistics 10, 1–35
> John Swales 1990 Chapter Seven: Research articles in English. In *Genre Analysis: English in academic and research settings.* Cambridge University Press.

Establish as your research site articles selected from scholarly journals in sciences, psychology, business, criminology, economics, education, history, anthropology, communications, literary criticism, or other fields which are relevant to your own academic goals and interests. You could concentrate on just one field, or you might find comparision of two or more fields more revealing. You might also consider an historical inquiry, investigating changes in a discipline's typical discourse over a period of decades.

Or you might compare scholarly accounts of a topic with popular accounts of similar matters. Still referring to the features listed above, you might compare a sample of the public discourse in the popular media on immigration to the account offered in

> Leo R. Chavez 1994 The power of the imagined community: The settlement of undocumented Mexicans and Central

Americans in the United States. *American Anthropologist* 96, 1, 52–73

or a sample of the public discourse on crime to

John M. Hagedorn 1994 Neighborhoods, markets and gang drug organizations. *Journal of Research in Crime and Delinquency* 31, 3, 264-94.

or popular description of eating disorders to

Alan Apter et al. 1994 Cultural effects on eating attitudes in Israeli subpopulations and hospitalized anorectics. *Genetic, Social, and General Psychology Monographs* 120, 1, 85-99.

# 8.6 Preparing a proposal

Proposals (also called "abstracts" or "abstract proposals") are a widely used genre in academic communities. Seeking a place on a conference programme, or a spot in a collection of essays that will be published on a particular topic, scholars answer "Calls for Papers" with a proposal. Conference chairs or the editors of collections evaluate the submissions they receive on bases we have become familiar with. They look for the Big Issue — topics that excite interest in the research community. They look for evidence that the author of the proposal is in touch with established positions on the topic — statements reported from recognized sources. They look for mention of a knowledge deficit — an estimate of the limitation of what has been said so far. They look for some account of method — how knowledge will be constructed on this topic. Chairs and editors also try to estimate the proposal's feasibility: can the researcher actually accomplish what he or she promises? Is the research site appropriate and manageable? Will it yield relevant data that can be usefully interpreted?

So, if I were interested in the Big Issue "gender and language," I might compose a proposal which identified the issue and cited some previous research on the topic —

As Coates (1986) and others have observed, there is a long history of commentary on women's speech, commentators having, through the centuries, detected and interpreted features which they believed to peculiarly feminine. More recently, studies such as Sheldon (1990) and Eckert (1990) have attempted to interpret identifiable features of women's speech in relation to the social context in which they occur, referring to larger theories of power and dominance in the social order. Christian-Smith (1991) has added reading practice to speaking practice in looking for significant patterns in the gendering of language.

— and then identify a knowledge deficit and a research question:

Yet all these studies focus on one kind of social context: the school. We might wonder whether educational settings exert particular influence on the interactive styles of speakers, and whether the features identified in these studies occur in other institutional settings, such as the workplace, or other public contexts.

It is all very well to wonder about this, and my reader might feel a spark of interest, but he or she, as someone responsible for the success of a conference or a volume of collected papers, would need to know more before accepting the proposal. What am I going to *do*? My reader might accept the claim that

This paper will investigate language and gender in settings beyond the school.

but still not accept my proposal, having no idea how I will find my way in this vast research site called "settings beyond the school." But if I specify the research site, show that it is relevant to the topic, and explain how I will contruct knowledge from the data it offers, my reader will feel more confident that my project is feasible:

This paper will report data gathered from a public institutional setting with a decision-making goal: transcripts of two meetings of a municipal Board of Zoning Variance, on which two men and three women serve. I will examine conversational turn-taking, topic shifts, personal narrative contributions, and mention or reading of documents such as by-laws and site plans to discover whether the "cooperative" speech styles of girls and young women in school settings are also evident in this more overtly political context.

(Notice that I am not an expert on city planning or municipal politics: zoning decisions are only my research site, not my topic.)

Proposals have many of the stylistic and rhetorical features of scholarly introductions. And both genres — proposals and research articles — serve the values and routines of the research community. But they differ in fuction in that, in many disciplines, the proposal describes work that has not yet been completed — perhaps only planned, or just begun. If a scholarly paper were actually to come from my (fictitious) proposal, its introduction might differ significantly from the proposal, reflecting what I found when I actually carried out the research. Conference chairs and editors know this — they know that the work may not have been done yet, and that the actual product may differ from the one predicted by the proposal. (So at scholarly conferences, you can observe a by-product of the operation of the proposal genre: people standing up to present their work and saying, "First I have to tell you that my title has changed. . . .") But the proposal gives chairs and editors confidence in the *process* : the researcher is aware of relevant research in the area; has a specific research question in mind; has a manageable research site and productive techniques for constructing knowledge.

## assignment

Write a 200-300 word proposal for the paper you are working on to fulfill one of the assignments suggested above, or for another paper you are working on. Ask your instructor to go through his or her files to find examples of proposals he or she has submitted or received: inspect these examples to determine the salient features of the genre. Or follow this plan:

- Title (including major abstraction and reference to research site)
- Topic (the Big Issue or Prestige Abstraction which warrants this project)
- Existing knowledge (statements reported from other researchers)
- Knowledge deficit (limits of existing knowledge, and the research question which formulates these limits)
- Research site (the "place" where you will conduct this research — which does not have to be a geographical location but can be a "textual location" if you are examining documents)
- Method (how you will construct knowledge, how you will organize and interpret your data)

## 8.7    Making an oral presentation

A main event in the life a research community is the **conference**. Conferences — organized, programmed series of oral presentations of research results — abound in the academic world. Their abundance is a sign of their usefulness in the knowledge-making professions. Conferences summon several speech genres — the keynote address, the introduction of speakers, the roundtable discussion, the audience response to research reports, for example — but the most important one is the paper presentation.

Few professional scholars let a year go by without presenting a paper at a conference, or at least attending a conference and listening to other people present their papers. And few students get through a term without having to make an oral presentation in class. Professional scholars and students have in common the genre of the oral presentation. Although the oral presentation can seem to students to be a punitive or cruel assignment, arbitrary and nerve-wracking, it is in fact an authentic element of scholarly life.

Most people feel some anxiety at speaking formally in public. If you are among this majority, you should not see your anxiety as a bad sign: totally relaxed people often seem to give the worst presentations, offhand and pointless. Maybe they underestimate the real and undeniable challenges in making themselves interesting for ten or twenty uninterrupted minues.

yah, well, I haven't really got anything prepared. I thought I'd just give you some of my ideas....

Feeling a little stress on these occasions is probably not only normal but productive: it will make you work harder at getting ready. What follows is some advice on preparing for an oral presentation.

## 8.7.1 *Make your material fit the time available.*

Few presenters of papers have too little to say; many have too much. If their presentation reports work that is in preparation as a written paper or essay, they are especially likely to have too much to say. And many presenters underestimate how much time it will take to deliver their material.

Although other factors contribute to the success or failure of an oral presentation, I have come to believe that *making your material fit the time available* is just about the most important task in preparing for a presentation. If you have too much to say, you will rush, and talk too fast — and listeners will have a hard time following. Or you will have to stop before you have made your most important points. Or you will edit as you speak —

*OK ... well, I'll have to skip this, there isn't time ... let's see ... OK ... another point is that ...*

— and risk leaving out parts of your reasoning that are necessary to making the whole comprehensible and meaningful.

Some long-winded presenters get mad when their time is up. Maybe they are overcome by the stress of the situation. Maybe they have mistaken the oral presentation for some other genre, like the article or essay. Maybe they feel that their thinking is so important that it should not be subjected to limitation. But the typical 20-minute allotment for a conference paper is fair enough both socially and cognitively: it shares time among more speakers than longer allotments would do; it pretty nearly matches a listening audience's capacity for attending to a complex argument. Equally, if you are assigned a five- or ten-minute presentation in class, this allotment will neither impose on your listeners nor confound them. Take comfort in time restrictions and work within them.

As a general rule, eight double-spaced typed pages becomes a twenty-minute presentation.

## 8.7.2 *Keep in mind that written and spoken English differ*

The eight-page rule assumes that presenters write out their materials and then read their writing to their listeners. In the first edition of this book, I argued against this practice for several reasons, all developing from the inescapable fact that writing and talking are not the same, and neither are reading and listening. While people have many strategies for understanding the spoken genres (conversations, for example, or class discussions, or consultations with doctors or loans officers), they have few strategies for understanding written genres read out loud (legal contracts, to take an extreme example, or, closer to our concerns, university essays). The different situations in which speaking and writing come about produce different styles.

We could say that, at the most basic level, written and spoken genres separate from each other along the lines of differences between **planned** and **unplanned** discourse. Situations served by writing include time for planning and revising; situations served by spoken genres — although they will be informed by habit and established routines — do not include time for planning and revising. The presence or absence of planning results in different communicative styles.

The oral presentation lies between writing and speaking. While it is spoken, it is certainly not unplanned. As *listeners*, people are used to the styles that arise in unplanned discourse. But, hearing an oral presentation, they are faced with a planned text. To accommodate their listeners' predicament, presenters can take certain steps. They can

- repeat main points frequently (maybe more often than they think they should) to help their listeners keep important material in mind. We know that articles and essays use repetition, too, to confirm readers' interpretation of detail. But readers have further means of confirming their understanding of the material that is being presented: they can *slow* the pace of their reading, dwelling on important points to get them firmly positioned on their mental desktop. Listeners can't do this. So oral presentations should be more repetitive than articles and essays.

- introduce frequent messages about the argument. Unlike readers, listeners don't know where they are in the discussion — near the end, or a long way from it; at a division between one section and another or in the middle of something; in the middle or at the end of a series of examples. Presenters can orient their listeners by frequently signalling their position in the argument and forecasting its progress: "I will begin by giving some background. . . ," "Later I will . . . ," "To show you what this means, I will describe . . . ," "To conclude, I am going to . . . ."

- shift their emphasis from the abstract and general to the concrete and specific. By concentrating on examples, presenters can leave a more enduring impression, replicating the tendency of conversation to turn to the interesting anecdote, the particular case that attracted attention.

- unload the heavy nominal expressions typical of scholarly writing. Noun phrases are much lighter in speech: whereas writers have time to plan heavy nominal expressions, speakers are more likely to scatter attributes and agents across several clauses. So, while the long noun phrase in

    <u>Extensive longitudinal and cross-cultural research including interviews with and observations of hundreds of children</u> led Kohlberg to conclude that moral development moves through three levels.

is characteristic of written scholarly expression, these unpacked, lighter versions more closely resemble the noun phrases typical of speaking:

    <u>Extensive research</u> led Kohlberg to conclude that moral development moves through three levels. <u>This research</u> was both longitudinal and cross-cultural. <u>It</u> included interviews with hundreds of children, and observations of them, too.

Although listeners may be used to coping with heavy nominal expressions in their reading, they won't be used to hearing them.

- use visual aids, like handouts or overhead projections. Lists of figures, important quotations, or key terms and phrases can turn listeners temporarily into readers, and support their efforts to understand.

In the first edition of this book, I also recommended that presenters compose their material in *note form* — words and phrases. By using note form instead of sentences and paragraphs, presenters activate their own natural competence as speakers, using language in ways characteristic of speaking rather than writing. I still think this can be a good idea, but I now also have reservations.

For one thing, note-form materials can balloon and drift over time boundaries. As we expand and explain, we can risk longwindedness, saying more than needs to be said. And, for another thing, many of the very best papers I have heard at scholarly conferences have been read from prepared pages of prose — not notes. If reading a paper out loud works so well at conferences, it may also offer some benefits to classroom presenters, too.

If your classroom situation is informal and colloquial, you might be better off with note-form materials. If, on the other hand, your classroom is a more formal setting, a *brief* and well-prepared paper read out loud can be very successful. And if you are in fact preparing a presentation for a conference or other public, scholarly occasion, it is probably best to have your eight pages of prose typed out and right in front of you. Just remember that the oral presentation is *not* an essay or article. And even if the essay or article is already written and ready to submit to a teacher or a journal, *don't* be tempted to just read it out loud. Make a new, reduced, and simplified version for presentation (offering your audience copies of the essay version if they are particularly interested in your argument). Essays and presentations are different genres.

---

## assignment

Prepare a ten-minute oral presentation on the research you described in your proposal (Section 8.6) or on research you are doing for another assignment. Include in your plans time for discussion: ask your audience to respond to your work with questions, advice, insights — even criticisms.

Position yourself as a researcher reporting on work-in-progress and offering a scholarly community a contribution to knowledge. Attend to the voices of the scholarly community.

Good luck with your paper.

# Using *Academic Writing*

## Courses of studies

This book begins at a fundamental level — with advice on summarizing what many call "sources" — and ends at an advanced level — with advice on preparing proposals for presentations on scholarly occasions. If we were to map a student population across this span, we could locate beginning students principally in the book's first chapters and more experienced writers in its last three. Still, the categories of this developmental range are not strict. Lots of "beginning" writers are ready to confront the problematic nature of scholarly style ("can I use 'I' in my essay?;" "why is academic writing so complicated?"), and, in any case, by the end of an introductory course, beginners are no longer beginners. They are often ready to undertake the kinds of reasoning provided for in the later chapters. Equally, experienced writers — even graduate students — can benefit from the summary practice in Chapters Two and Three, or Chapter Five's practice of defining abstractions. And Chapter Four, which elaborates a cognitive model of reading, is useful for any writer, at any stage.

Nevertheless, despite these overlaps, in my own classes I use the materials in this book in a roughly developmental way. Our one-semester course "Introduction to University Writing" begins with summary assignments and proceeds through assignments based on definition and comparison. Our one-semester course "Advanced University Writing" begins with a critical-summary assignment, combines definition and comparison (5.3.3), assigns an ethnographic project at week 8 of 13, and devotes the last weeks to in-class analysis of scholarly styles in different disciplines (consulting Chapters Six and Seven, and working on exercises in those Chapters, including those which ask students to reflect on their own work) and a research project (often students choose to do a second ethnography). This final assignment includes a proposal and a presentation. In both courses, all assignments are based on scholarly readings — with the exception of the final assignment in the advanced course, where some students find their own "readings," ones relating to their work in their own disciplines.

## Suggested assignments

All articles referred to in this section are collected in *Academic Reading*, the anthology which accompanies this textbook.

When students have warmed up with the practice summaries in Chapters Two and Three, they are ready for a full-size **summary** project. While all the selections in *Academic Reading* are, of course, summarizable, some are more accessible than others. In my estimation, both

Alan Apter et al. 1994 Cultural effects on eating attitudes in Israeli subpopulations and hospitalized anorectics. *Genetic, Social and General Psychology Monographs* 120, 1, 85-99.

and

Reed Way Dasenbrock 1987 Intelligibility and meaningfulness in multicultural literature. *Periodical of the Modern Languages Association* 102, 10-19.

present clearly organized arguments susceptible to brief summary (400 words). Five that might call for longer summary and present a slightly greater challenge (but still not overwhelm beginning academic writers) are

Maykel Verkuyten, Wiebe de Jong, and Kees Masson Similarities in anti-racist and racist discourse: Dutch residents talking about ethnic minorities. *New Community* 20, 2, 253-267.

Dorothy Counts and David Counts "They're my family now"; The creation of community among RVers. *Anthropologica* 34, 153-182.

Nick Tiratsoo and Jim Tomlinson 1994 Restrictive practices on the shopfloor in Britain, 1945-60: Myth and reality. *Business History* 36, 2, 65-84.

Mary Lynn McDougall 1983 Protecting infants: The French campaign for maternity leaves, 1890s-1913. *French Historical Studies* 13, 1, 79-105.

More challenging are

Cheshire Calhoun  1994  Separating lesbian theory from feminist theory. *Ethics* 104, 558-581.

Min-Zhan Lu  1992  Conflict and struggle: The enemies or preconditions of Basic Writing? *College English* 54, 8, 887-913.

Harriet Baber  1994  The market for feminist epistemology. *The Monist* 77, 4, 403-423.

Despite the escalating challenges in these listings, most students — with lots of encouragement, consultation and collaboration — could produce worthy accounts of these articles. (It can be useful to have different students working on different articles. Then, when they exchange drafts for feedback, they find out how readable their summaries are for people who have not studied the original.)

All of these articles are also suitable for **critical summary**. So, for example, a student might compose a summary of Dasenbrock as a first assignment, and a critical summary of Lu for a second assignment.

As students are drafting their second assignments, they will be ready to approach the cognitive model of reading presented in Chapter 4. The suggestions for think-aloud protocols at the end of that chapter can provide them with a guide for reading and responding to one another's work — as they draft their second assignments, and throughout the course.

Practice in **definition** (Chapter 5) can be expanded by asking students to identify a relevant abstraction that arises from their reading, and to use definition of that abstraction to develop an account of published research. So, an account of

Leo R. Chavez  1994  The power of the imagined community: The settlement of undocumented Mexicans and Central Americans in the United States. *American Anthropologist* 96, 1, 52-73.

could be structured around a definition of *community*. An account of

Rebecca J. Scott 1994 Defining the boundaries of freedom in the world of
cane: Cuba, Brazil, and Louisiana after emancipation. *American Historical Review* Feb. 70-102.

could be structured around a definition of *labour relations*. A **comparison** assignment could develop by adding Counts and Counts "They're my family now" to Chavez, on the grounds of a shared focus on *community*. Similarly, a student who has worked on Scott and *labour* could, for comparison's sake, consider

Naila Kabeer 1994 The structure of 'revealed' preference: Race, community
and female labour supply in the London clothing industry. *Development and Change* 25, 307-331.

in a subsequent assignment, paying attention to the way both articles regard labour as not simply an employer's requirement but also a worker's decision.

Once students have worked on summarizing, on developing a critical stance, and on defining and comparing, they can head into a *ethnographic* project (Chapter 8). Counts and Counts is a fine example of ethnography, and other articles in *Academic Reading* also use ethnographic methods: Eckert (adolescent "girl talk"), Chavez (undocumented immigrants), Kabeer (London clothing industry), Verkuyten, de Jong and Masson (anti-racist and racist discourse).

Instead of, or in addition to ethnography, students could explore some of the many connections between the articles collected in *Academic Reading*. For example, Baber (feminist epistemology) and McDougall (maternity leaves) both refer to "scientific" conceptualizations of maternity. Students looking at labour (not the maternity kind) as it is represented in Kabeer (London clothing industry) could add Baber's analysis of the "vicious circle" of women's position in the workplace, or even the brief account by Apter et al. (eating disorders) or women and work on the kibbutz. Lu (Basic Writing), Dasenbrock (multicultural literature) and McKenzie (literacy in early New Zealand) all apply some form of post-colonial analysis to their subjects, Lu and McKenzie both reflecting on education. Lu and Counts and Counts (RVers) both refer to "margins," and life there (some students might find Calhoun on lesbianism relevant here). Race and ethnicity are issues for Lu, Kabeer, Verkuyten, de Jong and Masson, and Dasenbrock. Both Chavez and Verkuyten, de Jong and Masson examine aspects of immigration and the discourse which surrounds it. While instructors can guide students toward these research opportunities, I think it is best for students to develop their own research questions, discovering for themselves a "knowledge deficit" and a way of addressing it.

Finally, students could make the articles in *Academic Reading* their research site. They could, for example, compare the ethnographic methods of Counts and Counts, Kabeer, Eckert, Chavez, and Verkuyten, de Jong and Masson, possibly using Apter et al. as a contrasting methodological case. Several writers talk about the past. Scott and McDougall are historians; McKenzie looks at "early New Zealand"; Tiratsoo and Tomlinson examine 1945-1960 in Britain. How do their methods of constructing knowledge of the past differ from or resemble one another? And a number of articles in *Academic Reading* deal with "gender" issues. Using Baber's account of "feminist epistemology" as a guide, students could examine the range of means of constructing knowledge of gender issues, from the psychological methods of Apter et al. through the historical methods of McDougall to the ethnographic methods of Eckert and Kabeer.

# Index